ESCAPE

FROM

CORPORATE AMERICA

Pamela Skillings

BALLANTINE BOOKS · NEW YORK

ESCAPE

FROM

CORPORATE AMERICA

A PRACTICAL GUIDE TO CREATING
THE CAREER OF YOUR DREAMS

A Ballantine Books Trade Paperback Original

Published in the United States by Ballantine Books,
an imprint of The Random House Publishing Group,
a division of Random House, Inc., New York.

BALLANTINE and colophon are
registered trademarks of Random House, Inc.

Library of Congress Cataloging-in-Publication Data
Skillings, Pamela.
Escape from corporate America : a practical guide to
creating the career of your dreams / Pamela Skillings.
p.   cm.
ISBN 978-0-345-49974-5 (pbk.)
1. Career development.   2. Vocational guidance.
3. Entrepreneurship.   I. Title.
HF5381.S6215 2008
650.14—dc22   2007043429

Printed in the United States of America

www.ballantinebooks.com

2 4 6 8 9 7 5 3 1

Book design by Liz Cosgrove

For Alex

CONTENTS

PART III
Going Over the Wall

Does your corporate career leave you stressed out, burned out, or just plain bummed out?

Believe me, you're not alone. But you don't have to stay stuck in a job that doesn't inspire you. You don't have to choose between paying the bills and enjoying a fulfilling career.

Been There, Done That, Wrote the Book

I wrote this book because I know exactly how you feel. After twelve years on the corporate fast track, I walked away from a six-figure salary and a VP title to start my own company. Along the way, I rediscovered my creativity and my confidence and learned that it really is possible to love your work.

Making the leap wasn't easy. It took me years of trial and error to escape from Corporate America. Once I left, I was amazed at people dying to know how I did it and whether they could, too.

This book is about exploring your options. It's not a bitter anti-corporate rant. In fact, chapter 5 looks at some of the corporations that people love to work for. These are companies that offer entrepreneurial cultures, innovative work–life balance programs, and even free lunches. They almost made me want to update my résumé. Almost.

Unfortunately, your corporate home probably isn't that warm

and fuzzy or you wouldn't be reading this right now. You need an exit strategy. Aren't you glad I'm here to help?

I spent the last three years talking to more than two hundred amazing people who successfully made the transition from corporate servitude to careers they love. I spoke with entrepreneurs, filmmakers, nonprofit leaders, restaurateurs, corporate VPs, teachers, singers, and a reality TV star. And that was only the beginning.

I found corporate escape artists everywhere I went. In my clients' offices, at my volunteer gig, in my writing workshop, at the gym, online, and on vacation. Along the way, both my brother and my best friend from college quit their corporate management jobs to pursue their dreams.

Memoirs of a Corporate Misfit: The Early Years

My personal story is just like thousands of others in cubicle land. I was a creative person who stumbled into the corporate world for a "temporary" gig that lasted twelve years.

I had always wanted to be a writer, ever since I composed my first prose masterpiece in crayon in the first grade (my mother laminated it for posterity). Even as an idealistic young thing, though, I never believed I could actually make a living as a writer. I majored in journalism because I thought that was the only way I could get paid to write, even if I was writing obits and puff pieces.

Unfortunately, entry-level journalism doesn't provide much of a living, especially in New York City. The editorial jobs I was offered didn't pay enough to support a lifestyle that included both regular meals and a roof over my head.

Luckily, I could type. While I was interviewing for pittance-paying editorial assistant positions after graduation, a temp agency sent me to work in public relations at an investment bank. I was dazzled by this new and foreign world—the fast pace of the financial markets, the fun of company parties and expense-account dinners, the hobnobbing with the rich and powerful. Ah, the honeymoon phase.

When my glamorous new boss offered me a healthy salary to come aboard full-time, I put my creative career dreams aside. After all, I had no trust fund to tap into and I had to pay rent on my roach-infested apartment somehow. I decided that writing press releases was a valid alternative to running the copy machine at a magazine.

Then a funny thing happened—I kept getting promoted. At first, it was fun because there was a lot to learn. Earning raises and promotions fed my hungry ego, and it was nice to be able to buy new shoes once in a while.

I can't pinpoint exactly when it got ugly. Maybe it was when I first encountered the joys of middle management. At some point, I stopped learning and started stagnating. My job became much more demanding and much less stimulating. My energy was sapped by the effort required to appear interested through hours of boring meetings each day. To my credit, I'm pretty sure I nodded off only once.

Nothing about my work was meaningful or exciting anymore. I'd been through countless reorgs, mergers, layoffs, and management changes, and I was exhausted. It turned out that I had finally climbed far enough up the ladder to realize that the view sucked despite the panorama of the New York City skyline outside my office window.

Worst of all, I started to get the sinking feeling that there was no way out that didn't require moving into my parents' basement. So I sucked it up and hoped things would get better after the next promotion.

☕ Breakdown in the Fast Lane

After twelve long years, I had all the things that I'd always thought
I wanted: a sweet paycheck, a fancy title, and an expense account.
I had a "good job," but I was miserable. My spacious office with its
mahogany desk and its view started to feel like a jail cell. Every
morning, I rose early, put on my sensible business casual uni-
form, and braved an hour-long commute to do my time in climate-
controlled conference rooms.

Okay, maybe the prison metaphor is a bit melodramatic. After
all, I didn't have to worry about getting shivved in the exercise
yard, but that was only because we weren't allowed outside very
often.

If you picked up this book, you can probably relate to my feeling of being trapped in a job, and a life, that wasn't working.

I certainly wasn't alone in feeling frustrated. Most of the people
around me hated their jobs, too. In fact, I had started to wonder if
that was just the way things worked. Maybe I was naïve to think I
should get any sort of satisfaction out of my daily grind. Maybe I
should just grow up, shut up, and collect my paycheck.

I tried that for a while. But I didn't like the person I was turning
into. I was tired, I was cranky, and I was fat. I was tired from working endless hours, cranky about feeling trapped, and fat because
the highlights of my day had become lunch and happy hour.

Next, I tried following the advice in those other career books
that insisted I could learn to love my job if I just tried a little harder.
I volunteered for new projects and proposed new ideas, but just
ended up working longer hours and feeling like more of a failure. I
tried interviewing for positions at other companies, but they all
started to sound the same after a while. I had grown cynical and
could see the grim truth behind the happy interview-speak.

The professional career advice wasn't working and I blamed

myself. What was wrong with me? Why couldn't I find a happy home in Corporate America?

How I Escaped

As my midcareer crisis worsened, I started to think seriously about making a radical change. An acquaintance of mine had started a consulting business and seemed to have the perfect life. She worked on interesting projects for lots of different companies and never got bored. What if I tried the same thing?

Until then, I had never considered the idea of launching my own business. Who was I to think I had what it took to succeed as an entrepreneur? Twelve years in Corporate America taught me to avoid risks and always cover my butt.

But I knew I had to do something. I asked the freelancers and consultants I knew for advice, and they gave me the inspiration and encouragement I needed to get serious. The funny thing is that as soon as I seriously considered the idea and gave myself permission to think big, I realized that striking out on my own was the perfect solution.

I knew how to write a good business plan, so I decided to write one for myself. Step 1 involved taking small freelance projects on the side and socking away some of my salary for future rainy days.

When I was ready for step 2, I put together a proposal for my boss and pitched the idea of leaving my job with a signed agreement to work twenty hours a week for my old company as a consultant. It was a ballsy idea, but I had crunched the numbers and found that the arrangement could save my company money while saving my sanity. It was a "win–win," as they say in corporate-speak.

My boss seemed open to the idea, but before the conversation could get very far, my best-laid plans fell to pieces when the latest round of corporate layoffs was announced.

While my co-workers prayed that their names wouldn't be on the hit list, I found myself fantasizing about getting downsized. I approached Human Resources and asked if they were accepting volunteers. I knew I was taking a major risk. If they said no, I would be exposing my carefully maintained façade as a happy corporate camper for nothing. I decided the risk was worth it for the potential payoff—a decent severance package that would help me get my new business up and running.

Thanks to the approval of my supportive and surprisingly open-minded boss, I was able to make a deal. Unfortunately, that meant no part-time consulting work, so I walked out the door with exactly zero prospects. I was so excited about my fresh new start that I hardly cared.

When I told my co-workers I was leaving, most of them thought I was insane. "Are you sure?" was the most popular response to my thrilling news. They could understand the impulse, but they couldn't believe I was going through with it.

I felt like I had already waited too long. Fortunately, I have never regretted the decision for a minute, not even during those scary first months on my own when money was tight.

☕ I Got Out with a Little Help from My Friends

Later, I realized how much I owed to those freelancers and entrepreneurs who took the time to help me. When I was at my lowest and had resigned myself to thirty-odd more years on the corporate hamster wheel, hope came to me in the form of these successful corporate escapees who were living the dream. Their stories showed me that escape was possible if I was willing to get creative.

Now I want to pass on the favor and share the lessons I learned the hard way. This is the book that I so desperately needed when I was standing in your shiny but painful corporate shoes.

I spent three years talking to corporate all-stars and escapees—from entry-level college grads to millionaire managing directors. I asked them about what they liked and disliked about the corporate grind. I grilled them about the challenges of leaving and the secrets they discovered along the way. I learned a lot about how and why the best and the brightest employees are leaving Corporate America, and I'm sharing it with you.

Whether you want to start a business, follow a passion, or simply find more time and energy for your personal life, this book can help. I wrote it for all of you who can't bear the thought of another Monday in a cubicle; for everyone who has ever fantasized about a different career.

Trust me. You don't have to stay stuck in a job you hate, and you don't have to starve to find work that you love. All you need is a plan and a little bit of nerve.

Do you really need this book? Are you just having a bad week or are you at the end of your rope?

Take this quiz to find out if you need to make an escape from Corporate America.

1. Rate your general job satisfaction:

   a. I love what I do.

   b. I have more good days than bad days.

   c. It could be worse, I suppose.

   d. I hate my job.

2. If you won or inherited a million dollars tomorrow, would you continue on the same career path?

   a. Definitely. I'd take a great vacation and buy a few toys, then get back to work.

   b. Probably not. With a financial cushion, I would likely take the time to explore my options.

   c. Hell, no! Are you crazy?

3. Which statement best expresses your feelings toward your job?

   a. I enjoy what I do for the most part.

   b. Sometimes I fantasize about quitting to do something else.

c. I am actively exploring other career options.

d. I only stay in my job for the paycheck. If money weren't an issue, I would leave.

4. What are your long-term career goals?

a. I am on a good career path, and my current job is a step along that path.

b. I feel a bit stuck and unsatisfied, but I'm not sure what I want to do instead.

c. The idea of staying on my current career path for the rest of my life gives me the cold sweats.

5. Are you pursuing your dream career?

a. Yes.

b. I'm not sure.

c. No.

6. Do you get the Sunday-night blues?

a. Not really.

b. Sometimes.

c. I get the every-night blues.

7. How do you feel at the end of an average workday?

a. Proud and happy.

b. Tired, but satisfied.

c. What was the point?

d. Miserable.

8. Where do you see yourself in five years?

a. In a bigger job at my current company or at a similar firm.

b. On a different career path within the corporate world.

    c. Out of corporate life. I know I need to make a change, but I'm not ready yet.

    d. Stuck in this hellish job or one like it. I'm miserable, but I can't see a way out.

9. Do you feel energetic and positive at work?

    a. Most of the time.

    b. Occasionally, but not as much as I'd like.

    c. Rarely or never.

10. Which of the following are among the positive aspects of your current job? Check all that apply.

    _____ Interesting work.

    _____ Growth opportunities.

    _____ Great boss.

    _____ Pleasant co-workers.

    _____ Fair pay.

    _____ Good benefits.

    _____ Flexibility.

    _____ Fulfillment.

    _____ Pride in what I do.

    _____ A company that cares about me and/or treats me well.

11. Which of the following are among the negative aspects of your job? Check all that apply.

    _____ I spend excessive amounts of time in meetings, documenting meetings, and scheduling follow-up meetings.

    _____ I can't remember the last time I felt truly excited about a work project.

    _____ I put in long hours mostly because of other people's ego trips. This includes face time, cleaning up messes, or staying late because others screw up or delay decisions.

_____I need at least two levels of approval on any decision.

_____Knowledge and ability are less important than who I know and how well I can BS.

_____I'm not quite sure what my job accomplishes, aside from making money for shareholders and senior management.

_____I don't feel passionate about anything I do at work. It feels like I'm putting in time for a paycheck.

_____I dread going to work most mornings and come home exhausted.

_____I don't see a future that I can get excited about.

_____I have been a victim of or a witness to bullying or blatantly unfair treatment.

Calculating Your Score

- For questions 1–9, give yourself 3 points for every A answer, 2 points for every B answer, 1 point for every C answer, and 0 points for every D answer.

- For question 10, give yourself 1 point for every item you checked.

- For question 11, deduct 1 point for every item you checked. Deduct 2 points each for checking either of the last two items.

What Your Score Means

28–37 **You are ridiculously satisfied.** Against all odds, you love your corporate job. You might want to read on for a true appreciation of just how good you've got it.

17–27 **You are on the fence.** Your corporate job is okay, but something is missing. If your current career isn't your true calling, what is? This book can help you explore your options.

6–16 **You are disgruntled.** You don't like your corporate job, but you're trying to make it work. Unfortunately, your feelings of frustration and rage may be starting to take a toll on your personal life. Read on for some solutions.

Less than 5 **You need an intervention. Stat.** Your corporate job is making you miserable. You desperately need to read this book and figure out your escape plan.

PART I

PLAN YOUR ESCAPE

ONE

This Is Not Your Father's Job Market

If you cannot work with love but only with distaste, it is better that you should leave your work.

—Kahlil Gibran

So I was sitting in my cubicle today, and I realized, ever since I started working, every single day of my life has been worse than the day before it. So that means that every single day that you see me, that's on the worst day of my life.

—Ron Livingston as Peter Gibbons in *Office Space*

Some of the most seemingly successful corporate movers and shakers have a dirty little secret. They hate their jobs.

Bob in Accounting is burned out and on the verge of going postal—better stay away from the mailroom. Diane the VP of sales just got downsized for the second time in two years, and Ted the new marketing guy is counting the milliseconds until five o'clock.

The corporate career path can be exciting, well paid, and highly prestigious. On the flip side, Corporate America can also feel like a creativity-destroying, soul-deadening maze of politics and bureaucracy.

While some thrive in the rat race, others feel trapped. If you're sick of trying to conform to the corporate dress code, the corporate mind-set, and the corporate "culture," you're not alone.

If you picked up this book, it's because there's a part of you that dreams of a career more fulfilling than your current nine-to-five rut. A little voice inside has been telling you that something has to change.

So why haven't you made a break for it? Wiggling free from the golden handcuffs of a "good job" that's making you miserable isn't easy. The idea of walking away from a steady paycheck and health benefits can be terrifying—especially if you're not 100 percent sure what you really want to do with your life.

That's how millions get stuck in lives of quiet corporate desperation. But it doesn't have to be that way. You don't have to choose between cubicle slavery and abject poverty.

Today there are plenty of job options beyond the corporate ladder. And there are plenty of ways—both practical and radical— to make the leap from a life of daily distress to a career that inspires you.

☕ I Hate My Job

Recent surveys show that a record 50 percent of American workers are dissatisfied with their jobs and 80 percent fantasize about leaving their current gigs. Surprisingly, despite higher salaries and better benefits, corporate workers are more miserable than those in other types of jobs.

Studies have revealed that employees of small companies are more than twice as satisfied as employees of large corporations. Meanwhile, free agents and entrepreneurs are even happier, with 87 percent reporting they are satisfied with their jobs.

"Corporate America is not aligned with the needs and require-

> "Sometimes I fantasize about getting hit by a car," confides Dina P., a midlevel manager for a large financial services corporation. "Nothing too serious. Just bad enough that I have to miss work for a while."

ments of its increasingly diverse workforce, and radical changes in attitude mean that a growing number of young Americans are dissatisfied, disengaged, and unproductive," according to a report by researchers from The Concours Group, who conducted a survey of more than seven thousand U.S. workers.

Of course, millions of people in other professions experience similar issues, but corporate types face unique challenges. After years of ascending the corporate ladder, most have attained a certain salary level and a certain degree of career success. Feelings of identity, self-worth, and belonging are all tied up in their job titles. They feel like they have a lot to lose by walking away.

Suck It Up, Cry-Baby

So what's wrong with these people? They're not ditch diggers or sweatshop laborers. Dina and David have cushy office jobs, make good money, and enjoy generous 401(k) plans. They should be happy, right?

Your grandparents would have scoffed at the concept of job fulfillment. Previous generations mostly saw work as a necessary evil—you weren't supposed to like it. They felt lucky just to earn enough money to feed their families and pay the rent. After all, does anybody really like his job?

The answer today is a resounding yes. There is a fortunate segment of the population made up of people who love what they do for a living. Their eyes light up when they talk about their work, and they're proud of the contributions they make.

> "I was always in a sour mood on Sunday nights because I had to wake up the next day and live a bad, bad nightmare all over again," says David R., a corporate attorney. "I felt like I was trapped in the movie *Groundhog Day.*"

Today work is more personal than ever before. Who you are is what you do. Sure, it's important to maintain perspective and not take opportunities for granted. With so much poverty and suffering in the world, the ability to choose a career that brings joy and fulfillment is a privilege. But for those who have the option, why waste the majority of your waking hours in a job that makes you miserable?

The average American spends more than one hundred thousand hours at work over the course of a lifetime. And that's a very conservative estimate, given ever-increasing workloads and later retirement ages. If you truly believe that work shouldn't be fulfilling or interesting, that it's just a means to a paycheck, then you're missing a lot.

Realistic Expectations

No job is all fun and free beer. That's why they call it work. Let's face it, even the most tedious corporate job beats cleaning toilets at the bus station or running the deep-fryer at Mickey D's.

And not every corporate job is a pit of Dilbertian despair. Some corporate executives love their work. They believe in their products and services and get a charge out of helping their companies succeed.

All jobs have both positives and negatives—and the negatives are different for every individual. One person might find number-crunching financial reports tedious while another thrives on the challenge. One employee may love the excitement of a demanding, competitive work environment while another gets ulcers just thinking about it.

Executives with seemingly great jobs can be just as unhappy as anyone else if their work lacks the elements that they value. For those looking primarily for financial gain or prestige, high-level corporate gigs can be very rewarding. For others who prioritize flexibility or exercising their creativity, corporate life can be hell.

It's not just about the money. A recent survey by The Conference Board found that 17 percent of those making $15,000 a year say they are satisfied with their jobs, compared with just 14 percent of those who make more than $50,000.

Marcus Buckingham, the author of *The One Thing You Need to Know* and an expert on employee satisfaction, told *USA Today* that some of the most disengaged people he's encountered were senior executives running empires and earning millions of dollars.

But My Job's Not So Bad . . .

Not all of the escape artists that I interviewed hated their jobs. In fact, many enjoyed their work, but still felt that there was something missing.

"I had the greatest corporate job ever," says Tracy Dyer, who worked for an internal innovation consulting group at Best Buy and was instrumental in the launch of Geek Squad. "But I always really wanted to work for myself."

For Tracy, it wasn't about escaping from Corporate America, it was about living her dream of becoming an entrepreneur. "My father always told me, 'You're only truly free if you work for yourself,'" she recalls. And Tracy's father, the bestselling author Dr. Wayne Dyer, spoke from experience. Dr. Dyer was on the tenure track as a university professor when he left to take a chance on a career as an author and a speaker.

Tracy followed in his footsteps when she abandoned the

> "Oh, you hate your job? Why didn't you say so? There's a support group for that. It's called EVERYBODY, and they meet at the bar."
> —**Drew Carey**, *The Drew Carey Show*

corporate career path to start Urban Junket, a handbag and accessory company, with her friend and former colleague Tracy Arnold.

☕ The Price of Job Satisfaction

Torn between a well-paying job that doesn't inspire you and a less lucrative dream job? A study by economists John Helliwell and Haifang Huang at the University of British Columbia found that money is not as critical to life satisfaction as many think. Moving all the way from the bottom of the income scale to the top is only likely to boost your overall satisfaction with life by about 10 percent.

This finding is backed up by numerous other studies showing that across-the-board increases in the standard of living haven't made people any happier. The disposable income of the average American has increased by about 80 percent since 1972, but the percentage of Americans describing themselves as "very happy" (about one-third) has barely budged in that same time frame.

So unless it's a matter of necessity, think twice before taking that higher-paying job for the money alone. Having more cash to buy more stuff won't really make you happier.

The Corporate Balance Sheet

THE BENEFITS OF CORPORATE JOBS	THE DRAWBACKS OF CORPORATE JOBS
• Steady paycheck.	• Excessive workloads.
• Benefits.	• Grueling commutes.
• Paid vacation days.	• Endless meetings.
• Prestige.	• Cubicles.
• Free office supplies.	• Fluorescent lighting.
• Open bar at the holiday party.	• Tedious work.
• Résumé building.	• Sense of worthlessness.
• Mom's approval.	• Bad coffee.
• Structured career path.	• Neckties and panty hose.
• Friendships forged in shared misery.	• Mean and/or idiotic bosses.

Bad Corporate Versus Good Corporate

Good Corporate Jobs

There are extremes in the corporate world—the very good, the very bad, and the mind-numbingly tedious in the middle. Not all corporations are hell. Even in today's world, there are some that people actually enjoy working for.

These businesses recognize that employees who are treated fairly do a better job. Companies with high rates of employee morale are more productive and more profitable, primarily due to reduced turnover and more engaged workers.

Toward that end, some large companies have established on-site day care, flexible work arrangements, career development training, and other innovative programs. These benefits can make a huge difference in employees' lives. Flexible work arrangements, for example, can mean the difference between chronic exhaustion and a healthy work–life balance. Training programs can prevent burnout by offering new challenges. Read on in chapter 5 for more about corporations that get high ratings from their employees.

Interesting work, good management, and a sense of contribution are other factors that can transform corporate drudgery into job satisfaction. Many workers will gladly put up with bureaucracy and other headaches as long as they find their work interesting. And even in an otherwise unfeeling corporate monolith, a good manager can create a fair and rewarding work environment.

Bad Corporate Jobs

For many, however, the term *Corporate America* still conjures up images of zombies in suits shuffling dead-eyed from meeting to cubicle to meeting. Okay, that's a little overdramatic. Corporate workers may *look* like zombies, but the majority don't actually eat brains.

Despite offering good salaries and decent health plans (though this has been changing in recent years, sadly), Corporate America has gotten a bad rap. Can thousands of *Dilbert* cartoons really be wrong?

The truth is that for some corporate workers, the bureaucracy and BS are annoying but tolerable parts of the job. For others, the drawbacks of corporate life cause unbearable stress and frustration.

Bait and Switch

How did you end up in corporate hell? Many smart young things were raised to aspire to the life of the hotshot business exec, to the Holy Grail of a snazzy job complete with fancy title and nice suits. It all looked very exciting on TV. It was a shock to find out that corporate life rarely includes hot sex in the mailroom.

Instead you found overwork, corrupt management, mass layoffs, and layers and layers of insane bosses.

For most, corporate dissatisfaction is not about laziness or reluctance to work hard. On the contrary, the majority have worked their butts off to pay their dues—only to get stuck in the no-man's-land of middle management, wondering what the point is.

Those who hate their corporate jobs generally stay—and ignore their real career dreams—for practical reasons. You'd have to be crazy to walk away from a stable job with a steady paycheck, right?

But the supposed stability of a corporate job is an illusion. In Corporate America today, you can be sent packing with little no-

> "Without work, all life goes rotten. But when work is soulless, life stifles and dies."
>
> **—Albert Camus**

tice no matter how well you perform or how long you've been loyal to your employer.

This painful realization has inspired a widespread change in attitude. If all jobs have risks, why not go for one that inspires you? There are no guarantees.

Today's top performers don't want to be enslaved by a faceless company. They want work that is meaningful. They want to feel excited about what they do every day—or most days, anyway. They want to leave a legacy in this world beyond landfills of old memos and obsolete cell phones.

The Rules of Engagement

The problem with many corporate environments is that they are still patterned after the work world of the 1950s. The system worked back in the days when employees pledged undying loyalty in return for guaranteed jobs for life.

But in today's work environment, most employees have already lived through numerous layoffs, downsizings, and reorganizations. Everybody knows that working hard is no guarantee of advancement or even continued employment.

At the same time, companies heap more and more work on the employees who survive the purges. This guarantees that many of those who remain are burned out and fed up.

They are no longer engaged at work, which is bad for their mental health and bad for the company. HR types define *engaged employees* as "those who feel a strong sense of personal accomplishment in what they do and are willing to invest discretionary effort to see that the organization succeeds."

In 2005, Towers Perrin surveyed approximately eighty-six thousand people working full-time for large and midsize companies in sixteen countries. This global study found that a vast majority was moderately engaged at best, and nearly a quarter were actively disengaged.

STAYING SANE IN CORPORATE AMERICA

The Practical Way

Take a mental health day tomorrow. Do something that you love that you usually don't have time for.

The Radical Way

Negotiate a flexible work schedule with your boss (see chapter 6 to find out how).

The survey also identified the top drivers of employee engagement—including several that are often lacking in large companies:

- **Opportunities to learn and develop new skills.** In bureaucratic corporate environments, smart employees frequently feel stuck performing duties below their ability level. Without opportunities to learn, workers swiftly become bored and uninspired.

  Most are seeking out jobs where they can be challenged to grow. Instead, they are challenged by having more to do—overwhelming workloads of mundane tasks and busywork.

- **Input into decision making.** Large organizations tend to be extremely layered and political. As a result, the average employee has very little real decision-making ability. Multiple approvals are needed for even the smallest decisions. Managers waste their days on cover-your-ass (CYA) tactics to avoid being blamed in the event something goes wrong.

- **Reputation of the company as a good employer.** The American corporation in general is experiencing a major reputation crisis. In the wake of Enron, Worldcom, and plenty of other embarrassments, employees are cynical. Many have trouble believing that any company has their best interests in mind or that any managers can be trusted.

WORDS OF WISDOM FROM THE CORPORATE SAGE

Dilbert Creator Scott Adams's
Top Five Tips for Corporate Burnouts

What book about corporate dysfunction would be complete without insights from the creator of *Dilbert,* Scott Adams? Adams parlayed his time in the corporate world into a multimillion-dollar business. More than ten million copies of *Dilbert* books are currently in print; Adams has also published two novels and launched a natural foods company.

He not only escaped from Corporate America, but also became a hero to all the rest of us downtrodden wage slaves. He almost made corporate cool. Okay, maybe not cool, but definitely funny.

I asked him to share his advice on kicking corporate and building an empire.

Tip 1: Don't Settle

Even as a kid, Adams wanted to be a cartoonist. But he looked around and noted that "most people seemed to end up in dead-end business jobs" and figured he would probably have to settle for a similar future.

After college, Adams landed a job as a teller at Crocker National Bank in San Francisco. He worked his way up the ladder to middle management over the next eight-plus years before moving on to

Pacific Bell. Along the way, he came close to giving up on his dream of becoming a cartoonist entirely.

"People are unhappy day-to-day, but if you ask them if they're satisfied, they'll say yes," says Adams. "It's a rationalization process to convince yourself that you made the right decision."

Luckily for Adams, he eventually found the courage to go after the career he really wanted.

Tip 2: Seize Opportunities

The character Dilbert was born as a doodle during a boring meeting. Adams soon began drawing Dilbert's continuing adventures to entertain his co-workers and mock his superiors. The enthusiastic response gave Adams the idea that he might be on to something.

"During the period when *Dilbert* first launched, there was a lot of downsizing and everyone was disgusted with corporations," explains Adams. He had a feeling people would be able to relate—and he was right.

If Adams hadn't had the confidence and the determination to take his office in-joke to the next level, he might still be sitting in staff meetings today.

Tip 3: Be Persistent

While working on bringing Dilbert to life, Adams saw a TV show featuring a successful cartoonist's advice for beginning comic artists. Adams wrote a letter asking for additional tips and received an encouraging reply that advised him to keep trying, even if he didn't succeed at first. The more experienced cartoonist saw potential in Adams's work.

But Adams didn't heed the advice. After he sent his sample strips out to a few publishers and was rejected, he decided to forget about his dream.

A year later, out of the blue, Adams received a second letter from the successful cartoonist. "He was cleaning out his office, found my original letter, and wanted to make sure I hadn't given up," says Adams.

The letter gave Adams the push he needed to commit to getting his work published. Soon after, United Media gave Adams his big break and syndicated the comic strip.

Tip 4: Consider Your Job a Learning Experience

"People who spend time in Corporate America come out knowing so much more," says Adams. "You have more connections and skills and ideas." He credits the explosive success of *Dilbert* to lessons he learned in business school and during his stint in the cubicle maze. For example, he was one of the first cartoonists to use market research and actively solicit feedback from readers.

"People told me constantly that they enjoyed Dilbert most in the office," he says. Early strips focused more on Dilbert's home life, but readers thought his job was funnier. Adams took the suggestion and began to focus the strip on Dilbert at work. Good choice.

Tip 5: Don't Be Hasty

Following your dream doesn't mean leaping without a net. Even after landing a deal with United Media, Adams didn't immediately quit his day job. "Part of it was that I still needed the money," he explains. "The strip was only in a hundred or so papers at first, and I wasn't confident that I could do it for the rest of my life."

Adams found that his corporate day job became much less depressing once he had another plan in place. As soon as he knew he wouldn't be trapped in his cubicle forever, the frustrations were a lot easier to bear.

Besides, every day at the office provided a wealth of material for the comic strip. Of course, as soon as he started making some serious bucks, Adams quit his day job. Wouldn't you?

Corporate History 101

The good news is that the traditional corporate grind is going the way of the brontosaurus and affordable health care. The regimented corporate structures of the last millennium are not working anymore for anyone. Not Generation X and Generation Y

workers who value balance and passion above power and prestige. Not the aging Baby Boomers who are looking toward retirement and the prospect of more time with their families, less at
work.

Corporate Malaise: A Brief History

1288	The oldest surviving business corporation in the world, Sweden's Stora Kopperberg, is founded.
1628	"Corporations cannot commit treason, nor be outlawed," writes the great English legalist Edward Coke, "for they have no soul."
Late 1600s	The corporation emerges as a popular business structure. Previously, companies were formed by small groups of men who both owned and managed their businesses. In the corporation, one group of managers runs the firm, while another group, the shareholders, owns it.
1720	The English Parliament bans the corporation after the collapse of the South Sea Company (a precursor to Enron, et al.) and a proliferation of corporate hijinks. But no law can hold the modern corporation back for long.
1776	In *The Wealth of Nations*, legendary economist Adam Smith writes that "negligence and profusion" will be the inevitable results when businesses organize as corporations. Smith feels strongly that managers should not be trusted to steward "other people's money."
1813	The first significant American industrial corporation, the Boston Manufacturing Company, is established.
1886	In the landmark Supreme Court case *Santa Clara County v. Southern Pacific Railroad Company*, corporations are granted "artificial personhood," subject to protection under the Fourteenth Amendment.
1956	*The Organization Man*, a book by William H. Whyte extolling the virtues of the good corporate soldier, is published.
1968	The cubicle is invented by Bob Propst of office furniture company Herman Miller. Originally viewed as an improvement over the open office plan, Propst's design is adapted in order to cram more employees into smaller spaces. Propst will come to regret his invention: "They make little bitty cubicles and stuff people in them. Barren, rat-hole places. . . . "

1989	The first *Dilbert* cartoon is published, starring powerless corporate schlub Dilbert and his dangerously stupid pointy-haired boss. Dilbert strikes a major nerve with corporate workers and will go on to appear in two-thousand-plus newspapers and on millions of cubicle walls all over the world.
1991	Douglas Coupland's generation-defining book, *Generation X,* coins a new term for the cubicle—"a veal-fattening pen."
1999	*Office Space,* the classic film about modern work life, is released. TPS cover sheets and Milton's stapler feel like cinema verité to millions of downtrodden cubicle dwellers. The movie will go on to become a cult classic and gross millions in video and DVD sales.
	Thousands of corporate workers flee their boring jobs for dot-coms.
2000	The NASDAQ crashes and the tech bubble bursts. Thousands of dot-com workers return to corporate cubicle farms with their tails between their legs.
2001	The United States enters a recession, ending the longest economic expansion in history.
	Enron collapses, unveiling the biggest corporate scandal in US history.
2002	The Worldcom scandal continues the parade of corporate crooks on the front pages.
2005	The number of corporate workers fired in mass layoffs reaches 5.4 million since 2001.
	Cornell University announces that Americans now work more hours per year than even the Japanese, who invented *karoshi,* or "death by overwork."
2007	Surveys show American job satisfaction has hit a record low, with more than 50 percent of workers saying they are dissatisfied.

☕ RIP Organization Man

The Organization Man, published by William H. Whyte Jr. in 1956, defined *career success* for American generations past. Whyte's Organization Man believed in denying his own goals and interests in service to a large company. He was unfailingly loyal to his employer in exchange for complete job security for life.

The Organization Man was declared dead years ago—killed by changing times and corporate greed. It was a painful but necessary mercy killing.

The change began in the 1980s and 1990s. Layoffs and downsizing became more and more common. Loyal Organization Men (and Women) who had sacrificed for their companies found themselves unexpectedly let go to fend for themselves in an unfamiliar job market.

Many of today's Generation X and Y workers watched their parents go through it, only to experience the sting of downsizing themselves years later.

Corporations decided to stop living up to their end of the loyalty bargain. In addition to downsizing, some companies started cutting benefits, eliminating pension funds, and even stealing from employee 401(k) plans.

Employees had little recourse but to put up with it when the job market was tight. Interestingly, the tables were briefly turned in the late 1990s during the dot-com boom. Dot-coms and technology firms lured the most qualified people with stock options and cool perks. Workers left Corporate America in droves, and it wasn't just about the stock options. Those of us who felt stifled in corporate bureaucracies jumped at the chance to do more interesting, creative work. Unfortunately, when the bubble burst, both corporate and dot-com employees found themselves in the unemployment lines.

Things went from bad to worse on September 11, 2001. It was a day that changed everything for everybody. Faced with incredible tragedy, we were all forced to reevaluate what was really important. Did we really want to spend our lives on work that wasn't meaningful?

	BABY BOOMERS born 1946–1961	GENERATION X born 1961–1981	MILLENNIALS born 1982–2003
Life stage	The Boomers are nearing the traditional retirement age and wondering what's next. Many are thinking about their legacies and the dreams they have yet to fulfill.	Cynical Gen Xers don't want to work for "the man" the way their parents did. Many have become parents and are fighting the epic battle to balance work, family, and a rewarding life.	Fresh-faced Millennials are shying away from the old-school corporate career track. These fussed-over kids grew into self-analytical adults who are not willing to settle for boring, ordinary jobs.
Work philosophy	Driven to succeed.	Success is a balanced life.	Work should be meaningful.

The New Work Order

Now three generations of disgruntled corporate employees share the same conference rooms and watercoolers. The Baby Boomers, the Generation Xers, and the Millennials have very different priorities and personalities. However, they all seem to have one thing in common—they're fed up with Corporate America and looking for more meaningful work.

Luckily for everyone, a world of new work options has opened up, driven by these changing attitudes and the possibilities of technology.

People are starting their own businesses in record numbers. There are more than twenty million small businesses in the United States today, 25 percent of them technology-driven. Many of these are part of the "solopreneur" trend—one-person businesses, freelancers, side and weekend ventures, eBay storefronts, and more.

Technology has also enabled new job options such as telecommuting and job sharing. Most jobs can now be performed from anywhere, even if Corporate America continues to try to keep us in cubicles.

The changes we've seen so far are only the beginning. In their book, *Workforce Crisis: How to Beat the Coming Shortage of Skills and Talent*, human resources consultants Ken Dychtwald, Tamara Erickson, and Robert Morison predict a bigger shakeup ahead. "As the massive boomer generation begins to retire and fewer skilled workers are available to replace them, companies in industrialized markets will face a labor shortage and brain drain of dramatic proportions," the authors caution.

According to writer and business futurist Joyce Gioia, there will be approximately nine million more knowledge worker jobs than knowledge workers by 2010. That means the power will be in the hands of the best employees. Corporations will be forced to change to attract and retain talented workers.

But what if you don't have the patience to hang on that long? Are you merely temporarily burned out or are you ready to plan your escape from Corporate America—for the sake of your sanity?

We Are All Entrepreneurs Now

The age of the employee is over. No matter whom you work for or how many stock options you own, the future of your career is ultimately up to you.

Back in the day, you went to work for one company and trusted that the firm would take care of you for life, or at least until you were presented with a shiny gold watch at your retirement banquet. I have seen photos of both my grandfathers posing proudly at their retirement parties after fifty years of work at their respective companies. It's no wonder they always seemed mildly alarmed when I announced I was changing jobs again.

Today we all know that there are no guarantees. Your career is a business and you are already something of an entrepreneur even if you sell your time and services to just one company in exchange for a salary and benefits.

You may have found a good business model for You, Inc., in Corporate America. But that doesn't mean that you don't have other options or that you can't find a better deal if you get fed up with your current client. After all, your employers won't hesitate to cut you loose if your position stops making business sense for them.

BREAK UP WITH YOUR JOB

Do you secretly fantasize about more attractive jobs? That's a pretty good sign that the thrill is gone at the office. Or maybe your relationship with your current gig has always been a little bit dysfunctional. Bad jobs can have a lot in common with bad relationships. It might be time to listen to the advice of your well-meaning friends and make a clean break. Here's a list of jobs you should ditch like that mouth breather you met on Match.com.

The Job You're Settling For

It's not a bad job. It could be a lot worse. There are things you like about it—maybe you have a nice office, or a good dental plan, or a prestigious title. But something major is missing. That spark. That passion. The idea of waking up and going to this job for the next thirty years makes you: (a) queasy; (b) depressed; or (c) suicidal.

Would you tell your best friend to stay with a boring partner just in case nothing better comes along? Your job is exactly like a character in a predictable romantic comedy—say, Bill Pullman in *Sleepless in Seattle*. You know the heroine's going to dump him for the dashing but risky hero by the end of the third act. Don't you want a happy ending, too?

The Clingy Stalker Job

This is the job that, much like the brilliant Glenn Close in *Fatal Attraction*, refuses to be ignored. Working around the clock is de rigueur. Vacations are for losers. Extra-long bathroom breaks are frowned upon.

Like a clingy stalker boyfriend, this job has an addictive quality. It makes you feel important and needed. For a while. But these situations never end well. Eventually, you'll find a bunny boiling on your stove.

Wouldn't you rather have a job that you pursue instead of one so desperate and neurotic that it won't leave you alone? You'd tell a friend to step away from the drama (and maybe get a restraining order), right?

The Job That You're Using for the Money

It's all about the benjamins with this one. This job buys you nice things and foots the bill for your sweet little love nest, but is there anything else to love? If you hit the numbers in the lottery, would you even call in the morning?

Material things are nice. But when money is your only reason to stay, you will quickly start to resent the fact that you're enslaved by a paycheck. You deserve better, and your job deserves better.

Do you really want to be the shameless gold digger clinging to the rich old geezer who thinks you love him? Your job is never going to conveniently keel over and leave you millions. The smart move is to find a career that can pay the bills without making you feel dirty.

You Don't Have to Settle

If you are truly unhappy in your corporate job, you owe it to yourself to make a change. Too many people resign themselves to staying in unsatisfying jobs because they don't see a way out. They don't think they can make a living doing what they love, so they set aside their dreams. Others stay because they fear they don't have the talent or the ability to succeed. Instead they stay stuck, grow more bitter by the day, and medicate their unhappiness with tequila and Twinkies.

This is tragic because escaping from Corporate America doesn't have to mean quitting your day job. At least not at first.

Are you willing to spend the rest of your working life in corporate purgatory? If now isn't the right time to make a change, will it ever be? You've already wasted enough time. Stop trying to love the job you hate. Stop trying to convince yourself that you don't deserve more. Stop making excuses and make a change.

> **Why I Got Out: Corporate Escapees on the Worst Aspects of Corporate Life**
>
> The worst thing is if your boss has control over your future and control over whether you fail or succeed. He's both judge and jury. It's not your good work that makes a difference.
>
> **—Scott Adams, creator of *Dilbert* (and former middle manager)**
>
> What bothered me the most was that I just didn't care what I was doing for twelve hours each day. There was no passion. . . .
>
> **—Sarma Melngailis, successful restaurateur (and former investment banking analyst)**
>
> I felt completely empty at the end of the day. I came home and felt like I had done nothing important in the world.
>
> **—Andrea Beaman, chef/reality TV star (and former administrative assistant)**

TWO

The Trouble with the Rat Race

The trouble with the rat race is that even if you win, you're still a rat.

—Lily Tomlin

Bureaucrats: they are dead at thirty and buried at sixty.

—Frank Lloyd Wright

Staying in a job that makes you miserable can take a serious toll on your mental and physical health. Job stress has been linked to ailments including anxiety, depression, ulcers, chronic back pain, high blood pressure, and heart conditions.

Overall, these ailments add up to $300 billion in health care costs each year. Is that 4 percent raise you're working so hard for really worth it?

The Phases of Corporate Disillusionment

Chances are your job wasn't always a soul-sucking pit of despair. There was a time when your hopes were as bright and shiny as your brand-new stapler.

But for most of us, it was all downhill from there.

Phase 1. The Honeymoon: "I Love My New Corporate Job!"

During the honeymoon phase, there are endless possibilities. Maybe you're a fresh-faced newbie to the corporate world or maybe you're a seasoned veteran making a change from another company. Either way, a new job is your chance to start over with a clean desk and a clean slate.

You have new people to meet, new things to learn. Your boss is still on her best behavior. There is still a chance that this will be the job of your dreams.

This giddy enchantment might last for months or it might be over by noon on your first day. Inevitably, though, the honeymoon phase has to end. Your boss and co-workers will eventually show their more annoying sides. The new and different evolves into the same old, same old.

If you're lucky, the good outweighs the bad and the honeymoon phase transitions into a happy marriage. Sure, you occasionally have bad days at the office, but you're basically content.

If you're not so lucky, the honeymoon phase is just the first step in the corporate disillusionment spiral.

Typical Honeymoon-Phase Behavior

- E-mailing your friends and former colleagues to brag about your great new job.
- Inviting your boss out to lunch to discuss your brilliant ideas for improving the department.
- Volunteering for high-profile projects to show your value.
- Writing a five-year plan to document your impending meteoric rise to senior management.
- Feeling smug.

Phase 2. Denial: "My Job Is Great, I Tell You, Just Great."

As the honeymoon glow fades, many continue to cling to the hope that good times will return. During the denial phase, you can't quite face the fact that your new job sucks. You're certain that your boss is just "demanding," not psychotic. You feel sure that you'll love working eighty hours a week once you get used to it.

It can be tough to admit that you've made a mistake, especially if you had high hopes for your new position. It's much easier to believe that you're overreacting or that the danger signs you're seeing aren't real. After all, if you admit that your new job is a lemon, you may have to do something about it.

Typical Denial-Phase Behavior
- E-mailing your friends and former colleagues to assure them that the new job is still just great, seriously, you mean it.
- Ignoring the writing on the cubicle wall.
- Laughing on the outside.

Phase 3. Bitching: "This Job Sucks."

During the bitching phase, the anger you suppressed during the denial phase comes out in full force. You're finally ready to admit that your job is miserable. In fact, you can't seem to shut up about it.

Everybody likes to vent sometimes, but corporate malcontents turn complaining into an art form. You can't really blame them for taking advantage of one of their few creative outlets.

At first, it's a huge relief to be able to vent your frustrations to your co-workers. Just keep in mind that getting stuck in the bitching phase can be hazardous to your health. Spending five days a week in an intensely negative environment makes a bad job worse. On those rare days when you're feeling okay, one of your co-workers is sure to bring you down with a bitch session.

The other problem with the bitching phase is that your negative attitude often doesn't quit at five o'clock. Most likely, you continue to moan and complain about the office to your friends and family. For a while, they will be sympathetic. But even those who love you will eventually get tired of hearing about your troubles at work.

Typical Bitching-Phase Behavior

- E-mailing your friends and former colleagues to tell them you hate your job and want to die.
- Taking long lunches with your co-workers to complain about the latest outrage.
- Inventing insulting nicknames for your boss and other members of the management team.
- Rolling your eyes.

Phase 4. Bargaining: "I Can Make It Work Somehow."

Once you've grown bored with constant bitching (this might take awhile), you'll probably spend some time in the bargaining phase. Nobody wants to stay miserable, but the prospect of finding a new job (or—even scarier—a whole new career) is often just too daunting.

This is true especially for those who are suffering in jobs that have some redeeming qualities. Particularly if those redeeming qualities include a nice salary and benefits. During the bargaining phase, you will search desperately for some way to make things work. If you're bored, you might volunteer to take on a new project. If you have a difficult boss, you might look harder for common ground. If you're overworked, you might try scaling back or finally schedule your overdue vacation. You might even look into the idea of making a move within your department or company.

The good news is that these tactics often work. Sometimes a small change is all you need to make a bad job good again. It's certainly worth a try, especially if you're at a point in your life when making a larger change would be very difficult.

Still, there are times when it's impossible to drive a good enough bargain. Maybe your boss will shoot down your idea, or maybe you'll actually get what you want—only to find that it's not enough.

Typical Bargaining-Phase Behavior

- E-mailing your friends and former colleagues to pick their brains about your new plan.
- Searching internal job listings daily.
- Making pros and cons lists.
- Justifying.
- Stockpiling good karma.

Phase 5. Depression: "What's the Point? There's No Way Out."

After bargaining fails, many fall into job depression. You might get a mild case of the blues, or you might feel severely bummed out.

Until now, you were clinging to a sliver of hope that things could improve. No longer. During the depression phase, you may start neglecting your personal hygiene and compulsively start playing solitaire just to spite your boss.

This is rock bottom. Everything looks hopeless.

Typical Depression-Phase Behavior

- Ignoring e-mails from your friends and former colleagues.
- Muttering "It's just a job" over and over and over again.
- Hiding in the bathroom.
- Calling in sick and making up dead relatives.
- Regular Sunday-night sob-fests.

Phase 6. Acceptance or Change: "I Guess Things Could Be Worse" or "It's Time to Make a Change."

After you've wallowed in depression for a while, it's time to make a decision. Are you going to accept your corporate lot in life and try to make the best of it, or are you going to make a change?

Most of us are not gluttons for punishment and instead opt for a change of some kind. That could mean finding a job at a similar company or even a different department within your current organization. Any change is a move in the right direction. And who knows? Maybe a change of scene will be enough to get the sparkle back in your eye.

Or you may just be prolonging the agony. A small change is a whole lot easier than a big one, but sometimes it's not enough. You may temporarily relieve your symptoms only to find yourself back in the honeymoon phase, destined to begin the cycle of corporate disillusionment all over again. Sometimes it's just a matter of "same shit, different office."

Typical Change-Phase Behavior

- E-mailing your friends and former colleagues to ask for external job leads.
- Taking long lunches to interview or plan your next move.
- Fantasizing about your resignation scene.
- Rediscovering your happy place.
- Developing nostalgia for the good old days.

What's Your Damage?

So what exactly is it that you're so disgruntled about anyway? Before you can find a cure for your corporate blues, you'll have to take a good hard look at what's making you miserable.

Think about your misery as a learning experience. If you can understand what you don't like about your current situation, it will be much easier to determine what type of career change will make you happier.

Maybe you're overworked or maybe you're understimulated. Maybe you're pining for a true calling that seems unattainable. Maybe you're stuck working with a bunch of morons who don't appreciate you. Usually it's a combination of several factors.

Whatever your angst is, you can be sure there are others who have been through it. My research on corporate malcontents has identified six common reasons for dissatisfaction with cubicle life. Which ones are you suffering from?

1. Corporate Burnout
2. Terminal Boredom
3. Square Peg Syndrome
4. Balance Disorder
5. Meaning Deficiency
6. Toxic Workplace Blues

1. Corporate Burnout: "Stick a Fork in Me, I'm Done."

In today's Corporate America, burnout is an epidemic. Maybe that's because working long hours is a badge of honor in most firms. Throw in the constant stress caused by looming layoffs, excessive workloads, and other factors, and you've got a recipe for disaster.

The Mayo Clinic defines *burnout* as "a state of physical, emotional and mental exhaustion caused by long-term exposure to demanding work situations." And it's no joke. Dealing with extreme work stress and frustration on a long-term basis can have a serious impact on your health.

According to the American Psychological Association, burnout can cause depression, anxiety, and physical illness. People self-medicate with drugs, alcohol, or Krispy Kremes. Extended periods of burnout can even lead to physical and mental breakdowns, which include suicide, stroke, and heart attack.

Sometimes burnout is the result of being overworked, over-stressed, and just plain exhausted. You can get burned out even in a job you love if you push yourself too hard.

Another cause of burnout is simply being in the wrong career. It's exhausting to put on a happy façade every day, to summon the energy to care (or at least appear to care) about tedious busywork, to pretend to be someone you're not. In fact, suffering from any of the other five issues described in this chapter can also push you over the edge into burnout.

Many cope with corporate burnout by disengaging and doing the bare minimum to justify their paychecks. Ironically, they are so exhausted from working too hard that they start working too little.

Symptoms of Corporate Burnout

- You work nights and weekends. A lot.
- You feel tired and stressed out most of the time.
- You don't have time for the hobbies and social activities that you once enjoyed.
- You no longer feel much satisfaction from your achievements at work.
- You are irritable and impatient with co-workers or clients.

COMMON CAUSES OF JOB BURNOUT

- **Control issues.** Do you feel that you have little or no control over your work hours, your workload, or how you do your job?
- **Unclear expectations.** Is your job poorly defined? Do you struggle to understand what your boss expects of you?
- **Workplace drama.** Do you work with a bullying boss or conniving colleagues?
- **Value judgments.** Do you disagree with the values of your company or the way it does business?
- **Wrong job.** Do you feel you are working in a job that doesn't utilize your abilities and interests?
- **Excessive workload.** Do you work too many hours?
- **Monotony.** Do you struggle to stay focused in a job that doesn't engage you?

Cures for Burnout

Schedule your next vacation *now*. Even if you can't take off right away, knowing that there is relief on the horizon can do a lot to lessen your day-to-day stress. Take as much vacation time as you can get away with. Remember, there is never a good time to take a vacation. There will always be a project or a meeting or a boss who doesn't want you to go. Sure, be responsible and work around major commitments, but don't let yourself be bullied into putting your vacation off indefinitely. And don't feel pressured to take fewer days than you deserve or agree to be on call while you're away.

Use your vacation to decompress and spend quality time with your neglected friends and family. But also set aside a little time to really think about how you got so burned out in the first place. Were you just overdue for a break or do you need to make a change?

Take advantage of this time away from the office to consider your long-term career goals and what sacrifices you're willing to make. Away from the daily grind, you may be surprised at how much clearer your perspective becomes.

NEED A VACATION?

Experts say regular vacations can help ease even extreme job stress. Unfortunately, Americans live with the stingiest vacation allotment in the industrialized world—an average of 8.1 days annually after a year on the job and 10.2 days after three years, according to the Bureau of Labor Statistics.

Compare this with the French (twenty-five vacation days per year), the Germans (thirty vacation days), and even the Japanese (eighteen vacation days).

Surprisingly, half of US workers don't even take the vacation days they're given. US workers forfeited approximately 421 million vacation days in 2005. Are we gluttons for punishment?

Some of us are so tied up in our jobs that we can't bear the thought of time away. Or we just can't imagine that our colleagues could possibly manage without us.

But there are many more who actually fear taking a vacation. They feel the pressure from management: *There's so much work to do. What if something goes wrong and we need you?*

Nobody wants to risk leaving during a "critical" time for the company, or to take the chance that the bosses might realize they're replaceable. Maybe that's why 42 percent of those who take vacations perform some form of work while they're away. Others just fear the mountain of work they'll face when they return.

Edward W., a computer programmer for a major bank, says vacations "aren't worth the trouble." He works late for weeks before a planned vacation, preparing for any possible contingency during his absence. And when he returns, it's to an avalanche of e-mails and a towering inbox. "The first week back from vacation is hell," he says. "You're supposed to feel refreshed, but for me it's more like, *Oh yeah, it's still as awful as I remembered. And now there's no vacation to look forward to.*"

DARING TALES OF CORPORATE ESCAPE

Sarma's Story

Name: Sarma Melngailis

Former occupation: Investment banker

Current occupation: Owner of trendy Manhattan raw food restaurant Pure Food and Wine and CEO of One Lucky Duck, a company that manufactures and sells products for the raw and organic lifestyle through oneluckyduck.com and retail outlets.

Sarma Melngailis developed her passion for cooking at an early age. "My mother was a chef, so it was always a part of me," she recalls.

But in college, she also developed an interest in business and economics and ended up earning a dual degree from the prestigious Wharton School and the University of Pennsylvania.

After graduation, Sarma says she "just kind of fell into investment banking." It was what all of the other Wharton stars were pursuing, so she applied to the big investment banks and landed a position at Bear Stearns in New York City.

She compares her experience there to doing time in the marines. "Bear Stearns kicked my ass. I worked really, really hard." She spent late nights, every weekend, and marathon fifty-hour stretches in the office.

At first, she found the work exhilarating. "I liked the excitement of working on big deals." But the grueling schedule eventually caught up with her. "I used to go into the stairwell and cry because I was just so tired. I had to keep my game face on in front of people, but I would just hide away in the bathroom to escape and find peace."

She spent the next few years working for a top private equity firm and a leading hedge fund manager, but something was always missing. One day, a colleague volunteered some advice: "You always talk about food and restaurants. Why don't you do something in the food business, maybe work for a cooking magazine?"

Sarma was struck dumb. This person who barely knew her saw what she hadn't been able to see. "I realized that he was right. But I had already bought an apartment with a mortgage and I couldn't afford to take a pay cut. I almost cried, realizing I finally knew what I should do but I couldn't do it."

She soldiered on in her corporate job, but her heart wasn't in it. "I wanted to do something I was passionate about. What bothered me the most was that I just didn't care about what I was doing for ten hours every day," she recalls.

After she moved in with her then-fiancé and started sharing living expenses, Sarma felt she had more financial room to think about other job options. Eventually, she made a bold and brave decision. Sarma resigned from her well-paying job to attend the French Culinary Institute. She wasn't sure what she wanted to do after that, but she knew she had to pursue her dream of becoming a chef.

She never regretted her decision, but she did struggle a bit with the loss of her old identity. "For me, one of the hardest things was giving up the prestige of having a good job at a good company," she says. "It was hard to go out and not know what to say when people asked me, 'Oh, what do you do?' "

Cooking school was hard-core, but Sarma loved it. "I enjoyed those days in the hundred-degree heat of the kitchen, feeling the sweat drip down the back of my legs and into my shoes."

After cooking school, Sarma teamed up with a partner to open Pure Food and Wine, a popular New York City restaurant that serves only raw food (nothing heated over 115 degrees Fahrenheit). The restaurant has received rave reviews in the press and even inspired a book.

Sarma now runs Pure Food and Wine on her own, along with One Lucky Duck, her spin-off company that produces products for the raw food lifestyle.

Although she still works hard, Sarma doesn't cry in the ladies' room anymore. She is living her dream and pursuing her passion every day. If she hadn't gone through the misery of corporate burnout, she probably never would have found the motivation to completely change her life.

2. Terminal Boredom: "I Am Slowly Going Crazy."

Boredom at work can be more stressful and damaging than overwork. A recent research study showed that workers doing meaningless work with little opportunity for input were more likely to die young. That's right—your job could literally be boring you to death.

If your job is a snore, you're not alone. A poll by the Gallup Organization found that 55 percent of all US employees are not engaged at work. "Gallup found that these employees are basically in a holding pattern. They feel like their capabilities aren't being tapped into and utilized and therefore, they really don't have a psychological connection to the organization."

Bored workers don't necessarily have too little to do. Many have full schedules of meetings and tasks—the problem is that none of the work challenges or interests them.

Corporate jobs can be repetitive and tedious. Days get bogged down with endless meetings and hours spent filling out forms, seeking approvals, and documenting procedures. There's often a lack of autonomy that makes corporate cubicle dwellers feel like rats in cages.

Senior managers make the important strategic decisions. Centralized groups control such matters as hiring and purchasing. It takes a village to get anything approved in most corporations.

Terry F., a corporate marketing manager, says she spends most of her time on paperwork and politics. "I actually spend more time justifying and reporting on my projects than I spend on my actual projects! It takes three levels of sign-off just to get a brochure color scheme finalized."

The tedium of her work left Terry extremely frustrated. "I was learning nothing and creating nothing. I could just feel my brain cells dying, day after day."

Symptoms of Terminal Boredom

- You rarely feel intellectually challenged by your daily work duties.
- You're not learning anything new at work.
- You don't see an interesting career path ahead of you.
- You don't have the resources or authority you need to do your job well.
- You can almost feel yourself getting stupider every day.

On-the-Job Cures for Terminal Boredom

There are plenty of ways to make work more interesting without quitting your job.

- **Find a new project.** Think about what kind of project would energize you and see if you can find or create one at your company. Get inventive if nothing immediately springs to mind. Look outside your department if you have to. Volunteer to write for the company website, to lead training in your area of expertise, or to join product brainstorming sessions for another division.

   You may have to sell the idea to your boss. After all, he wants you focused on the work he hired you to do. Still, most bosses will be receptive as long as you demonstrate that you will continue to do your primary job well.

- **Learn something.** If you aren't learning and growing on the job, you may have to take your professional development into your own hands. Many large organizations have formal training programs and standard policies for reimbursing employees for outside training and education.

   Find a training course that intrigues you and forces you to step outside your comfort zone. If your company doesn't offer training that meets your needs, do some research on programs available from other sources. Many professional organizations offer interesting training courses in specialized areas. You can also look at adult education institutions and the continuing education departments at local colleges and universities. There are plenty of online training courses if you can't find something in your area. (See the Escape Tool Kit at the end of this book for some recommended options.)

   If you want your company to foot the bill, you'll probably have to make a case for how the training will improve your job performance. That isn't as limiting as it may sound. Learning any new business-related skills can make you a better-rounded professional. Most likely, your company will pay at least part of the cost if you can get your boss's approval.

   If your company shoots down your request, consider investing your own money, especially if you'll learn new skills that will make you more marketable for your next job.

Off-the-Job Cures for Terminal Boredom

If you can't find a way to make your job more thrilling but aren't yet ready to quit, you may have to get your intellectual stimulation after hours. It's certainly not ideal to stay for long in a job that bores you silly. However, if you feel temporarily stuck thanks to financial or personal needs, there are ways to liven things up by finding outside interests to keep your brain cells firing. You may be surprised how much more tolerable a boring job becomes when you have other passions that provide the meaning and challenge that are missing between nine and five.

- **Volunteer for a good cause.** There are thousands of organizations—from charities to schools, local cultural institutions, and professional groups—out there that would love to have your help.

  The key is to find a way to get involved that will energize you and leverage the skills you aren't using at work. While working the ladle at the soup kitchen and helping to paint the local school are worthy activities, they probably won't alleviate your boredom at work for the long term.

  What you need is an ongoing volunteer project that is challenging and fulfilling. Ideally, your volunteer gig will also help you develop skills and experience that will qualify you to land a nonboring job at some point down the road.

  Find an organization that you believe in and think about the ways that you could help. Could you manage a committee, spearhead a fund-raising or PR campaign, or help reorganize facilities? You may just discover a new career in the process.

- **Find time for your passion.** It's amazing how many of us give up treasured hobbies and interests when we get sucked into the corporate world. That's probably because there's often little extra time for sleep, let alone hobbies, when working the typical corporate grind.

When we do have time, we're usually so exhausted that we end up vegging in front of the TV instead of participating in activities that truly excite us. What would you do if you had a whole week free with no responsibilities? Take a minute to close your eyes and imagine your ideal week. Don't be practical; this is fantasy time. Would you take a trip, work on your novel, or just spend the whole week playing with your kids?

Whatever activity you imagine, you've got to find a way to get more of it in your life. When you're stuck in a boring job, it's particularly important to make time for the outside interests that recharge your batteries.

The truth is that no job can provide complete fulfillment. If you've gotten stuck in the rut of living to work, it's no wonder that you're frustrated. Take a class, join a club, get a life. Set aside time on a regular basis to indulge your love for impressionist art, hide-and-seek, scuba diving, or heavy metal guitar playing. You'll be a happier and more interesting person and may eventually find a way to make a living from one of your passions.

3. Square Peg Syndrome: "It's Not Your Job, It's You."

The world of cubicles just isn't a good fit for all personalities. Most corporations are rife with political hierarchies, bureaucracy, and the pressure to conform. People with creative, entrepreneurial, or individualist personalities often feel suffocated.

Even those who adapt well to Corporate America can find themselves in situations that don't work for them. Working in a job that doesn't utilize your skills or engage your interest gets old fast. It's also no fun to stifle your true personality to fit in.

In some corporate cultures, you have to be aggressive and

confrontational to get ahead. Other companies reward brown-nosers and yes-men. We all make small compromises to get along. It's perfectly okay to save your spandex shorts and yodeling hobby for after hours.

The problems arise when the culture at your company requires you to change your personality and become someone you don't like. You may be able to play the game for a while, but eventually the stress will start to wear on you.

Authenticity may sound very new-age, but it's a real issue. If you spend fifty hours each week pretending to be someone you're not, it will take a toll.

Daniel Nahmod was a talented musician who found himself ignoring his artistic side to climb the corporate ladder. He stopped making time for his first love, music, and tried to conform to the conservative corporate culture. Soon he was earning big money and traveling the world as an IT executive for a *Fortune* 100 company. Unfortunately, he was miserable.

"I was so sick of pretending to care," says Daniel. "It was all a game for money. I was sitting in meetings for hours debating whether the cover of a report should be white or blue."

Daniel turned to ice cream to ease the pain. He'd visit the Dairy Queen in the building lobby each day to drown his sorrows in hot fudge. He gained forty pounds in less than nine months.

Part of Daniel's struggle was his guilt. He knew plenty of people who'd love to have his job and his salary. So why was he so hard to please? Therapy and prescribed antidepressants didn't solve the problem. Daniel struggled for years to convince himself he should be happy. Finally, an epiphany came in the men's room of a corporate office park, where he had fled to escape a boring training session. "This isn't my life," he realized as he gazed at his reflection in the mirror. "It's a dream job in someone else's dream."

That was the beginning of a major change in Daniel's life. He didn't storm into his boss's office and quit that day, but he did make a plan. Over the next several months, he built up his savings and worked toward preparing for a career in music.

Now, seven years later, Daniel has a thriving career as a singer-songwriter. He lost the forty pounds and reclaimed his old personality. It took a little time to get established, but Daniel started earning more than he had in his old corporate job by his third year as a musician.

Symptoms of Square Peg Syndrome

- You spend more than 50 percent of your time on tasks that you don't like, aren't good at, or both.
- You struggle to find the energy to care about your work projects.
- You find yourself keeping your true thoughts to yourself just to fit in.
- You are frequently frustrated and mystified by the activities and opinions of your co-workers.

Cures for Square Peg Syndrome

Something's got to give. You need either a new job or a lobotomy (the lobotomy may be covered by your health plan if you use an in-network provider). There's no reason to keep torturing yourself.

The solution could be as simple as finding a different job at your current company or at a similar firm in the same industry. If you think you need to make a more dramatic change, see chapter 3 for guidance on finding a career path that better fits your personality.

4. Balance Disorder: "Who Has Time for a Life?"

Achieving a better work–life balance was the number one resolution on 2007 New Year's resolution lists, according to a global survey by research group ACNielsen. More than half of respondents resolved to spend less time at work, while only one-third wanted to go on diets and only one-fifth aimed to quit smoking.

These results are hardly surprising when 42 percent of us work more than fifty hours per week and most good corporate citizens are left with little time for their families, friends (what are those?), or outside interests. You can quickly learn to hate even a job you once loved if it leaves no time for a life.

Balance disorder is a bit different from good old-fashioned corporate burnout. You don't have to be completely fried to feel like you're neglecting your personal responsibilities.

The longing for balance is symptomatic of a change in attitudes. A large percentage of today's workers have rejected the idea of devoting their lives to work. Members of the Baby Boom generation used to brag about "living to work." But many Baby Boomers have come to the painful realization that the old saying is true—nobody on their deathbed ever wishes that they'd spent more time at the office.

Meanwhile, Generation X and Y professionals are more cynical about work. They've witnessed too many corporate scandals and layoffs to believe in job security or employer loyalty. They're not willing to give up their lives to companies that don't play fair.

Companies have acknowledged their employees' desire for more balanced lives. *Work–life balance* has become a favorite buzzphrase in recruiting spiels, but not enough corporations back the idea up with programs that provide real relief.

Working parents face some of the toughest challenges when it comes to balancing home and office. With long corporate workdays stacked between long commutes, parents have limited hours for their children. For many couples, having one parent drop out of the workforce to become a full-time caregiver isn't economically feasible. Instead, in most cases, parents make do by running between the office and day care and trying to squeeze in a few hours of shut-eye when they can.

Balance isn't just about getting a full night of sleep once in a while, though many working parents would settle for that. Balance is about being a complete and multifaceted person. It's about making time for fun and reflection and connection.

All work and no play really does make Jack a dull boy. That's bad for Jack and bad for Jack's company. Research shows that true business innovation comes from diversity of ideas and fresh ways of seeing things. If you have no work–life balance, you're not doing yourself or your company any favors.

Symptoms of Balance Disorder

- You often feel guilty that you're not spending enough time with your family or friends.
- You are spread so thin that nothing is getting done right.
- You find it difficult or impossible to set boundaries around your work.
- You wish you had more time for outside interests and hobbies.
- You have missed important family or social events because of work-related conflicts.

Cures for Balance Disorder

You don't necessarily have to leave a demanding job to achieve greater balance. If you generally like your job, but don't like how it has taken over your life, there are options you should explore before you do anything hasty.

Many of us unwittingly contribute to creating an out-of-balance work life. We are so eager to succeed that we buy into unreasonable expectations or imagine unreasonable expectations where they don't even exist. Would your boss really write you off if you stopped working weekends? Would your career really go down the toilet if you asked to work from home once a week to lessen the pain of a killer commute?

If you find that your workload is excessive no matter what you do, it may be time to have a chat with your manager. This can be tricky, because so many corporate rules and expectations are un-spoken. Bosses rarely come right out and tell you that you should take work home every night. They just make it clear what needs to be done and expect you to find a way.

Most people suffering from balance disorder hesitate to speak up because they don't want managers and colleagues to think they can't hack it. They don't want to be branded as a whiner or an incompetent. Handled correctly, however, a request for boss in-tervention could pay off in major quality-of-life improvements.

Before you schedule that meeting with the head honcho, spend some time documenting the current situation and coming up with ideas for how to improve it. You're not going to make much headway by simply complaining that you have too much work and expecting your boss to provide a magical cure. You want to present a real business case for scaling back your workload, along with some viable solutions.

List your responsibilities and the time you spend. If you can, document the source of any workload increases—have you inher-ited extra responsibilities from downsized colleagues or has there been a significant increase in new projects? Remember, this should be a business conversation. What you need to demon-strate is that one person can't realistically do all this work and do it well. Don't deliver premature ultimatums; be sure to anticipate objections that might come up, and prepare to address them.

Propose more than one solution, especially if you can clearly demonstrate why your preferred answer is the best one. By pro-viding choices, you give your boss the ability to take ownership of the final solution and also show that you have taken the time to explore all alternatives.

5. Meaning Deficiency: "I'm Just Collecting a Paycheck."

The quest for meaningful work has gained momentum as the job market has improved and more opportunities have opened up.

For years, high unemployment kept people trapped. We felt lucky to have any job at all. The idea of work with meaning seemed a luxury for the lucky few who didn't have bills to worry about.

But meaningful work is not a new concept. For decades, people have searched for their true callings and sought out work that makes a difference. That's why so many educated and passionate individuals choose to labor for peanuts in the nonprofit sector when they could be raking in big bucks in Corporate America.

Meaningful work isn't just about saving the world, though. Any work can be meaningful if it aligns with your values and priorities and makes you feel that you've accomplished something valuable.

If you ask people why they work, many will say it's for the money. However, survey after survey has shown that people list money behind priorities such as interesting work, meaningful work, and work–life balance when considering a new position.

Many do find meaningful work inside corporations. They love what they do and believe strongly in their company's mission. These lucky people get the best of both worlds—work that has meaning *and* a dependable paycheck.

For others, looking for meaning in a cubicle proves to be a wild goose chase. "People find themselves working for corporations with values that are diametrically opposed to their own personal values," says Joshua Rosenthal, who worked for a medical supply company before founding the Institute for Integrative Nutrition, a professional training organization for health counselors that boasts faculty members such as Deepak Chopra and Dr. Andrew Weil.

"People are finicky about who they sleep with or who they marry, but they end up spending years, and even decades, in careers they don't like."

At the same time, the modern corporate workplace often takes meaningful decisions away from junior and midlevel employees.

In a schedule jam-packed with meetings and bureaucracy, there is little room for fulfillment.

"I wasn't creating anything, I wasn't helping anyone. I was basically just helping to make more money for rich guys," says Andrea Beaman, formerly a corporate administrative assistant and currently a nutritionist and TV personality.

Both job satisfaction and productivity increase when workers feel that their work makes a difference to others, even in tiny ways. A recent experiment at the University of Michigan found that telemarketers who believed their work had a positive impact on others were more satisfied with their jobs and actually had more sales per hour.

THE VIEW FROM THE TOP—IS IT WORTH THE CLIMB?

What's the supreme reward of working around the clock, surviving layoffs, and battling discrimination? The lucky winners get promoted to management. Too late, many of them realize that it wasn't worth the struggle.

In the corporate world, you're conditioned from day one to aspire to the next rung of the ladder and keep climbing. For many, promotions and titles become proof of their value and ability.

Nobody likes to publicize the fact that management jobs are often more stressful and less rewarding than lower-level corporate gigs. Managers spend even more time on tedious tasks such as budgets, plans, and project reports. And they often have very little power, serving mostly to carry out the decisions from above.

"The higher I moved up in the organization," says David T., "the less control I seemed to have over anything. It was just more paperwork, more meetings, more crap."

Middle managers also become the messengers for delivering

bad news to their employees. They deal with tears and anger during layoffs. They shoot down hoped-for raises and promotions. They announce budget cuts and hiring freezes and canceled projects.

No wonder the boss is always in a bad mood. But nobody in Corporate America wants to admit that joining the managerial club isn't always worth the dues. After all, who really wants to hear that moving up can be a downer? What would all those slaving peons have to look forward to?

A survey by workplace consultants Age Wave/Concours Group found that only 62 percent of managers strongly or moderately agree that "I really care about the fate of this organization," and only half were glad they chose to work at their company over another. Moreover, just 35 percent of managers said their organization inspired the best in them. Is it any wonder corporate life sucks when the people responsible for engaging and leading others are themselves completely disenchanted?

Symptoms of Meaning Deficiency

- You feel vaguely embarrassed when you tell people what you do for a living.
- You're not particularly invested in your work.
- You rarely feel a true sense of achievement at the office.
- A good portion of your time is spent on busywork.
- At the end of the day, you often wonder if you've achieved anything of value.

Cures for Meaning Deficiency

Is there a way to create meaning in a job that isn't fulfilling? You can certainly try. Sometimes we lose sight of the meaning of our work due to other job annoyances. And sometimes we don't realize the impact we're having.

Take a few moments to think about your work and the people it affects. Do you help make your customers' lives easier? Do you contribute to keeping the company afloat and making sure your co-workers get paid? Do you delight your boss with well-written memos?

List everything you can think of, no matter how silly it may seem. If you're stumped, try talking to a co-worker or friend about it. *Quick tip:* "What the hell is the point of this job anyway?" isn't the best conversation starter.

Once you have your list in front of you, read through it and see if you've uncovered anything new. Are there items on the list that excite you? If you spend even a small percentage of your time on work that is truly meaningful, you're off to a good start. You may be able to find ways to expand that part of your job and scale back other responsibilities.

If your list only depresses you, don't despair. You are not your job. Maybe you need to focus on finding more meaning outside the office. For you, the primary meaning of your job may be that it allows you to support the people you love or helps you to finance other pursuits. (For advice on adding more meaning to your life through volunteer work and other passions, see page 37.)

That doesn't mean you shouldn't keep striving to find a career that both supports you and provides you with meaning.

LIVING IN FEAR

In Corporate America today, we're always watching our backs. Approximately 5.4 million people lost their jobs in mass layoffs between 2001 and 2006. These layoffs go on in good economic times and bad, spurred by a rise in outsourcing and rampant mergers and acquisitions. Downsizing has become a standard corporate practice, a go-to tactic when the quarterly numbers miss the mark or a new management team wants to change the guard.

As a result, many corporate professionals live in fear—waiting for the next round of seemingly arbitrary firings and playing aggressive defense to avoid getting the ax. Over time, the survivors of layoff bingo may suffer as much as or more than those let go. Experts in organizational behavior say that those left behind often go through a sort of post-traumatic stress effect.

Even if management has a rationale for the restructuring or the layoffs, the list of victims can seem random. Those who stay wonder if they are more valued than those who were fired—or just luckier. In the wake of seeing good workers sent packing for no apparent reason, survivors become cynical and defensive, worrying that they will be next on the hit list.

Meanwhile, they work harder and longer to take up the slack for those who have left. "After they laid off half of my department, I ended up with the equivalent of three full-time jobs," says Nick C., a midlevel financial services manager. "With that much work, I can't do any of it well. I'm being set up to fail."

When the threat of layoffs looms, we all start running on fear and adrenaline. When there's a threat—whether it's to our bodies, our livelihood, or our self-esteem—the mind kicks into overdrive to prepare for fight or flight. This may be helpful in the short term, but if the brain stays in racing gear for too long, the inevitable result is burnout.

6. Toxic Workplace Blues: "I Deserve Hazard Pay."

Most offices are a little dysfunctional. Challenges arise whenever you bring a bunch of different people together to work in close proximity. There's the guy in the next cubicle who smells like tuna and conducts every inane conversation on speakerphone at full volume. There's the woman down the hall who decorates her office with pictures of George Clooney and her eleven cats.

Without a little dysfunction, work would be boring. A toxic workplace is a different story.

Discrimination and Disrespect

Forty years after the passage of the 1964 Civil Rights Act that forbade workplace discrimination, many companies still practice their own subtle brand of favoritism. Just look at the rash of recent discrimination lawsuits settled by America's biggest and best-known corporations.

Despite the progress made in recent years, women and minority managers are still paid less than white males. They're also less likely to be promoted to the executive suites of *Fortune* 500 companies.

It's not just about race and gender. People are also discriminated against for other reasons—such as not being friends with the right people. Bad managers often promote the people who make them feel comfortable, whether they deserve it or not. Their frat buddies and brothers-in-law, say, and the cute intern who laughs at their jokes.

Too often, hard work and talent are not enough to get promoted in today's corporate environment. Getting ahead more often seems a matter of who you know and how much they like you. It's kind of like running for Homecoming Queen.

Today's cynical workers have come to expect this sort of behavior from management. More than half of American workers question the basic morality of their organizations' top leaders and say that their managers do not treat them fairly, according to recent studies.

The result is a culture of constant political maneuvering. This type of environment is not conducive to results, teamwork, or good morale. Instead, it leads to backstabbing and rampant CYA behavior.

When people don't trust that they will be treated fairly, they spend a lot of time trying to protect themselves by creating paper trails and cc'ing the entire free world on e-mails—just in case they someday have to prove their innocence in a corporate blame game.

In the long run, it's a big waste of time that hurts both employees and the company.

Working with Morons

Corporations can also be a prime breeding ground for personality disorders. Bad bosses can be particularly hazardous. In a hierarchical organization, your boss is often the master of your destiny. Unfortunately, most employees say that their managers, far from driving the business forward, actually hamper progress.

A survey by consultancy Sirota Survey Intelligence questioned 3.5 million staff over three years at a range of firms including Shell, Microsoft, and Dell. What they found was an ingrained belief among employees that managers simply get in the way and hinder the natural enthusiasm of their workers.

THE BAD BOSS HALL OF SHAME

The cast of bad boss characters can range from the simply annoying—like the Self-Important Twit and the Holy Office Martyr—to the truly toxic.

The Bullying Boss—aka "the Rageaholic" or "the Psycho"

The bullying boss is the grown-up version of the schoolyard bully—this time in a suit. Bullying bosses use verbal and even physical abuse, along with indirect sabotage, to control employees. The tactics of a workplace bully often include falsely accusing someone of errors, nonverbal intimidation, and even the good old kindergarten silent treatment.

Kim B.'s boss threw a Lucite paperweight at her head. Luckily, he missed. Edward H. worked for a notorious yeller who seemed to revel in calling him nasty names on a daily basis.

The Workplace Bullying & Trauma Institute (no, I did not make this organization up) estimates that 62 percent of American workers have witnessed workplace bullying—including yelling and verbal abuse (33 percent), the damaging of office equipment in fits of rage (22 percent), and physical violence (7 percent).

Putting up with an office bully can be more than annoying. Studies have found a strong association between workplace bullying and depression and mental illness. Bullying has even been linked to suicides in Australia, the United Kingdom, and elsewhere.

If you find yourself working for a bullying boss, your best choices are to inform higher-ups and/or get out of the situation. Most good companies won't stand for this type of behavior—if only because a bullying boss is a potentially huge legal liability. See page 54 for more advice on where and how to report bad behavior at work.

The Micromanager—aka "the Babysitter" or "the Prison Warden"

The micromanager always makes careful note of who left "early" at five o'clock and closely monitors personal calls and bathroom breaks. A favorite afternoon activity is tiptoeing around the cubicle maze, hoping to catch someone socializing or otherwise having a good time.

"My old boss spent hours reviewing the reports from the key-card security system to see when people were entering and leaving the floor," says Joanne H., an IT manager. "These were VP-level employees and he was treating us like children!"

Sarah L. sat with a camera installed overhead and pointed at her desk. Her bosses wanted to make sure she wasn't slacking off. She was a fashion assistant, not a bank teller.

The micromanager boss always has a long list of "important changes" to every memo or e-mail. "Don't you think 'extremely' would be better than 'significantly'? And I'd definitely do bullet points instead of numbers. Frank loves bullet points."

Don't bother to disagree or question the importance of these inane comments. It will only lead to a long meeting to discuss the issue and your "attitude problem."

Micromanagers spend all their time monitoring irrelevant details because it makes them feel important. They often have little else to contribute.

The Clueless Boss—aka "Captain Dumbass" or "the CEO's Nephew"

Everyone knows that connections and political savvy can help even the most useless employee land a managerial position.

According to Laurence Peter's classic 1969 business book, "The Peter Principle," people in business organizations rise to their level of incompetence. Sometimes these idiots are ultimately unmasked and sent packing. But clueless bosses are usually very good at pretending to be competent. They accomplish this by delegating all actual work to their staff and mastering the art of BS. They learn all the buzzwords, they pass the buck, and they kiss boss butt like pros. What goes around ultimately comes around when new management is hired or yet another reorganization flushes the clueless boss out of hiding.

A lame manager often gets promoted because she is unlikely to be a threat to her own boss's job. These incompetent managers then stay on top because the people who promoted them don't want to admit they made a huge mistake.

Symptoms of Toxic Workplace Blues

- The overall atmosphere at your office is consistently negative or stressful.
- Inappropriate behavior is endorsed or ignored by management.
- You avoid spending time with your co-workers outside work at all costs.
- You feel uncomfortable about going to your boss with concerns or issues.
- Your friends respond to your work war stories with horror.

Cures for Toxic Workplace Blues

Can one person clean up a toxic workplace? Or should you just get out and save yourself?

It depends on the level of dysfunction. If you like everything else about your job, there are ways to adjust to working with minor annoyances such as a clueless boss or obnoxious colleagues. With some patience and a good therapist, the experience might just make you stronger.

However, if the offending behavior clearly violates company policies (or even worse, criminal law), you should consider reporting it through the proper channels. Generally, that means going to your boss first if you can. If your boss is part of the problem, you may have to go directly to Human Resources. Check your employee handbook to find out the company's recommended course of action.

Before you file an official complaint, you need to be prepared. It would be nice if we could rely on our employers to do the right thing on our say-so alone, but it doesn't always work that way. Remember, those folks in Human Resources work for the company, not for you. There *are* people who fabricate stories, and it would probably make life much easier for them to believe that you're one of them.

If you are making a serious accusation, especially against a senior person at the company, you need to gather whatever evidence you can before you go on record. You should save copies of e-mails or voice-mail messages and compile a written record of the events in question, complete with dates and details. You might not need the proof, but it's better to be prepared.

You also should be aware that, unfortunately, there may be some unpleasant fallout from standing up for yourself. Even if your accusations are taken seriously, there's no guarantee that the offending person will be fired. You may have to continue to work with him, which will be extremely uncomfortable at best. Although complaints are generally supposed to be kept confidential, corporate grapevines are very efficient, and word often gets out. As a result, some whistle-blowers might get praised as heroes while many others will be labeled as troublemakers or worse.

Sadly, these potential pitfalls discourage people from reporting bad behavior at the office. Sometimes it's easier just to find another job than to open up a can of worms.

Those who step forward are to be commended. They perform a true service for other employees by drawing attention to bad behavior and forcing toxic undesirables out of the company.

However, every situation is different. What if you don't have the stomach to take on Big Corporate? Or what if the behavior of your toxic tormentors falls just short of being against the rules? It's hard to reform grown adults, especially if they don't want to be reformed. You can either wait for the bad guys to get laid off (it will usually happen eventually), or you can find a new job.

A CUBICLE WITH A VIEW

Recent research has shown that having a view of nature from your work space can improve your job satisfaction, diminish stress, and boost your overall physical health.

Looking out at buildings and parking lots won't do the trick. However, gazing at trees and grass can provide relief from mental fatigue and enhance competence. Employees with nature views also took fewer sick days and said they felt more productive.

For those of us who gaze at nonrejuvenating human-made scenes such as brick, concrete, and other people's offices, it's particularly important to make time at lunch or after work for a trip to the nearest park or other green space.

☕ Your Best Hope Is Early Intervention

If you've been suffering from any or all of the afflictions described in this chapter, the good news is that there's hope. None of these syndromes is truly terminal. The important thing is to take immediate steps to lessen the pain. There are no Purple Hearts awarded to those who suffer on the corporate battlefield.

THE CORPORATE MALCONTENT'S iPOD PLAYLIST

When office life gets you down, block out your boss's yammering and the tortured noises from the next cubicle with the sweet sounds from your iPod. Here are some song picks to add to your rotation.

Songs for Wallowing in Your Misery

- "Back on the Chain Gang" by the Pretenders
- "Sixteen Tons" by Tennessee Ernie Ford
- "Bang on the Drum All Day" by Todd Rundgren
- "Cubicle Love Song" by Sam Bisbee
- "I Wanna Be Sedated" by the Ramones
- "I Hate My Job" by the Butthole Surfers
- "Manic Monday" by the Bangles
- "Working 9 to 5" by Dolly Parton

Songs for Daydreaming About Leaving

- "Take This Job and Shove It" by Johnny Paycheck
- "Sweet Escape" by Gwen Stefani
- "Freedom" by George Michael
- "Goodbye to You" by Scandal
- "Na Na Hey Hey Goodbye" by Steam
- "You Only Live Once" by the Strokes

THE CORPORATE MALCONTENT'S MOVIE NIGHT

Steal some microwave popcorn from the office pantry and spend an evening at home wallowing in the insanity of corporate life with these DVDs:

- *Office Space*, 1999
- *Nine to Five*, 1980
- *The Corporation* (documentary), 2003
- *Clockwatchers*, 1997
- *The Temp*, 1993

THREE

True Callings and Wrong Numbers

You have to have a dream so you can get up in the morning.

—Billy Wilder

To love what you do and feel that it matters—how could anything be more fun?

—Katharine Graham

Now that you know exactly why your corporate job is driving you bonkers, it's time to decide what you want to do instead. I only wish it were as easy as it sounds.

If you're one of the lucky ones who already knows what you want to do with your life, feel free to skip ahead to the next chapter and read about how to develop a plan for making it happen.

However, if you're still struggling to figure out where you're going to escape *to* when you escape from Corporate America, rest assured that you're not the only one. I have talked to dozens of unhappy corporate types who stayed for years in jobs they hated because they didn't know what career change to make.

The Myth of the True Calling

What is your true calling? Your life's mission? Your reason for being? If you don't know and get tense just thinking about it, you're not alone.

A popular myth floating around out there says that there's one perfect career for each of us—a job soul mate. I blame this intimidating idea for causing way too many smart people to sit around in cubicles for years waiting for a blinding flash of insight or for Frankie Avalon to appear in their dreams and serenade them with a few bars of "Accounting Department Dropout."

The truth is that you may not have one true calling, one perfect career. If you're like most people, you have a complex collection of interests, talents, and priorities.

At the same time, as you grow and evolve and your life circumstances change, your criteria for what makes a true calling may also change. That's why the ideal career for you at twenty-two may make you miserable at forty-two.

This is especially true if you're the type of person who is motivated by curiosity and challenge, always looking for the next mountain to conquer or skill to learn. If you read the previous chapter and diagnosed yourself with terminal boredom, you probably fall into this category.

It's time to let go of the fantasy that you have one true calling and won't be happy until you find it. You don't have to feel paralyzed by the daunting task of trying to figure out your one mission in life, the end-all and be-all of what you were put on this earth for. There are likely many careers out there that could make you happy right now.

The bad news is that you no longer have an excuse to keep waiting around for your destiny to reveal itself. You've got to stop hoping for an epiphany and take some action to find a career path that inspires you. Epiphanies don't usually show up until you've done the prep work.

How Will I Know?

Whitney Houston said, "Trust your feelings," but she also married Bobby Brown, so she may not be the most reliable guide. There is something to be said for intuition, for paying attention to your instincts. Whether you're talking about careers or relationships, sometimes you just "know."

When I first met my husband, I just "knew." It wasn't that old cliché premonition that *This is the man I'm going to marry,* just a hard-to-describe but definite sense that we had places to go together.

When an idea resonates at a very deep level, it means there's something there that merits exploration. Sometimes your intuition will lead you to a specific career path, and sometimes it only provides hints that you'll have to decipher on your own.

The Gut Feeling

We have all known those annoying people who came out of the womb knowing exactly what they wanted to be when they grew up and never looked back. They got the message early. So why didn't you? It's entirely possible that you did and you just didn't trust it. Maybe somebody told you it was a silly idea or maybe you just got distracted.

I knew from a very early age that I wanted to be a writer. After college, however, I turned away from writing and toward corporate marketing. I was motivated by the practical need to make money, but there was more to it than that.

Quite frankly, I was scared that I would never be good enough to be a "real" writer and thought it would be a lot easier to succeed in a corporate job. More importantly, the coward in me knew that it would never be as devastating to fail in Corporate America because I would never truly be personally invested. I always planned to go back to my writing "someday," but that someday began to seem more and more unlikely as I climbed farther up the ladder.

The Epiphany

There are others who really do figure out their missions in life in a blinding flash of inspiration. Genevieve Piturro, founder of the nonprofit organization the Pajama Program and a recent Oprah guest, was sitting on a New York subway train when she was struck with the idea to form a charity dedicated to providing pajamas to kids in shelters and foster care.

The idea was sudden, but Genevieve immediately knew that she had discovered what she was put on this earth for. It may sound like it was easy, but Genevieve had already spent more than ten years working in corporate marketing and volunteering in homeless shelters in her spare time when she had her "sudden" epiphany. She had put in the time and effort to get to know herself and explore her interests. She didn't just sit around hoping for a sign.

The Hands-On Approach

Experience is the best teacher when it comes to finding your true calling. How can you know that you'd love to be a marine biologist if you don't truly understand what that means? You can make assumptions based on your knack for science and your interest in the ocean, but you can't really be sure until you've done your homework.

Our schools don't do enough to prepare us for choosing a career. Unless you're lucky enough to stumble into the right college major when you're seventeen (and let's face it, very few of us are thinking clearly at that point), you may never be exposed to the career options that are best for you.

Instead, we graduate with our expensive degrees and our student loan debt and let inertia take over. We start sending out résumés and looking at job postings. We go with the most attractive offer we receive and, unless we get inspired somewhere along the way, we end up following the structured path in front of us within our chosen company or industry.

We may have every intention of finding our "real" career path someday soon. Unfortunately, too many of us get caught up in the day-to-day routine and let our dreams fade away.

You owe it to yourself to step back and spend some time thinking about what it is you really want. Otherwise you run the risk of letting your career "just happen" to you. That's probably how you ended up in your current job and, since you're reading this book, we know how well that's been working out for you lately.

The Perfect Career for You

Fortunately, the process of identifying your true calling(s) can be a lot of fun. That may surprise you if you associate career planning with those boring standardized tests you took in high school.

Career interest and aptitude tests can be useful in some situations, but they don't always give you the full story. The results of the test I took in high school indicated that I could have a stellar career as a furrier (I was a vegetarian at the time and completely obsessed with writing, so this idea was memorably ludicrous).

The method I'm proposing is more like a game than an academic exercise (don't worry, Type A personalities, I promise you'll get real results and not just a lot of fluffy nonsense). It's designed to help you quickly generate a list of solid ideas, then investigate your most promising possibilities.

My method is divided into three steps:

1. Career Fantasy
2. Detective Work
3. Try on Your Dream Job(s)

1. Career Fantasy

The first step is the most fun. You get to put aside all your precon-
ceived notions and doubts and give yourself permission to loosen
up a little. The goal is to come up with a list of career ideas that
you can start researching. Your list might include specific job
titles, skills or talents you enjoy using, industries or fields that
you're drawn to, locations or people that intrigue you, and other
random brainstorms.

Later on, you're going to put on your detective hat (it's a sharp
deerstalker number à la Sherlock Holmes) and weed out the ideas
that don't make sense. So for now, there is no editing allowed. If
the idea pops into your head, write it down. If you can, jot a line or
two about what appeals to you about the idea or where it came
from. Don't get caught up in analyzing right now, though. You
don't have to defend your ideas at this point.

Think big and don't limit yourself to jobs that are practical or
actually exist. You're not going to show this list to anybody, so it
doesn't matter if you feel ridiculous writing that you want to be
Julia Roberts, or Spider-Man, or a *Solid Gold* dancer. A truly
kooky notion may end up inspiring a related idea that's perfect
for you.

Don't worry, I'm going to help you with this fantasy process.
Most people need a little bit of structure to really let loose with
their best ideas. I've included a series of exercises for you, some
based on established career counseling techniques and others inspired by creativity and innovation exercises that have worked for
me and my clients.

Read through and start with the first one that inspires you (or
sounds like it might be fun). You can try them all, but you probably won't have to.

Fantasy 1. Time Travel

These three exercises take you back in time to rediscover what you loved to do in the past.

Back to Childhood

What were your childhood career fantasies? Fireman? Princess? Madonna? Think back to what you wanted to be when you grew up. Who were your role models?

_____

_____

_____

_____

_____

Back to Adolescence

What were your adolescent career fantasies? What jobs inspired you when you were in high school and college? Veterinarian? Professional athlete? Madonna?

What were your dreams when you were old enough to know your own mind but still young enough to not be too bogged down with practical considerations?

_____

_____

_____

_____

_____

Success Inventory

Look back at your greatest successes throughout your life—acting the lead in the school play, serving as president of the senior class, landing that prestigious internship, earning that award. What are the achievements and skills that you're most proud of?

By exploring the achievements that you value, you can gain a better understanding of what kind of future work would be most meaningful.

_____

_____

_____

_____

_____

Fantasy 2. Money Is No Object

What could be more fun than fantasizing about being filthy rich and doing whatever you please with your days and nights? What would you do? Go ahead and start out by jotting down all the cool trips you'd take and stuff you would buy. Your list might even provide some helpful clues on the career front.

Once you've gotten that out of your system, start thinking about what you'd do for a career once you got bored with shopping. Remember, you don't have to worry about pesky concerns like earning money anymore. Your job doesn't have to be practical, and you don't even have to be particularly good at it.

_____

_____

_____

_____

_____

Fantasy 3. People Are Talking

What are people saying about you? What do they think you're good at? What do they always ask you for advice about?

You have a reputation with your co-workers, friends, and family. Sometimes it's well deserved and sometimes it's not. Take the information and opinions that are useful and throw the rest away. Just because your mother always wanted you to be a lawyer doesn't mean you should be. But if she came up with the lawyer idea because you've always been such a persuasive speaker, that could point you toward some other job options.

Make a list of all of the compliments that you can remember. Imagine what your best friends or biggest fans would say if I called them up and asked what you're good at. It doesn't matter right now if you agree with their opinions or not. Write it down.

If you get stumped, ask a trusted ally (or two or three) to tell you what they think you'd be good at if you decided to change careers. You might get some answers that surprise you.

This exercise has the added benefit of giving you a nice ego boost if you happen to be feeling a little down.

_____

_____

_____

_____

_____

Fantasy 4. Create Your Own Dream Sequence

Let the screen go fuzzy and fade into your own personal dream sequence. Imagine your perfect day. Where do you wake up? Who's beside you? What do you put on to go to work? What does work look like? Where do you go for lunch? Revel in the details.

Don't worry: You don't have to commit to one vision at this point. Try it one way and then do it again. Imagine your day as a supermodel, and then switch to a fantasy about your life as Speaker of the House. Write it all down and make careful note of the details that are most vivid for you.

_____

_____

_____

_____

_____

Fantasy 5. Career Envy

Who gives you career envy? Who have you met, heard about, or read about who made you think, *Wow, I would love to have* her *job*. Jealousy can be a beautiful thing if it helps you identify what you want.

Who would you love to trade places with for a day? What is it about that person's job that leaves you chartreuse with envy? It's okay to be petty and shallow. Get it all out on paper.

_____

_____

_____

_____

_____

Fantasy 6. Job Site Safari

Job sites (such as Monster.com and HotJobs.com) are great tools for exploring career ideas. Just come up with a word or phrase that intrigues you, enter your term into the job search keywords field, and go. Read the listings that come up and see if any of them sound interesting. If the jobs themselves don't inspire you, click through on some of the company names and see what other openings are listed at that firm.

Don't limit yourself to established job or industry descriptions. Get creative. If you're fascinated by medieval history, plug "medieval" into the keyword field and see what comes up. When I ran the search, I found job listings for professors, research assistants, music engravers, and managers for the Medieval Times restaurant chain. Type in "music" and find listings for music teachers, music therapists, account executives for music publishers, music directors for radio stations and mobile phone companies, and lots of other interesting gigs.

_____

_____

_____

Fantasy 7. Your Grand Obsessions

What do you love to talk about/read about/think about? What magazines do you subscribe to? What websites do you visit daily? What topics do you love to debate with friends?

Again, don't even think about editing yourself here. You may think that your love of *American Idol* or Welsh corgis has no bearing on your future career direction, but it very well could spark an idea or help you identify a theme in your areas of interest.

Fantasy 8. Go with the Flow

Psychology professor Mihaly Csikszentmihalyi (that's *CHIK-sent-me-high*; say it three times fast) wrote a great book called *Flow*. He defines *flow* as "the state by which people are so involved in an activity that nothing else seems to matter." When you're in flow, you lose track of time. You forget to eat, sleep, or call home.

Have you ever been in flow? If so, it's a pretty good indication of an activity that inspires you. When's the last time a day flew by in a flash because you were so caught up in a project? What were you doing?

Fantasy 9. Your Career Sweet Spots

Can you remember a time when you were in a career sweet spot? Did you have a job, project, or class that totally energized you, however briefly? What aspects inspired you? Did you love the fast pace of your dot-com job before it crashed and burned? Did you get a charge out of managing a high-profile product launch?

If you get stumped, look for career sweet spots that happened outside the office. Did you organize an event for your child's school? Star in a community theater production? Make a killing on eBay?

_____

_____

_____

_____

_____

Once you've completed the exercises that appeal to you, you should have a nice long, disorganized list of intriguing ideas. You're probably looking at a jumble of job titles, skills, talents, areas of interest, and random likes and passions. We're going to call this your Big Brainstorm List (or BBL if you're one of those corporate types who just loves your acronyms).

The list doesn't have to make sense yet. During the detective work step, you're going to organize, identify themes, ditch ideas that don't make sense, and build on your initial brainstorms.

2. Detective Work

If you're a fan of mystery novels or any of the nine million _Law & Order_ or _CSI_ franchises, you're going to love this part of the process. It's got all of the intrigue and a lot less mess. You might even discover that your true calling is to follow in Miss Marple's or Lennie Briscoe's footsteps.

The first thing you're going to do is look at your list and see if any ideas or job titles jump out at you. If not, that's okay. We're just getting started.

Next, you're going to create three new lists based on the big one. On separate pages, you're going to create an Interests List, a Skills & Talents List, and a Job Titles List. On each list, make plenty of room for notes under each item. Keep in mind that calling it a Job Titles List doesn't mean you're limited to careers working for somebody else. Open your mind to entrepreneurial ideas as well.

Copy each idea that you jotted down to the appropriate list. You're still not allowed to edit! Don't make me deduct points from your final grade. I know you're going to look at some of these items and wonder what the heck you were thinking. I don't care how stupid an idea may seem to you now—move it to the appropriate list(s). Would that *CSI* dude with the bug fetish ignore a piece of evidence just because it seemed incongruent? No, he would not. He would put it under the special lights and give it the full treatment.

As you sort your ideas into their appropriate categories, keep thinking and brainstorming. If new thoughts pop into your head, add them to the lists, too. Expand on the ideas you already have. *Like how?* you ask. Read on.

Your Interests List

On your Interests List, you can include industries, topics, geographic regions, or anything else that catches your fancy but isn't a job title or a skill or talent.

Then drill down and get more specific. For example, if you wrote down "animals," can you break that down into any particular subcategories? Do you have a special love for cats, or just Siamese cats—or is your love for animals all-encompassing?

Interests List

_____

_____

_____

_____

_____

_____

_____

_____

_____

_____

_____

_____

_____

Your Skills & Talents List

As you went through this chapter's exercises, you should have come up with quite a few skills and talents that you may have forgotten about. There might be some overlap with your Interests List. However, just because you're good at something doesn't mean it's the right career for you. You're probably reasonably adept at the duties that you perform in your corporate job, but that doesn't mean you enjoy them.

If you don't have a good long Skills & Talents List, you haven't been trying hard enough. Go back and take another look at the Success Inventory, People Are Talking, and/or Career Sweet Spots exercises if you need to come up with more.

As you review your Skills & Talents List, remember to be as specific as possible. Make a special note of those you consider your most distinctive or best-developed abilities.

Do any of these impressive skills and talents suggest job titles you haven't thought about? Add them to your Job Titles List.

Skills & Talents List

_____

_____

_____

_____

_____

_____

_____

_____

_____

_____

_____

_____

Your Job Titles List

Now you're ready to dive into the Job Titles List. In the notes section under each title, you're going to create a Pros section and a Cons section. The pros and cons list is a tried-and-true method for making any decision and will be invaluable in helping you to prioritize your results.

For each job title, ask yourself what you find most appealing and write it down under Pros. As you're going through this process, consider whether there are other job titles that might offer some of the same advantages. If so, add them to the bottom of your list.

Once you have accentuated the positive, you're going to think a bit about the negative and fill in your Cons section. Up until now, this process has been all about the shiny and the happy. However, you're not going to get anywhere if you're not a little realistic. For each job title, what are the potential drawbacks? Are there aspects to the job that you know you would hate, or that you don't know the first thing about? Does it require extensive education or training? Is it an extremely competitive field?

Make note of all of the *Yeah, but . . .* thoughts that sprang into your mind when you came up with each job title idea. If you're still not satisfied with your list of job titles, you may want to go back to the Job Site Safari exercise, plug in some of your interests or talents, and see what jobs come up.

Job Titles List

Job Title 1

PROS:

_____

_____

_____

_____

CONS:

_____

_____

_____

Job Title 2

PROS:

_____

_____

_____

CONS:

_____

_____

_____

_____

Job Title 3

PROS: _____

_____

_____

_____

CONS: _____

_____

_____

_____

Job Title 4

PROS: _____

_____

_____

_____

CONS: _____

_____

_____

_____

Job Title 5

PROS: _____

_____

_____

_____

CONS: _____

_____

_____

_____

Research Your Job Titles

Now that you have a nice long list of job titles, your detective work will get a little more focused. You're zeroing in on your prime suspects, and you'll start to eliminate those that don't fit with the evidence.

Go back to those job titles that you were tempted to delete earlier. Do you still feel they don't belong on your list? Are there other jobs that better represent the Pros you noted for these potential rejects?

If you're tempted to delete only because the Cons seem daunting, don't be too hasty. You owe it to yourself to at least take the time to research career options that really inspire you. You may be wrong about some of the Cons—for example, maybe the salary isn't as low as you assumed, or maybe there are creative ways to get into the field without investing the time in a graduate degree. Or maybe you really are good enough to succeed, even in a very competitive field, despite your insecurities.

If you have a long list of potential job titles, it can be intimidating to know where to begin. Use your instincts. There are probably at least one or two job titles on your list that are calling out to you.

You can do a good bit of your research online from the privacy of your own home or office. Once you identify your top choices, you'll want to branch out and do some more advanced fieldwork. For now, however, all you need is a computer with an Internet connection. Of course, if you happen to have a friend or acquaintance in one of the fields you're studying, you should most definitely take advantage of that connection. Still, it's best to at least do a little preliminary research online first, just to make sure you ask the right questions.

For each of your job title targets, you're going to look for information in several categories:

- **Job duties.** What are the day-to-day responsibilities and activities?
- **Job qualifications.** What levels of education, training, and experience are required?
- **Compensation.** What is the average salary for this job in your area or in the areas where you would consider relocating?
- **Skills and abilities required.** What talents would you be using?
- **Work context.** What is the typical work environment like? Is the job structured or unstructured? Would you work primarily alone or with people?

Some of these job titles will require more follow-up field research than others, but you should be able to learn enough online to understand if you want to investigate further.

The following are some great resources for finding information about specific careers:

- **O*NET OnLine** (http://online.onetcenter.org). This free online database provides a wealth of information on a wide variety of jobs and career paths. Job reports are based on data gathered from surveys of workers in each occupation.

   You can search by keyword or browse by categories including Work Activities, Interests, and Work Values. Each job report includes detailed information on typical job tasks, knowledge and abilities required, median wages, and much more. You'll also find links to descriptions of related jobs at the end of each job report.
- ***Occupational Outlook Handbook*** (www.bls.gov/oco/home.htm). This online handbook is published by the US Department of Labor and has information on more than 250 occupations—from able seamen to zoologists. Each entry includes descriptions of job duties, required training, earnings, demand outlook, and more.

- **Industry associations.** You'll find a professional association out there for practically every industry and occupation that you can imagine. These groups can be great sources of knowledge about a potential career path's opportunities and challenges. Most of them have websites with articles and resources online for members and prospective members. Many of these organizations also have online job listings so you can read about the types of opportunities available in the field.

    Go to your favorite search engine and type in "association" and the name of the job or the industry you're interested in. Another resource for finding professional associations is *The Encyclopedia of Associations,* which can be found at most libraries.

- **Salary.com.** At Salary.com, you can enter a job title and a zip code and get detailed data on salary ranges, bonuses, benefits, and even how much you might take home in an average paycheck. It turns out that a zoologist in New York City typically makes between $46,909 and $103,647 in annual salary. Basic information is free, but you'll have to pay if you want a custom report tailored to your background and your company or industry details.

- **The job boards.** The job boards can be excellent sources of information about the kinds of positions that are actually out there in a given field. It's easy to search for job listings, and you can see exactly what companies are looking for in terms of skills and background. Sometimes you can even see compensation ranges and benefit information.

3. Try On Your Dream Job(s)

Hopefully, your research has led you to at least one or two possibilities that excite you. If you've got a longer list of possibilities, it's time to prioritize. That doesn't mean you have to give up on any of the other options entirely. You can always come back to them later if you wish. For now, though, you're going to focus on the one or two ideas that either (a) make the most sense based on your research, or (b) are the most fascinating to you. Or, ideally, both.

Trying on is extremely important. Don't skip this phase even if you think you already know what career path you want to pursue. You've done a lot of research and learned a great deal about yourself and the careers that interest you. However, it's not until you try on a career option that you can truly understand if it's right for you. Some careers look beautiful on the hanger, but feel tight and unflattering when you put them on.

The try-on phase will take you from thinking to doing. It can have the added benefit of helping you develop skills and experience to use when you're ready to make your move.

Try-On Techniques

- **Pick someone's brain.** Do you know someone in the field you're researching? Or do you know someone who knows someone? Invite him to coffee or lunch and get the inside scoop.

  Mike Marriner is one of the founders of the Roadtrip Nation movement that has sent dozens of college students on cross-country adventures to interview leaders from all walks of life about their career paths (and filmed most of them for a PBS series). His crews have scored meetings with CEOs, celebrities, and plenty of other busy people.

  "More often than not, people are happy to speak with you because they can relate to the idea of being lost and trying to figure out the next step," Mike says. "We've talked to thousands of people and everyone has gone through some form of career confusion."

Be considerate and professional and make it as convenient as possible for your prospective mentor to say yes to your invitation. It may be a bit nerve racking to reach out at first. Don't make this a bigger deal than it is. People like to talk about themselves and their interests, but people are also busy. If someone does say no, don't take it personally.

- **Volunteer.** Find a volunteering opportunity that will allow you to get involved in your field of interest or network with people in the professional community. For example, industry organizations are often searching for people to help out at events. You can do a good deed, strengthen your résumé, and get hands-on experience in your prospective career. See chapter 11 for tips on finding the best volunteer opportunities to achieve your objectives.

- **Go back to school.** Take a class and get a deeper knowledge of what the career's all about. Scope out continuing education programs in your area for courses targeted to professionals in your desired field. You don't have to commit to a lengthy course of study. One or two classes may give you what you need. You can make valuable contacts while you increase your knowledge.

Building Momentum

Remember, this whole process is about building momentum. Don't put too much pressure on yourself to figure it all out right away. But don't be too easy on yourself, either.

The exercises in this chapter will absolutely help you get the ball rolling. If you feel that you need a more structured approach, check out my recommendations in the Escape Tool Kit at the end of this book for more ideas.

FOUR

Let's Get Practical

One of the greatest discoveries a man makes, one of his great surprises, is to find he can do what he was afraid he couldn't do.

—**Henry Ford**

Money is better than poverty, if only for financial reasons.

—**Woody Allen**

I know what you're thinking. You'd love to change careers, but it just doesn't seem practical. Everybody says you would be foolish to give up a steady paycheck and corporate job security to take a chance on something new. What if you fail?

First of all, stop fooling yourself that your corporate job is secure. You've seen enough layoffs and reorganizations to know that your seemingly stable cash flow could evaporate tomorrow.

"I met someone recently who got laid off after thirty-two years of service just six weeks before her retirement," says Dr. Janet Scarborough, a psychologist with seventeen years of experience counseling clients on career issues. "I cannot think of a story that highlights better how important it is to shape your own destiny instead of trusting that a company is going to do it for you."

If you're going to take a career risk anyway, wouldn't it be better to go after what you really want? I'm not saying that you should leap blindly. I don't want you to storm into your boss's office and tell him to take this job and shove it. Please feel free to indulge that fantasy on a regular basis, complete with embarrassing boss sniffling and undignified begging for you to stay. Just don't make any sudden moves in the real world until you've done your planning.

I probably don't have to tell *you* to be cautious. People who get trapped in corporate jobs are generally practical people. You are well aware of the challenges you'll likely face in making a dramatic career change. The good news is that the picture isn't as bleak as you may have imagined. Most of the financial concerns and insecurities that have held you back can be overcome with a bit of planning.

My approach to escaping from Corporate America is based on what has worked for me and the dozens of successful escapees that I've interviewed. It's all about planning well to minimize risk and looking before you leap. In fact, you can do most of your preparation—and even start making money at your new vocation—before you quit your corporate day job.

Your Money or Your Life

Unfortunately, many of the best-laid corporate escape plans never even get off the ground because of fears about money.

When you work in a corporate job, you become very accustomed to that regular paycheck being direct-deposited into your bank account. You know that money is going to show up no matter what you do. You can plan your spending and always know where your next meal is coming from, even if it's usually coming from the break room vending machine.

The new career you're contemplating may not be as predictable. Some of you want to start your own businesses. Others are considering careers that pay much less than your current gigs, either because you're starting at a lower level in a new field or because you're moving to an industry that doesn't pay as well.

Hey, don't worry. Just do what you love and the money will follow, right? Unfortunately, it's not always that easy. If you love to watch reality TV and eat Cheetos, you're going to have a hard time getting paid for your passions unless the Cheeto factory is hiring.

It can be terrifying to trade predictability for something completely unknown that may or may not be as lucrative. You may be miserable staying in Corporate America, but at least you won't be broke. In fact, many of us frequently comfort ourselves with mantras such as *At least I make good money.*

We make good money so we can afford to have homes we rarely have time to enjoy, eat in nice restaurants while we complain about our jobs, and pay for good therapists to listen to our problems.

I strongly believe that people are more likely to be successful at work that they love. Most of the richest and most accomplished people in the world got that way by following their passions. Bill Gates and Oprah Winfrey didn't take over the planet by settling for jobs with steady paychecks. They were inspired by their passions, worked incredibly hard at what they loved even when everyone told them they were crazy, and the money eventually followed. And kept on following.

It didn't happen overnight, of course. Only those who are doing what they love have the persistence and the motivation to achieve incredible goals against the odds.

MONEY MATTERS

My survey of former and current corporate professionals revealed that compensation is a top concern, but not necessarily a major contributor to job satisfaction.

• Primary goal when starting your corporate career—62 percent said "to earn a good salary" (the number one answer).

- The best things about working in Corporate America—65.8 percent said salary (the number two answer among the top three, behind health insurance).
- Thirty-eight percent said compensation was "very important" to their job satisfaction, compared with 71 percent who cited intellectually challenging work and meaningful/fulfilling work.
- The biggest fear about leaving Corporate America—66.7 percent said they feared that they would not make as much money in their new career (the number one answer).
- Biggest challenge in establishing your new career—53.3 percent said financial instability (the number one answer).
- Finally, when asked why they stayed if they felt trapped in their corporate jobs, 51.4 percent of my respondents said they didn't think they could make enough money doing what they wanted to do.

But I Have Mouths to Feed

Money concerns stand in the way of a lot of potential corporate escapees—especially those who have others depending on them for financial support. Sometimes the decision isn't just about you. Someone has to pay for groceries, school clothes, and orthodontia.

Certainly, it's easier to make a dramatic career change when you're the only one who will have to pay a price. Once there are other mouths to feed, there are additional priorities to be considered.

Unfortunately, many people with family responsibilities give up on finding work they love because they jump to the conclusion that they just can't afford to leave the steady job they hate. "Maybe someday when the kids are out of school," they say, cringing at the idea of twenty more years of servitude at cubicle central.

I admire anyone willing to make personal sacrifices in order to be a good parent, spouse, or family member. But many of you are giving up too easily.

If children or other family members rely on you financially, it's important to make sure that they will be taken care of during the transition. Making an educated financial plan will be a top priority, and you will have to put more money aside to ensure that all essential costs are covered.

Still, while such preparations may take longer, the benefits can more than compensate. You may have more time to spend with your family as a result of your career change. You will definitely be more fun to hang around with once you're working in a career that energizes you.

Many of the successful corporate escapees I interviewed had families to support, and quite a few were the primary breadwinners. They approached their career changes a bit more cautiously than others, but they didn't settle for career drudgery just because they had responsibilities.

Worst-Case Scenarios and Bag-Lady Fantasies

In most cases, leaving Corporate America will require a financial adjustment. The idea of financial instability can raise all kinds of issues. People have baggage when it comes to money. For some, there's never enough. For others, money represents success or worth. For many more, money is a convenient excuse not to go after what they want. Don't discount the power of money as an excuse. Failure can be terrifying, and there are those who would rather never try.

Any potential change in the financial picture can freak people out. They get paralyzed by the fear of worst-case scenarios and torture themselves with visions of living on the streets and eating out of Dumpsters.

For some reason, this extreme-worst-case scenario is more common among women than men. Most of the women I spoke with related some version of the bag-lady fantasy. Even Oprah confessed to *Fortune* that she once kept $50 million in cash around as a "bag-lady fund."

The fantasy goes something like this: *I quit my job to start my business/go freelance/follow my dream and am an utter failure. I rapidly go broke, lose my house/apartment, and all of my loved ones abandon me. I am forced to sell my body fluids for spare change and sleep in the gutter with nothing but old newspapers and friendly rats to keep me warm.* The bag-lady fantasy is enough to make staying in your corporate job sound cozy.

No matter how much you may have socked away in savings, no matter how many safety nets you've put in place, you are not immune to bag-lady syndrome. Don't fight it. Trust me, I tried to ignore the bag-lady fantasy for a long time, but I couldn't shake it. The only way to defeat the bag-lady fantasy is through logic.

In fact, confronting your worst-case scenario can be extremely therapeutic. Go ahead and revel in it for a moment. What if your new venture fails miserably for the first few months? What's the worst thing that could happen, and what could you do now to avoid disaster? Usually that just means saving enough to feel comfortable that you'll be able to ride out any lean times.

Another thing to keep in mind when visions of doom appear is that leaving Corporate America doesn't have to be a permanent decision. You can always go back.

Nobody can take away the experience you've earned in the corporate trenches. You won't be punished with a black mark on your permanent record if you leave to pursue another career path. In fact, corporations concerned about impending talent shortages are launching programs designed to actively recruit and lure back people who have dropped out of Corporate America.

If all else fails, remember that Starbucks is always hiring. One of my interviewees soothed a stubborn case of paranoia with the thought that she could be reasonably happy as a barista for a while (at least they get health insurance and free coffee beans) if everything went terribly wrong.

☕ Don't Quit Your Day Job

However, you'll never have to blend Frappuccinos for a living if you follow my advice and do the prep work for your career change while you're still collecting your corporate paycheck. Think about your career change as a second job and get ready to start moonlighting.

For many corporate escapees, learning how to moonlight is an essential part of the plan. Moonlighting offers numerous benefits: You can get started planning and even earning income from your new career while you're still enjoying a salary and company-sponsored medical coverage. What could be better?

Moonlighting also lets you get a taste of what it will be like to work in your dream career. This hands-on experience can be extremely helpful for those still on the fence about making a change.

Turn that corporate captivity into an advantage and give yourself something to look forward to on Monday mornings again. Take whatever time you're currently spending on complaining, feeling miserable, and distracting yourself from feeling miserable and start spending it on a transition plan.

The Benefits of Moonlighting

- **Develop skills.** Your current job may offer you the opportunity to develop skills and experience that will serve you well in your new career. You can learn as you work by volunteering for projects that will increase your proficiency or at least look good on your résumé. Many corporations also offer training and tuition reimbursement for outside classes. Keep in mind that

> **Moonlight** (verb)—To work at another job, often at night, in addition to one's full-time job.
>
> *—The American Heritage® Dictionary of the English Language*

your company will generally only foot the bill for training if it is reasonably applicable to your job. Think about skills that would benefit you both in your current role and in your future career.

- **Build your network.** Your job is a great place to network, even if you are working toward a dream career totally unrelated to your current gig. Every day, you meet clients and co-workers who might become valuable contacts for your future career. They know people who know people who know people. On top of that, you can start making good use of all of those boring work functions. While everyone else is nodding off over industry chitchat, you can open up the conversation and ask about hobbies and previous careers. People love to talk about themselves, especially when the alternative is talking about the same old work topics again. Just keep it friendly and don't give anyone the third degree. You don't want to be too obvious. First of all, it's obnoxious to be one of *those* networkers. Second, you don't want to advertise to everybody at work that you've got one foot out the door.

- **Start generating revenue.** If you're savvy, you might actually be able to start generating revenue from your future career while you're disengaging from your present one. Thinking about making the move to freelancing or consulting? Start looking for projects that you can do on the side. Starting your own business? You can get it off the ground in your spare time. Start selling your new product on eBay or get a booth at the local flea market on the weekends.

- **Build momentum.** The sooner you can start taking action on your plan, the more likely you are to achieve success. Stay in the planning phase too long and you may never get started.

"When you can see concrete evidence that you're moving forward, even if the progress is slower than you would like, you

are much more likely to keep moving," says Dr. Janet Scarborough. "Just make some movement, any movement. You may
discover opportunities that you never knew existed and accel-
erate your transition greatly."

Ethical Moonlighting Guide

The caveat here is that you need to be fair to your corporate
employers—because it's the right thing to do and because you
may find yourself unceremoniously pink-slipped if you don't.

- **Keep doing your job well.** The fastest way to get busted is to
  start obviously neglecting your day-to-day duties. This may be
  challenging if you have a demanding job, but that's the price
  you pay for being able to collect a salary during your transition.
  Remember, this is a temporary situation.

  If your side project takes off, you have a very good problem
  on your hands. You will have to decide if you're ready to give
  your notice or if you need to slow down your moonlighting
  work until you are.

  In the meantime, make sure that you don't noticeably slack
  off. You don't have to be a superstar, but you do have to continue to fulfill your basic job requirements.

- **Be discreet.** Don't flaunt the fact that you've got a little something going on the side, even if it's only on your own time. If
  you've spent any time at all in the corporate world, you know
  that appearances are very important. Unless your boss is extremely understanding, you won't want to advertise the fact
  that your attentions are divided.

  If the culture at your firm is all work, all the time, you will
  definitely raise eyebrows by admitting to other career aspira-
  tions. This could jeopardize your chances for promotions or
  raises and could even make you more likely to be added to the
  next downsizing list.

- **Read the employee manual.** Some companies have rules about employees' outside activities, usually as a method of preventing conflicts of interest. Make sure you understand any regulations and how/if they are enforced.
- **Avoid conflicts of interest.** Even if there are no explicit rules against outside employment, it's in your best interests to avoid conflicts of interest. Don't freelance for your company's direct competitor. You'll only make yourself look unethical and alienate both companies if you're caught (and it's likely that you will be . : . most industries exist in very small worlds).
- **Don't poach clients.** Don't try to compete with your employer for clients. You'll only look shady to the clients and risk your company's wrath. If you work in a service business, some of your clients may very well follow you to your own shop after you quit. As long as you didn't sign a noncompete agreement, that's probably fine—though it won't win you any friends among your former colleagues.
- **Don't take advantage.** Avoid the blatant use of company resources for noncompany business. We've all made a few unauthorized copies in our day, but it's tacky to monopolize the color printer for your consulting proposals. Even if you don't have an ethical problem with using company resources, remember that e-mail and phone calls at large corporations are often monitored and that cubicle dwellers tend to be very nosy. Big Brother will be watching.

Feeling Divided

It's not easy to start a new career while working at a full-time day job. You're going to have less time for fun, socializing, and sleep. Make sure that it's worth it to you and that you really want it.

If things go well, you will eventually be able to quit your day job and hit the ground running with little to no ramp-up time without a paycheck. For those practical types among us, it's worth spending a few weeks or months doing double duty to reduce the financial risk.

Your Escape Plan

Your first project as a moonlighter is to develop your personal escape plan. I hate to be the one to break it to you, but the perfect time is never going to come unless you plan for it. You might even be surprised to find out that the impossible dream will be much easier to achieve than you realized. We often misunderstand how much money we need to enjoy a happy life.

Why not use all of that corporate planning experience you've gained so painfully to come up with a solid strategy for making the transition from cubicle blahs to career bliss? Your escape plan will have two components—a financial plan and a career plan. Both are extremely important. Those who fail to plan . . . say it with me, people . . . plan to fail.

Because your financial plan is going to depend in large part on the specific nature of your career change, the first thing you have to address is the steps required to start making money in your dream career. Once you clarify how you're going to get from Point A (job purgatory) to Point B (dream career), you'll have a much better sense of the financial implications.

The financial plan for taking two years off to go back to school will look a lot different from the one for finding a job at a smaller company that still pays well.

Your Career Escape Plan

If you went through the exercises in chapter 3, you already have a pretty good idea of where you're headed and what kind of skills and experience you need to get there.

There is no one pathway. You will likely have a variety of options. The road you take will depend upon your circumstances and your risk tolerance.

Every career change involves trade-offs. You need to clearly understand your priorities and what compromises and sacrifices you're willing to make.

A good way to start focusing your ideas is to ask yourself the following questions:

When will I be able to quit my day job?
Some possible answers:

- When I land a job in my new field.
- When I have the funding to start my business.
- When I have a steady income from other sources.
- When I have saved a certain amount in my emergency fund.
- When I get certification in my new career.

What do I need to work on before that can happen?
Some possible answers:

- Updating my résumé and calling recruiters.
- Writing a business plan.
- Signing a certain number of freelance clients.
- Relocating to a less expensive home.
- Completing a training course.

Make sure that your plan allows for some time to try on your new career and ensure that you're on the right track. See chapter 3, part three, for ways to try on careers and part 2 for advice on investigating particular career paths.

THE STEPPING-STONE JOB

If you've calculated that the degree of difficulty of leaping directly from your current job to your future career is just too high, it doesn't mean you should give up. A stepping-stone job may be the perfect solution.

For example, you may feel unprepared to start your own company with no experience running a business. Instead, you might do well to take a job at a start-up or small business in a related industry so that you can learn the ropes.

Alternatively, you might not be ready to pursue an acting career full-time, but could take on a less demanding day job to make ends meet while you audition for your big break.

Think about possible interim steps that can get you closer to your ultimate goal.

Your Financial Escape Plan

Think you can't afford to make a career change? I strongly encourage you to do the arithmetic and see if there's a way to make the numbers work. Get ready to put those math skills to the test and figure out what it would take to make the leap.

1. Understand Your Numbers

Before you can plan for the future, you need to get a realistic picture of your current financial health—your assets, your liabilities, and your cash flow. Many people avoid sitting down to work out the numbers because they fear what they will find. What if they add it all up and see—in horrifying black and white—that they will never, ever be able to follow that cherished dream? This is another of those unrealistic worst-case scenarios.

"You have to know what you're dealing with," says career

counselor Dr. Janet Scarborough. "I had a client who was on the verge of clinical depression because he felt trapped in his job, and it turned out he had plenty of money to fund his career transition and no need to stay in a job he hated."

Others do the math and realize they have much more challenging paths ahead of them. Either way, it's better to know the facts so that you can plan accordingly. "I was realistic enough to know that none of my potential careers were necessarily going to be lucrative ventures," says David Kucher, who left a high-paying executive gig in the music business to pursue a writing career. "And your dream is not always going to be lucrative, so you have to figure out a way to set up your life so that your dream doesn't have to be lucrative." For David, that meant buying and renovating some rental properties to create a stream of steady income to subsidize his other endeavors.

CONSIDER YOURSELF LUCKY IF YOU HAVE . . .

- **A spouse or partner with a good salary.** Does your spouse make enough to support the household financially? Could you get by on just one income for a while if you had to?
- **A spouse or partner with a good employee health insurance plan.** Health insurance is one of the biggest concerns for those considering careers outside Corporate America. Paying for your own health insurance is ridiculously expensive. The ability to get coverage under your partner's corporate benefit plan can make a huge difference for those considering starting a business, pursuing a freelance career, or taking some time off.
- **Savings.** Have you been putting money away for a rainy day? That financial cushion can give you the freedom to go after the career you really want.
- **Flexibility.** Do you have the flexibility to reduce your living

expenses? If you can scale back, even temporarily, you can afford
to consider more options.

- **A trust fund.** Most of us don't have the luxury of family money.
  But if you do have rich relatives, now's the time to start kissing up.
- **Resourcefulness.** Even if you have none of the above advantages, don't despair. Resourcefulness combined with determination will take you a long way.

Honestly, the financial trade-offs are the easiest ones to quan-
tify. You run the numbers and then you decide what you're willing
to give up. You may be able to make a career change without trading down in salary at all. When Tania Mulry was ready to leave her
senior corporate job after almost ten years, she was able to negotiate a great offer from a venture-backed start-up firm that was hungry for the experience she brought to the table. They matched her
compensation, gave her a piece of the company ownership, and
even kicked in moving expenses so she could relocate her family
of five.

Many entrepreneurs and freelancers make much more on their
own than they ever earned in Corporate America, though they often have to tolerate some financial instability while they get established. Other corporate escapees consciously choose careers that
pay less because they provide other rewards.

Whatever your goals, the key to a successful career change is to
start with a clear picture of where you stand. If you're not a financial wizard, it might be a good idea to hire a professional financial
planner while you're still earning a regular salary.

A financial planner can help you work through the numbers,
evaluate various what-if scenarios, and develop the best approach
for you. A professional can also help you validate your assumptions
and maybe even identify opportunities you haven't considered.

Commission-based financial planners make most of their

money from selling products to clients and work primarily with those who have more than $100,000 in assets. If you don't fit into that category, you might consider hiring a fee-only financial planner who charges by the hour. Fee-only planners have no vested interest in selling you anything but their services.

According to Sherrill St. Germain, a fee-only planner based in New Hampshire who specializes in helping clients plan for career changes, you can hire a planner to develop a comprehensive financial plan for you for about $2,500 and up. For a smaller fee, you can work with a planner on a more limited basis to validate your own planning or flesh out cash-flow scenarios.

If you're contemplating a dramatic career change and have no idea how to finance it, it may be smart to invest in a comprehensive financial plan. However, if you already have a pretty good idea of where you're headed and the financial implications, you might be able to spend a bit less and still have an expert advise you on whether your plans are realistic.

Visit the website of the National Association of Personal Financial Advisors (NAPFA) at www.napfa.org to learn more about working with a financial planner.

If you prefer the do-it-yourself approach, turn to page 101 for worksheets that will help you get started.

THE HEALTH INSURANCE QUESTION

Affordable health insurance coverage is one of the biggest attractions of corporate employment. If your career change involves moving to a smaller or more enlightened company or to a nonprofit organization, you will likely still be covered by an employer plan.

However, if you're thinking about working for yourself or taking a job that doesn't provide health benefits, make sure you calculate the high cost of monthly premiums into your projected expenses.

Health insurance is expensive, but you can find coverage that fits your budget if you know where to look.

Stay on COBRA

You can keep your corporate benefits for up to eighteen months if you're leaving a company that employs more than twenty people and you're not being let go for gross incompetence. The downside is that you'll pay much more for these benefits than you did as an employee. According to the Kaiser Family Foundation, the average employee covers just 28 percent of total health care costs. On COBRA, you'll pay the full amount unless your severance agreement includes insurance subsidies (they sometimes do). Even so, COBRA may be cheaper than buying insurance on the open market, and premiums are tax-deductible if you're self-employed.

If you know far enough in advance that you'll be leaving your job, switch to the cheapest plan your company offers to minimize your future COBRA payments.

Get on Your Spouse's or Partner's Plan

Your best bet is to get on your spouse or partner's plan if you can. It will likely cost less than any other options, but make sure you do your research. If your partner's company has a lame health plan, you might be better off with COBRA or buying your insurance through a professional organization.

Enroll in a High-Deductible Plan

One way to save on premiums is by enrolling in a high-deductible health plan (at least $1,000 for an individual). With a high-deductible plan, you'll pay for minor health care expenses such as doctor exams yourself. However, you have the comfort of knowing you're covered in case of serious illness or accident.

You can now also link a tax-advantaged health savings account (HSA) to your high-deductible plan. Simply enroll in an HSA-eligible insurance plan and you can contribute pretax dollars to your HSA and use them to pay for unreimbursed costs. Learn more about HSAs and compare rates for high-deductible health plans at www.ehealthinsurance.com.

Get Insurance Through a Professional Organization

Look into plans offered by membership groups, trade unions, or chambers of commerce. Freelancers Union, for example, offers health coverage to freelancers in thirty-six states. Just remember to check out any plan with your state's insurance commission to make sure it's legit.

2. Get a Grip on Your Expenses

To plan properly, you will need a true and complete picture of your expenses. This is not a fun exercise for most of us. You'll have to be brutally honest with yourself or you won't be able to identify where there might be room to cut back. That's the whole point for a lot of us. We don't want to feel guilty about our daily lattes or our shoe fetish. Just remember that you are in control. You don't have to give up anything that you don't want to give up. This financial plan is all about figuring out what trade-offs you're willing to make.

Your daily lattes aren't going to make the difference between financial servitude and financial freedom. You can hang on to them if you're willing to make compromises in other areas or wait a little bit longer to take the leap.

Until you run the numbers, however, you will never know what your options are. For me, doing the math on my expenses, was an eye-opening experience. I had been operating under the assumption that I had to make at least as much as I was earning in my corporate job to live comfortably. That limited my options significantly. I tried interviewing for jobs in my desired salary range, but none of them inspired me. What I really wanted to do was to work for myself on a flexible schedule that created plenty of time for my writing. I made the knee-jerk assumption that I would never be able to support myself that way.

Then I ran the numbers to see how many hours I would have to work as a consultant to equal my present salary and realized it was doable. After I threw in health insurance and start-up costs, the picture wasn't quite as rosy, so I had to bite the bullet and look at where I could cut back on expenses.

I always knew that I was wasting money on unimportant crap, but I had never wanted to look too closely at the situation. I was bored and cranky in my job and I deserved some indulgences, damnit. But if it meant the difference between being able to change careers and staying stuck? I knew I could give up my expensive blond highlights for a while. I knew I could cut back on cab rides and high-end sushi and new suits.

There were things that I didn't want to give up—certainly not permanently. My husband and I love to travel, so I built the cost of an annual vacation into my financial plan. I was willing to take less luxurious vacations, but I wasn't willing to cut them out completely. It turns out that I was so busy establishing my consulting business that we never took vacation that first year. We just put the money toward a bigger trip after my business was up and generating a consistent cash flow.

3. Set Up Your Escape Fund

Once you have a true picture of what you need to live on, you'll have a better idea of how much money you should sock away in your escape fund.

Financial planner Sherrill St. Germain, who herself left a fifteen-year corporate career in the technology industry to launch her planning practice, advises clients to set up a separate escape fund Roth IRA account and save enough to cover at least six months of expenses. St. Germain recommends that even those with steady incomes should maintain emergency savings equal to between three and six months' worth of expenses. Those making a dramatic career change should plan to set aside more. "You need to calculate how long it's going to take before you start generating income to replace your corporate income and cover all of your expenses," she explains.

RAISING YOUR ESCAPE FUND

- **Downgrade your living arrangements.** Several of the corporate escape artists that I interviewed funded their career changes by selling their homes or apartments and moving to less expensive abodes. Some even moved to cities with lower costs of living where their money would go further.
- **Use a home equity line of credit with caution.** If you own your own home, you may be able to qualify for a home equity line of credit that can serve as a financial cushion in the event of emergencies. Be smart about interest rates, though, or you might get caught off guard if rates increase.

4. Run the Scenarios

With your financial picture clearly in focus, you can confidently evaluate your options for moving forward. How long will you save? When will you quit your job? What will the coming months and years look like?

St. Germain evaluated several escape scenarios for an IT exec client who wanted to quit to go to law school. His wife was pregnant with twins, so he had some special concerns. Looking at his income loss plus the law school expenses, they evaluated the benefits of quitting in one year or waiting another year until the timing might be better.

"When you plan your transition, you have to consider what the impact will be on all of your financial goals—like retirement and your kids' college funds," says St. Germain. "Do you want to consider working part-time to generate more income or making other adjustments to your original plan?"

BEFORE YOU LEAVE YOUR JOB

- **Get a loan or a line of credit if you need one.** It will be infinitely easier to qualify for a good rate as a corporate employee with a steady income and a history at your current firm.
- **Line up that new lease or mortgage now.** Again, if you're planning a move, you'll have an easier time getting a mortgage or lease approval if you're employed. Just make sure that you can afford your future home on your future (realistically projected) income.
- **Take advantage of your health insurance.** Line up appointments for all of the checkups and treatments that you've been putting off while you're still on the company health plan.
- **Cash out all your perks.** Do your research and make sure you don't leave stock options, company 401(k) contributions, or other goodies on the table when you go.

St. Germain developed the worksheets on pages 101–107 to help career changers get started with cash flow analysis and net worth calculations.

Putting Your Plan into Action

Now that all of your escape plans are coming together, you're ready to learn more about what your escape route will look like. In part 2, you can explore seven exciting career alternatives to climbing the corporate ladder.

☕ Financial Planning Worksheets

Cash Flow Worksheet for Career Changers

In the worksheet below, the categories in which career changers are likely to see significant shifts are identified with one of the following notations in the left-hand column:

Most—Almost all career changers see shifts.

Bene—Those changing employee benefit plans.

Ed—Those returning to school.

Relo—Those relocating for the transition.

SE— Those transitioning to self-employment.

Time—Those who will experience more demands on their time post-transition.

	CATEGORY	ANNUAL AMOUNTS		
		PRE-TRANSITION	IN TRANSITION	POST-TRANSITION
	INFLOWS:			
Most	Wages and bonuses			
SE	Self-employment income			
	Interest income			
	Investment income			
	Alimony due to you			
	Child support due to you			
	Gifts			
	Other income			
	OUTFLOWS:			
Most	**Income Taxes Owed**			
	Federal			
	State and local			

	CATEGORY	ANNUAL AMOUNTS		
		PRE-TRANSITION	IN TRANSITION	POST-TRANSITION
	Social Security/Medicare			
SE	Self-employment tax			
Most	**Savings**			
Bene	Employer-sponsored retirement plan			
	Traditional IRA			
	Roth IRA			
	Savings/liquid account			
	Brokerage account			
	College account (529, Coverdell)			
	Housing			
	Mortgage payment			
	Property tax			
	Rent or lease payment			
	Home association dues			
	Homeowners/Renters insurance			
	Umbrella liability			
	Property improvements			
	Household supplies			
Time	Household help (yard, cleaner, etc.)			
Relo	Moving costs (if relocating)			
	Automobile			
	Car payment			
	Auto Insurance			
	Operating expenses (gas, oil, etc.)			
Most	Commuting (tolls, parking, bus, etc.)			

	CATEGORY	ANNUAL AMOUNTS		
		PRE-TRANSITION	IN TRANSITION	POST-TRANSITION
	Maintenance			
	Property tax			
	Food			
	Groceries			
Time	Dining out			
	Clothing and Personal Care			
	Clothing			
	Dry cleaning			
	Salon			
	Gym membership			
	Other (yoga, massage, etc.)			
	Utilities			
	Telephone			
	Cell phone			
	Water			
	Electric			
	Oil			
	Natural gas/propane			
	Trash removal			
	Cable			
	Entertainment			
	Vacation			
	Books			
	Newspaper			
	Movies (theater, video, plays, etc.)			
	Club dues (golf, music, etc.)			
	Other: _____			
SE	**Professional Expenses**			

	CATEGORY	ANNUAL AMOUNTS		
		PRE-TRANSITION	IN TRANSITION	POST-TRANSITION
Ed	Tuition and fees			
Ed	Books and supplies			
	Travel			
	Vehicle rental			
	Parking			
	Lodging and meals			
	Entertainment			
	Other: _____			
	Family obligations			
	Alimony you owe			
	Child support you owe			
Bene	Day care			
Time	Babysitting			
	Pet care			
	Food and supplies			
	Vet			
	Pet health insurance			
Time	Petsitter			
	Grooming			
	Gifts			
	Birthdays, holidays, etc.			
	Gifts to churches, schools, etc.			
	Other: _____			
Bene	**Medical expenses**			
	Doctor visit co-pay			
	Prescription co-pay			
	Dental care			
	Vision care			
	Other out-of-pocket			

	CATEGORY	ANNUAL AMOUNTS		
		PRE-TRANSITION	IN TRANSITION	POST-TRANSITION
	Other: _____			
	Other Insurance			
Bene	Medical			
Bene	Dental			
	Long-term care			
Bene	Life			
SE	Disability			
SE	Professional liability			
	Other: _____			
	Other Loans			
	Credit card #1: _____			
	Credit card #2: _____			
	Credit card #3: _____			
	Personal Loan			
Ed	School loan			
	Home equity loan or line of credit			
	Other: _____			

Net Worth Statement

CATEGORY	CURRENT VALUE
ASSETS:	
Cash	
Cash on hand	
Cash in checking accounts	
Savings and money market accounts	
Certificates of deposit (CDs)	
Money owed to me (rent deposits, etc.)	
Cash value of life insurance	
Savings bonds	
Investments (Nonqualified)	
Stocks	
Bonds	
Mutual funds	
Vested value of stock options	
Other investments	
Education Savings	
529 accounts	
Coverdell education savings accounts	
Retirement Assests	
Individual retirement accounts (IRAs)	
401(k) or 403(b) accounts	
Other retirement plans	
Real Estate	
Personal residence	
Other real estate	
Personal Property	
Cars/trucks (blue book value)	
Boats, planes, other vehicles	
Jewelry	

CATEGORY	CURRENT VALUE
Collectibles	
Furnishings and other personal property	
TOTAL ASSETS	
LIABILITIES:	
Mortgages	
Car loans	
Bank loans	
Student loans	
Home equity loans or lines of credit	
Credit card balances	
Real estate taxes owed	
Income taxes owed	
Other taxes owed	
Other debts	
TOTAL LIABILITIES	
NET WORTH (TOTAL ASSETS LESS TOTAL LIABILITIES)	

Prepared by Sherrill St. Germain, MBA, CFP. Copyright © 2007 New Means Financial Planning

PART II

EXPLORING ESCAPE ROUTES

FIVE

Corporate Jobs That Don't Suck

People are definitely a company's greatest asset. It doesn't make any difference whether the product is cars or cosmetics. A company is only as good as the people it keeps.

—Mary Kay Ash, founder of Mary Kay Cosmetics

Going to work for a large company is like getting on a train. Are you going sixty miles an hour or is the train going sixty miles an hour and you're just sitting still?

—Jean Paul Getty, founder of Getty Oil Company

Not all corporations are pits of bureaucracy and despair. Sure, I escaped from Corporate America, but that doesn't mean that everybody should.

Bad corporate jobs can suck for all of the reasons detailed in chapter 2 and many more. However, good corporate jobs can offer the best of all worlds—a steady paycheck, health insurance, *and* interesting work in a pleasant environment.

Some of us just aren't cut out for the corporate grind. But maybe you simply got stuck in a bad situation or at a bad company . . . or bad for you at the very least.

Obviously, there are many benefits to working at a large organization. Otherwise, your parents, guidance counselor, and college professors probably wouldn't have pushed you so hard to go work for one.

First of all, corporate jobs can provide invaluable education.

Most of the escapees that I interviewed for this book stressed how much they learned during their years in Corporate America. Everyone from entrepreneurs to founders of nonprofit organizations to filmmakers talked about the business skills they developed and the contacts they made while toiling in cubicle land. Several even said that they never could have succeeded in their dream careers without their corporate training.

Large companies can also offer opportunities to work on exciting, high-profile projects and collaborate with brilliant people around the world. Let's face it: A corporate job can be a major résumé builder. Even if you eventually want to work for yourself or for a smaller firm, a stint at Giganticorp, Inc., will give you added credibility. Hiring managers, investors, potential partners, and shallow people at dinner parties will all be impressed that you worked for a company with a real brand name.

However, the fact that you're reading this book is a pretty good sign that all of these lovely pros have not been enough to make up for the aggravating cons at your current house of ill employ.

Luckily for you, there are plenty of corporations out there that people actually love to work for. Seriously. You've probably seen the articles about Google offering free meals and massages to employees. Or maybe you have a friend who simply raves about her company, even though it doesn't spring for sandwiches and rubdowns.

Fortune publishes a list of the 100 Best Companies to Work For every year. "People should not settle for working in a lousy workplace," says Amy Lyman, cofounder and director of corporate research for the Great Place to Work® Institute, the organization that created and compiles the *Fortune* list.

To select the 100 Best, the institute conducts the most extensive employee survey in Corporate America every year. More than 105,000 randomly selected employees from 446 companies responded to the 2007 survey. Two-thirds of an organization's score is based on the survey; the remaining third comes from an evaluation of each firm's responses to detailed questions.

Over the years, Lyman has seen the number of companies that aspire to be great places to work increase significantly. Approximately 450 firms participated in the evaluation process to be considered for the 2007 list.

That's good news for those who have grown weary of toiling away at a not-so-great company to work for.

Defining Corporate Greatness

So what makes a company a great place to work? Yes, fair salaries are important, and cool perks don't hurt. According to Amy Lyman, however, it's the human factors that really make a difference.

"Policies and practices change over time, different concerns arise for different people at different life stages, but the fundamental issues that we hear time and time again revolve around how employees are treated," she explains. "Are they treated with respect? Are they supported to learn and grow? Do they have a sense that the workplace is fair?"

Great organizations aren't motivated purely by humanitarian impulses. There is demonstrated business value in becoming a preferred employer. "The best companies understand the benefits they get from being great places to work," says Lyman. "They see results in recruitment, in retention, in the quality of the work they inspire, and in the innovation that they are able to tap into."

What does that mean for a company's bottom line? For starters, the 100 Best Companies that are publicly traded consistently outperform major stock indices. A portfolio of stocks of corporations selected by *Fortune* as the Best Companies to Work For in America in January 1998 earned more than double the market return by the end of 2005, according to a study by Alex Edmans at the Wharton School of Business, University of Pennsylvania.

Employee-friendly policies also help corporations save money. Jeff Chambers, vice president of human resources at software company SAS Institute, estimates that his firm saves anywhere from $75 to $100 million each year because of its low turnover.

So why don't all organizations treat their employees like SAS does? "There are those companies that will wait until they have to change, and unfortunately, they will also be the laggards in creativity and innovation," says Amy Lyman.

TALES FROM THE CORPORATE TRENCHES

SAS Institute—Portrait of a Great Place to Work

Name: Jeff Chambers

Current occupation: Vice president of human resources of SAS Institute

SAS Institute is one of the largest software companies in the world and also a Best Companies to Work For all-star, having appeared on the list every year since it was launched in 1998.

Headquartered in North Carolina, SAS Institute has more than ten thousand employees in fifty-three countries and generates over $2 billion in annual revenue.

Vice President of Human Resources Jeff Chambers took the time to talk to me about how SAS Institute maintains its staggeringly low 4 percent voluntary turnover rate.

Providing Challenging Work

"Our model is to get people in and retain them for a long time by keeping them incredibly challenged and providing a great work experience," says Chambers. "We pride ourselves on that because the only way we make money is by having really engaged people."

The company helps to keep work interesting by investing 25 percent of its top-line budget into research and development every year. "Knowledge workers care about getting paid well, but it is more about the intellectual challenge of the work," Chambers explains. "We have set up a model that pays people to invent."

At SAS, experimentation is encouraged, and failure is okay as long as you learn from it. "When you fail and you learn, you become more valuable to us."

Investing in Retention

SAS Institute hires people with the expectation that they will stay with the firm for the rest of their careers. To make that happen, the company is willing to invest in the benefits that attract and retain the best talent.

Chambers admits that SAS doesn't offer the highest salaries in the industry, but notes that its phenomenal benefits more than make up for this. Some of those benefits include:

- **On-site day care.** The company provides on-site day care worth $1,200 a month to employees for just $150 per month. "Day care has an incredible retention effect," according to Chambers. "About half of our executives are female, and many will tell you they're still here because SAS helped them balance work and life when their families were young."

  SAS started its on-site day care program back in 1981 when it was still a small company. "We had a critical employee who was trying to decide whether she could come back to work after her child was born and we just did not want to lose her," Chambers explains. "So we started with 1 child and now have 610 kids at our day care center."

- **On-site health care.** SAS Institute covers 100 percent of employee health care premiums. The company also pays for an on-site health care center staffed by four doctors and nine nurse practitioners. "The on-site center saved us $5 million on our health care costs last year," Chambers reveals.

Respecting Work–Life Balance

At SAS, managers are encouraged to be flexible in allowing people to reformat their days based on their work–life needs. "It's okay for you to go home at four o'clock because your kid has a soccer game," says Chambers. The company trusts that those who leave early will hand any urgent tasks off to a co-worker, work extra hours the next day to get things done, or log in from home if necessary.

"We find that team members keep each other honest," says Chambers. "People realize that they have a pretty good arrangement and don't want anybody else to screw it up."

Employee Satisfaction Is Good Business

Chambers is quick to point out that SAS Institute is not a social welfare organization. "It is a for-profit business that makes a lot of money and will continue to make a lot of money because we are doing the right things," he says.

He cites estimates that the firm saves anywhere from $75 to $100 million a year because of its low turnover, far more than what it spends on benefits and perks. Chambers believes the money is well spent. "We are either going to spend it on chasing and training new employees or on keeping the ones we have."

The Voice of the People

The *Fortune* list and others like it are great resources for identifying good companies and best practices. However, it's word of mouth that will give you the real story.

During my research for this book, I asked more than two hundred people for their honest opinions about what makes a company a good place to work. Some trends definitely emerged.

Fair Treatment

Let's start with the basics. People want to be paid fairly, treated like adults, and rewarded for their good work. This shouldn't be a surprise.

Unfortunately, I have heard plenty of horrible stories about harassment, discrimination, shady dealings, and even physical abuse at companies that should know better.

Edwin T. summed up his best work experience: "The company promoted from within, valued employees that did good work, and provided nice benefits." It sounds simple enough, but far too many corporations fail to get these basics right.

Work–Life Balance

Today's employees rate work–life balance as extremely important. All work and no play leads to burnout and disengagement. Fried workers just don't perform well, no matter how much you beat them.

To retain their most valued human resources, smart corporations offer a range of benefits and programs to support employees in achieving that sought-after balance. The number of companies offering flextime, telecommuting, job sharing and compressed workweeks has increased dramatically in the ten years since the Great Place to Work Institute started tracking them.

Programs aimed at work–life balance can mean the difference between job satisfaction and exhaustion for many professionals. By demonstrating how much they value their employees, companies earn rewards in commitment, engagement, and loyalty.

Timberland, for example, offers a generous maternity leave policy, adoption assistance, lifestyle leave, and flexible work arrangements. At its headquarters, Timberland has an on-site day care center; it also offers services such as dry cleaning, car detailing, massage therapy, and more. "We recognize and support employees' lives outside of Timberland and we believe that helps make employees feel more positive about where they work," says Cara Vanderbeck at Timberland.

Meanwhile, Best Buy has implemented a Results-Only Work Environment[SM] (ROWE) in which employees are given the autonomy to work whenever and wherever they like as long as the job gets done. "The principle is to focus on the end results and outcomes, not on 'butts in seats,'" says Best Buy employee Kristen Witte, a director in the project resource group who specializes in change management. ROWE is more than just a flexible work arrangement; it's a culture shift. Employees are completely accountable for managing their time and delivering results.

"ROWE gives employees breathing room and eliminates some of the inherent stresses from Corporate America," says Witte, who often works from home on Monday mornings so that she can have some quiet time away from distractions to plan her week. "In general, my routine hasn't changed a lot, but my feeilng about work is much more positive because I feel more autonomous."

Corporate escape artist Karen L. recalls the joys of flexibility at a previous employer. "It was recognized that people had lives outside of work," she says. "It was not expected that you sell your soul, as it is at most companies now."

Entrepreneurial Cultures

For many, the key frustration is not having the autonomy they need to do good work. People are hired for their talent and experience and then promptly stripped of all power to use them.

While rules and processes are necessary in any large organization, the best firms have found ways to foster entrepreneurial cultures in which employees have ownership over their work.

"For me, the most satisfying and energizing work environment was in a company that operated on the premise that you hire the best person for the job and then get out of their way and let them do it," says Andrew W. "It was free of the bureaucracy that suffocates efficiency, creativity, and innovation. Not surprisingly, that company was also, by far, the most successful company in its market."

It can be difficult to maintain an entrepreneurial culture as a company grows, but some of the most successful firms have found ways to do it.

At Amazon, CEO Jeff Bezos believed that smaller teams were more innovative and more productive. He came up with the famous "two pizza team" rule, in which a working group must not grow too large to be fed by two large pizzas.

Google, *Fortune*'s number one best company to work for in 2007, has also found effective ways to foster an entrepreneurial culture that attracts and retains the best people in the industry. In one case, the firm learned from the best practices of Genentech, the biotechnology firm that has been ranked on *Fortune*'s list for nine consecutive years.

Genentech promotes the activities of its research scientists by giving them 20 percent of their time to work on anything they want to. "It has worked beautifully at Genentech in terms of their ability to develop products and their ability to attract and retain the best research scientists," says Amy Lyman.

Google has adopted a similar approach with its software engineers, allowing them roughly 20 percent of their time to try out new things. "They have structured within the workplace this ability to be creative and entrepreneurial," Lyman explains. "And lo and behold, the company benefits because they get great new products and ideas."

SO YOU WANT TO WORK AT GOOGLE . . .

Check out some of the coolest perks and benefits offered by the 2007 number one Best Company to Work For:

- Founders' Award programs, which recognize outstanding team accomplishments with restricted stock grants that vest over time. These awards totaled approximately $45 million in 2005, with individuals receiving up to several million dollars' worth.
- Free breakfast, lunch, and dinner for all employees. There are more

than eleven restaurants and eateries located on Google's Mountain View, California, campus.

- Twenty-seven days of paid time off after just one year of employment and unlimited sick days.
- A sabbatical program that allows employees to take a leave of absence of up to five years to pursue further education.
- Free commutes to the Mountain View headquarters in WiFi-equipped shuttles.

Ready to send your résumé? Make sure you put your best foot forward. Google is very selective. With those perks, it can afford to be.

Google is looking for the best of the best. And on top of demonstrating your qualifications for the job, you'll have to show your "Googleyness." Google hires people who work well in small teams and thrive in a fast-moving environment. The firm is also looking for well-rounded employees with interesting outside pursuits and a desire to make the world a better place.

Learning and Growth Opportunities

Nobody wants to be stuck in a dead-end job. In fact, modern career experts say that you'll get stale if you stay in the same role for more than two years unless your duties evolve and you continue to learn.

It is possible to forge a corporate career that lets you evolve and grow, but it requires creativity and risk taking. The corporate ladder is very structured and linear. Once you get on a particular path, you are generally rewarded for staying on it and avoiding risky or unconventional moves.

The best jobs allow you to stretch yourself and learn new things on a regular basis. And when employees are learning, they are happier and deliver better results for the company.

Great firms also promote from within based on merit and help steer valued employees onto the right career paths. Everyone has equal access to information about promotion and transfer opportunities to advance their careers.

THE CORPORATE INTRAPRENEUR

An "intrapreneur" is an employee of a large corporation who takes direct responsibility for the success and/or profitability of his work through assertive risk taking and innovation.

For example, many real estate brokers and financial advisors are intrapreneurs. Although he may ultimately work for a large company, each broker or consultant is responsible for establishing and growing his own practice within the firm. These opportunities can be excellent fits for those who are entrepreneurially minded but have limited appetite for risk.

Ken Shapiro is a wealth management advisor for the Global Private Client Group of a leading financial services institution. As a serial entrepreneur with an MBA in entrepreneurial management from the Wharton School of Business, Ken never imagined he would end up as an employee of a large financial services firm. In fact, early in his career, Ken turned down a plum job at Goldman Sachs to join the management team of a recycling company start-up in the Bronx.

Many years later, after helping to expand and sell that recycling company and launching a venture-backed software start-up, Ken was feeling a bit burned out on entrepreneurship and evaluating alternative career paths. When he was offered the position at the financial services institution, he was attracted to the idea of leveraging his own experience to become a financial advisor specializing in serving entrepreneur clients.

He accepted the job at the urging of his wife, though he had some doubts about how he would fit in. "My wife promised that if I tried it for a month and hated it, which I was sure I would, she would be okay with me quitting to start another company."

To Ken's surprise, he really enjoyed the work. "I liked it, I was good at it, and it was an opportunity to actually create my own business within a big company," he says. "I get paid by the corporation, but I am truly running my own company in my mind through my practice and my team."

Five years later, Ken the serial entrepreneur is still thriving as an intrapreneur. "I found out that the thing that made me happiest was having control over my own life and time," he says. "As an entrepreneur, I actually had less freedom in many ways than I do now."

The Chance to Make a Difference

The best companies have clear mission statements that employees can rally around. Everyone knows and respects what the company stands for and everyone understands how they are contributing to success.

Employees are happier when they believe that the work they're doing has real, tangible value—whether that means solving customers' problems, making great products, or helping people have more fun. They want to be proud of what they do for more than eight hours each day.

Some companies also help employees make a difference through community service initiatives and corporate foundations that strive to make the world a better place.

Timberland gives each employee forty hours of paid time to participate in community service activities every year. Nearly 95 percent of Timberland employees use their hours, and a large majority cite it as one of the top two Timberland benefits.

Salesforce.com founder and CEO Marc Benioff takes community service a step further. "We have a culture that has social responsibility embedded in its core," he says. Each year, the company is committed to donating 1 percent of company profits and 1 percent of employee working hours to community service through the Salesforce.com Foundation.

"Our employees are introduced to the foundation from the day they arrive," says Benioff. "The two-day orientation for all new hires includes a half day of volunteerism to demonstrate to newcomers that it is a true priority for the company."

After Hurricane Katrina, more than seventy Salesforce.com employees self-organized to combine all of the different survivor lists into a searchable online database to assist family members in locating their loved ones.

Benioff believes strongly that the company's philanthropy model helps it attract and retain the best talent. Approximately 85 percent of the firm's global workforce is active in philanthropy, compared with a national average of 18 percent.

"Employees tell us that the foundation is an inspiration in their daily work," says Benioff.

Good Management

A good manager can make a bad job tolerable, and a bad one can make even the best job a nightmare.

It all starts at the top. Senior management sets the tone. However, it is the immediate manager you work with every day who makes the biggest impact on your job satisfaction.

Great companies cultivate great managers. They also give them the tools and the autonomy to lead their teams effectively.

The People

Recent research studies show job satisfaction increases by nearly 50 percent when you have a close friend at work. It's a lot more fun to come to the office when you like and respect your colleagues.

"I really think that my best experiences were when I was working with a good team," recalls Daniel L. of his time in Corporate America. "As long as everything is okay in your immediate surroundings, going to work is great."

Many of those I spoke with echoed this sentiment. A good team can bring out your best and allow you to achieve results that would have been impossible on your own.

When I look back at my corporate experiences, I realize that my best jobs were rewarding because of the people. In fact, even my worst jobs were bearable because of the people.

How to Get a Corporate Job That Doesn't Suck: The Step-by-Step Guide

Whether you're looking to make a career change or simply to find a better job in your current area of expertise, you owe it to yourself to explore your options.

Step 1. Define Your Priorities

First, you have to get very clear about what you want and what you can't deal with. Google is a great place to work, but it's probably not the right employer for someone who feels overwhelmed in a fast-moving environment.

Step 2. Do Your Homework

Put in some research time to identify the right companies for you.

- **Read the lists.** The *Fortune* Great Companies to Work For list is a terrific first stop. You can browse through the hundred best companies and even sort by geography, or criteria such as "Best Benefits" and "Most Diverse." The entry for each company includes vital information like average salary, turnover rates, and job locations.

    Other lists worth checking out include the *Working Mother* Best Companies list and the Reputation Institute's Most Respected Companies list. See the Escape Tool Kit at the back of the book for more information on these lists and others.

- **Ask your friends.** Do you know people who love their jobs? Ask around and find out who in your circle is working for a firm that they adore. The official lists are great, but you'll get the most accurate information about a company by speaking directly with an employee.

    Step up your networking efforts and attend seminars and events where you can mingle with others in your industry. When you meet someone new, ask him what he likes about his company. You'll learn pretty quickly how to spot those who are truly enthusiastic and those who are putting a good face on things.

- **Listen to your gut.** What companies would you be proud to work for? Maybe you admire their technology, their products, or their way of doing business. Learn more about the firms that appeal to you to see if there's a match.

Step 3. Get Out and Interview
Put Yourself Out There

First, spiff up your résumé and post it on the online job boards. How else will hiring managers and recruiters know that you're out there?

If you're worried about your current employer finding out that you're on the market, most of the job boards allow you to keep your résumé anonymous and reveal your identity only if you choose to respond to an inquiry.

Honestly, though, it's no crime to keep your options open. Career experts recommend that even the happiest employees should always be passively job searching. Most employers have come to expect it. And even if you never find your perfect match through an online job board, it can be a nice ego boost to be wooed by recruiters.

Meanwhile, make sure to let people in your network know that you're looking. As always, use common sense. You don't want to advertise to your current colleagues that you have one foot out the door. However, let trusted friends and contacts know that you're exploring new opportunities and ask them to pass along any interesting leads. The vast majority of great jobs are found through networking, so don't be shy. Most people love to help out if they can. In fact, you may be giving someone an opportunity to be a star by hooking you up with another contact seeking the perfect job candidate.

Interview Around

If you haven't been out there interviewing in a while, don't waste another day. You'll want to get comfortable with interviewing again and to practice your spiel so you'll be ready when the company of your dreams comes calling.

Besides, interviewing is a great way to meet new people and learn about companies and jobs.

YOUR GUIDE TO INTERVIEW CODE

Ever notice that people never say what they really mean in job interviews?

What the Interviewer Says—What the Interviewer Means

- "This is a creative environment."—We have one guy who wears wacky ties on Fridays.
- "We work hard and we play hard."—We work hard and we get embarrassingly drunk at the holiday party.
- "We're looking for a real go-getter."—We need somebody who will work like a dog for little money and vague promises of promotion.
- "We're looking for a team player."—We want to hire someone who will take abuse and pick up our dry cleaning.
- "We need someone who can hit the ground running."—We will offer absolutely no training or guidance and expect you to read our minds.
- "The boss can be a bit demanding."—The boss is an unreasonable despot.
- "The boss is a bit of a perfectionist."—The boss is an anal-retentive freak show.
- "The boss is a real character."—The boss is an offensive jerk and possibly certifiable.
- "We're like a family here."—We are all dysfunctional messes with daddy issues.

Step 4. Evaluate Offers

Don't Ignore Your Instincts

The last thing you want to do is go through all the hard work of a job hunt only to land at a company that you dislike as much as your old one. I know how you feel. I used that as an excuse to avoid job hunting for years.

Look at the job interview process as a chance to conduct your own investigation. Yes, pour on the charm and show off your stuff. Ideally, you want an offer from every company you interview with. The more options you have, the better. That doesn't mean you can't be selective about which offers you accept.

Most likely, you already have a job, so you can afford to be choosy. Unless you're absolutely miserable, avoid the temptation of jumping to the first company that makes a decent offer.

Ask the Right Questions

I'm sure that your recruiter is very nice, but you can't trust her. She makes money only if you sign on, so it's in her best interests to gloss over any potential drawbacks of the job.

Years ago, I learned this lesson the hard way after naïvely accepting a job offer for a "great department" only to find out that the position was a revolving door because a difficult manager scared everybody off within a year or two.

Look for danger signs and ask the difficult questions. Why did the person you're replacing leave? What is the general turnover rate in the group?

If possible, ask to speak with others you would be working closely with before you accept a job. This accomplishes two goals: (a) You can get a sense of how crazy your potential co-workers are, and (b) you can draw them out about what it's like to work in the department. Most people won't come right out and tell you to run fast and far. They know that it could get back to their bosses, who would not be amused. However, do your best to read between the lines and pay attention to the general vibe and demeanor.

In today's connected world, you can even connect with ex-employees at your future company to find out the real scoop. Those who have moved on will have nothing to gain by keeping secrets. You can easily do a search by former employer name on LinkedIn.com and find people in the know.

Vault.com and WetFeet.com are also good resources for researching companies. You can find company profiles, staff surveys, and even message boards where current and former employees post.

What to Look For

CORPORATE CONDITION DIAGNOSIS	COMPANIES TO LOOK FOR
Corporate burnout	• Cultures that value quality of work over quantity. • Flexible work and time-off options. • Generous vacation allowances and the ability to take some time off before your start date. • Managers who support work–life balance. • Telecommute options. • Bosses and co-workers who look rested and recently showered.
Terminal boredom	• Entrepreneurial cultures in which autonomy is encouraged. • Small teams with limited bureaucracy. • Demonstrated openness to moving upward and laterally within the company. • Job duties that will require you to stretch. • Managers who value new ideas and challenging the status quo. • Opportunities for training, development, and on-the-job learning. • Bosses and co-workers who talk enthusiastically about their latest projects.

CORPORATE CONDITION DIAGNOSIS	COMPANIES TO LOOK FOR
Square peg syndrome	• Roles that truly leverage your skills. • Environments that feel comfortable. • Managers who encourage you to be yourself during the interview process and still offer you the job. • Bosses and co-workers who are interesting and value your ideas.
Balance disorder	• Flexible work options that people are actually allowed to use. • Sabbatical and family leave policies. • Cultures that encourage outside interests. • Job perks that help with your personal life—such as on-site day care, dry cleaning, or exercise facilities. • Bosses and co-workers who openly discuss families, vacations, and other nonwork topics.
Meaning deficiency	• Job duties that fully utilize your talents. • Small teams that allow for meaningful individual contributions. • Cultures with open communication styles so you can see where you're making a difference. • Clear corporate missions that you can enthusiastically support. • Bosses and co-workers who actually seem proud of their jobs.
Toxic workplace blues	• Zero tolerance for bullies, harassers, and sociopaths. • Cultures with open communication styles and the ability to air grievances. • Managers who aren't described by anyone as "demanding," "dynamic," "interesting," or "a bit of a character." • Reasonable turnover rates. • Bosses and co-workers whom you could see yourself having a beer with.

SIX

Take a Break

Absence makes the heart grow fonder.

—American proverb

Take rest; a field that has rested gives a bountiful crop.

—Ovid

Can this job be saved? Maybe you just need a little space—some time apart. If you're struggling with the symptoms of burnout or work–life imbalance, you may not have to escape from Corporate America after all. An adjustment to your current job may be enough to get you back on track.

This could mean temporarily or permanently changing or reducing your schedule, working remotely, or taking a sabbatical or leave of absence.

According to a study by Hewitt Associates, 75 percent of big companies now offer flexible work options. More and more frazzled and disgruntled corporate employees are taking advantage of these programs to construct more satisfying work lives.

Take Manya Chait. Manya had no intention of opting out of Corporate America. She just wanted to scale back her busy schedule as a vice president of public relations so she could spend more time caring for her young daughter. She loved her job, but had reached a point at which she could no longer handle both a full-time workload and her increasing family responsibilities.

When she approached her manager with a proposal to reduce her schedule to part-time, she was pleasantly surprised by the positive response.

Manya is just one of millions of corporate professionals struggling with the challenges of fitting a corporate career into a fulfilling life.

Luckily, there are a number of options to explore if you want to create more balance during a time when your personal life demands it—whether you need to take care of children or other family responsibilities, make more time for outside interests, or just slow down for the sake of your mental health.

Musician Laura Cantrell took a leave of absence from her VP job at an investment bank to open for Elvis Costello on tour. Marc Benioff, a former senior executive at Oracle, took a sabbatical to travel to India and Hawaii and contemplate plans for the next phase of his career. In fact, the trip helped inspire the idea behind his successful business, Salesforce.com.

The Flexible Revolution

Twenty years ago, even raising the idea of a flextime schedule or sabbatical would have been career suicide. A good Organization Man or Woman was expected not to have outside interests. If you wanted to spend more time with your kids or take a break of any kind, you had to resign. And good luck if you wanted to reenter the workforce a few years later.

Today there has been a shift in attitudes. A recent study cited in *The Wall Street Journal* found that 60 percent of all workers rate flexibility as a very important factor in retention. Having a life outside of work is no longer just for wimps.

Most people are in the workforce for more than forty years, and some never retire at all. Naturally, there will be times over the course of those decades when work is the number one priority and times when other aspects of life take precedence.

Luckily, more and more companies are recognizing the value of hanging on to their most valued employees throughout their careers. "Especially among the best companies, flexible work options have increased pretty dramatically," says Amy Lyman of the Great Place to Work Institute. "Telecommuting, job sharing, and compressed workweek offerings have really picked up. Less than 25 percent offered these in 1998, and now it is upward of 75 to 80 percent."

Why now? Because employees are demanding these options and it just makes business sense. During the recent economic downturn, big companies held all the cards. Work–life issues took a backseat to worries about just keeping your job. There weren't a lot of other options out there if you wanted to take your stapler and go home. The unspoken (if you were lucky) attitude was, *If you don't like it, you can leave.*

As the economy has improved, however, companies have been forced to compete for the best people—and the battle is only going to get fiercer. Remember the impending labor shortage that the futurists are predicting? Some companies have seen the writing on the wall and are actively looking for ways to retain their human resources. After all, turnover is expensive. Offering flextime options and sabbatical programs is often much less costly than recruiting and training replacements for the people who quit because of work–life balance issues.

At the same time, developments in technology have made it easier than ever to work from home and stay connected via cell phone, BlackBerry, and remote computer access. Face time has become less necessary (though not all managers seem to have received that memo). In fact, people working from home are often more productive because they skip the time-consuming and pollution-causing commute and avoid unnecessary meetings.

ARE YOU A VALUABLE EMPLOYEE?

If you can't answer yes to all of these questions, you'd better get busy sucking up if you want an opportunity to take a break:

- Do you have a history of positive performance reviews?
- Does your manager trust you and depend on you?
- Are you working on high-profile and/or important projects?
- Do you have skills and experience that are highly valued and hard to replace?
- Are you well liked?

If your reputation at work isn't stellar, that may be because your heart hasn't been in it. It can be hard to go above and beyond when you're miserable. However, if you think a flexible arrangement could be the answer to your prayers, it might be worth your while to actively reestablish your rep.

Not Just a Mommy Issue

Much has been written about the challenges of balancing career and family responsibilities. In many corporations, there is little flexibility for dealing with the often unpredictable responsibilities of parenthood. Need to leave early to pick up a sick child? Want to spend some quality time with your kids while they're actually awake? Let's hope your boss is feeling generous.

Traditionally, the majority of child care duties have fallen to good old Mommy. That remains true today, even in dual-career couples and despite the clear trend toward fathers getting more involved in childrearing and the welcome increase in the number of stay-at-home dads.

Many working mothers would be more than willing to scale back and find a happy medium between work and motherhood. Unfortunately, there have historically not been many legitimate opportunities for part-time or flexible work arrangements. Left with few alternatives, many women opted out of the corporate workforce either temporarily or permanently. This movement, dubbed the "opt-out revolution" by *The New York Times* in 2003, has led to a significant brain drain at corporations.

"Everything changes when you have kids," says Julie Smith, a former telecommunications executive. Julie went back to her full-time job shortly after the birth of her first child with every intention of making it work. She ran herself ragged trying to meet both the inflexible demands of her employer and the inflexible demands of her infant son.

When she got pregnant with her second child, Julie knew something had to give. She took some time off and eventually went back to work for McKinley Marketing Partners, an agency that places marketing executives at major companies on an interim basis. This new arrangement allows Julie to work more defined hours and take time off between assignments when she needs to.

Companies have started to recognize the value of the talent walking out the door with fed-up working mothers like Julie. In recent years, there has been a flurry of new programs designed to help with career "on-ramping" and "off-ramping" (HR-speak for taking time off from the workforce and returning). These programs include a range of options that allow workers to stay in touch while away from the job so that their skills remain fresh and marketable.

Booz Allen Hamilton, for example, has a gradual-return-to-work program to help women who have been out on maternity leave ease back into a full-time schedule. "They send a message to the woman that they want her to come back," says Amy Lyman.

Working mothers aren't the only employees interested in these programs. Many Baby Boomers have become caregivers for aging parents, and other workers are seeking time away for personal pursuits. "For anyone who works, flexibility is a big concern," adds Lyman. "It is now more acceptable to speak up and request flexibility."

TALES FROM THE CORPORATE TRENCHES

The Part-Time VP

Name: Manya Chait

Current occupation: Vice president of public relations, VistaPrint

Manya Chait has been a poster girl for flextime work ever since she started in her role as VP of public relations for VistaPrint, a printing and design firm that caters to individuals and small businesses (you or someone you know probably has some of VistaPrint's free business cards). She negotiated a four-day workweek schedule from the very start in order to have the flexibility to care for her young daughter.

"What attracted me was the incredible career opportunity," she says. "But I knew I could only do it on a flexible schedule, and my boss was open to that because we had worked together in the past and she knew what I could do."

On Fridays, Manya was out of the office, but would check e-mail periodically and be available via phone for emergencies. The arrangement worked well for everyone for more than two years.

Then Manya was forced to reevaluate. "My husband took on a new job with more responsibilities and my daughter's grandparents couldn't take her as often as they could before," she says. She realized that she would have to scale her work schedule back to twenty-five hours per week or leave her job altogether.

She went to her manager in March to present a proposal to start working part-time on June 1. She started the conversation by making it very clear that she did not want to leave the company. "I told her that I was really passionate about my work and

VistaPrint, but twenty-five hours a week was all I could do at that point."

Her boss responded very positively. The company wanted her to stay, and Manya and her manager worked with the Human Resource Department to put an agreement into writing.

"We adjusted my salary based on the number of hours I would be working and modified the benefits package based on my reduced schedule. I just had to pay in a little bit more," she says.

It helped that Manya gave three months' notice about her intentions so that her employers had time to figure out the best solution. "They had been very flexible for me, and I just felt like I wanted to be fair," she explains.

To make sure all her duties were covered, Manya delegated to her team members. "Many of the people who work for me were excited about the opportunity to take on responsibilities that they might not otherwise have had," she says.

"This experience has really renewed my faith in the work force. Moms and dads sometimes can't work full forty-hour weeks, and I was excited to see the company endorse flexible schedules as a way of keeping those people in the workforce."

Manya notes that it's not just working parents who have flexibility options at VistaPrint. For example, one of the firm's graphic designers takes time off to tour with his band. "Today it's much easier for people to start their own businesses, or jump to a different job, or take a few years off. So I think the organization sees it's in their best interest to work with the people they want to keep."

Manya Chait's Top Advice for Taking a Break

"As long as you have a good reputation and you work hard, then there is no harm in asking for the flexible arrangement that you want. The opportunity is not always going to be handed to you. No e-mail went out at my firm that said, *Please let us know if you want to work part-time.* I had to take the lead in making it happen."

The Realities of Flexibility

As more companies endorse these programs and more employees demonstrate their feasibility, the options should continue to expand. That's not to say that all corporations are shiny, happy, flex-friendly places to work. Unfortunately, some companies offer "flexibility" in name only.

If your company is late getting with the program, don't despair. Often flexible work programs start because someone is brave enough to defy company conventions and ask for what he wants.

How do you know if going flex will solve your problems? Let's review the options.

Flextime

Research shows that people are happier and more productive when they have greater control over their work hours. With a flextime arrangement, you will be working full-time, but you'll have more say over when you do it.

Flextime offers a range of options outside the typical workweek structure:

- You can adjust your starting and quitting times. For example, you could start your day at six and leave the office at three, in plenty of time to pick up the kids at school or take the schnauzer for a walk in the park.
- The compressed schedule allows for squeezing a forty-hour workweek into fewer than five days—For example, by working four days per week from eight to six and taking the fifth day off.

Flextime arrangements allow you to work when you are at your most productive. Most importantly, they also give you the freedom to take time for personal responsibilities when you need it.

It's probably no surprise that those with flexible schedules are happier and less stressed. They also tend to be more efficient.

☕ Telecommuting

Telecommuting allows you to work from home at least part of the week—using BlackBerrys, cell phones, and remote computer access to stay on top of your work. People, if you haven't asked for this setup, you're missing out.

In 2006, 12.4 million people worked from home for an employer at least one day per month, up 63 percent from just 7.6 million in 2004.

When you telecommute, you save time by skipping your annoying commute *and* any precious time normally devoted to dressing up for the office. You also get a good excuse for avoiding a lot of useless meetings.

Any meetings you do participate in will be via conference call. That means you can actually work while people are droning on about nothing. Just don't forget to put your phone on mute so they can't hear you typing happily away and yelling at the cat during their brilliant observations.

The biggest challenge in telecommuting is convincing your boss that you're actually working. Corporate managers are naturally suspicious creatures. They know that telecommuting is a sweet deal. Naturally, they worry that you'll spend your days watching Oprah if they're not there to keep an eye on you. After all, that's what they do when they telecommute.

The truth is you'll be able to make a lot more time for daytime TV and other important interests when you telecommute—and your boss will never have to know. Once you start working at home, you'll be shocked to realize the number of hours that you waste at the office between meetings, BS conversations with co-workers, and various other exercises in futility. Believe me, that time is better spent with Oprah or even Montel. Or you could devote those saved hours to your family, your friends, and/or your outside interests (like maybe launching a new career?).

Keep in mind that you will still have to get your job done. In fact, there will be added pressure to deliver. Your boss will be watching carefully to make sure you can be trusted to work at home. Don't ruin it for yourself or anybody else at the office. Make it a point of honor to be *more* productive on the days that you work from home.

So what's not to love about telecommuting? Well, the reduced face time with management can sometimes hurt your chances for promotions. Some people also complain that working from home is lonely. They miss the chat around the watercooler.

Both problems can be solved by using the time that you do spend in the office constructively. Make a point of socializing, glad-handing, and doing lunch on the days that you don't telecommute.

Of course, some people aren't cut out for telecommuting. If the socializing aspect of work is important to you, or if you have trouble managing and prioritizing your own time, you may be better off spending your days at the office.

Tips for Telecommuting

- **Get hooked up.** Do yourself a favor and set up a sweet home office with everything you need to do your job well. Don't forget the e-mail and Web-enabled PDA so you can stay in touch even when running errands. As long as you're responding to e-mails, you boss never has to know that you took a long lunch in the park. Your company might even spring for a new laptop or BlackBerry to keep you sufficiently connected. It doesn't hurt to ask, but don't push your luck. If your company won't pay for it, make a personal investment in the equipment and software that you'll need to do your job efficiently from home. If your home office is used regularly and exclusively for business needs, you may even be able to deduct some of the expenses.

- **Get out of your pajamas.** Yeah, I know it's fun to work in your PJs and bunny slippers. But do everybody a favor and start your days by showering and putting on some real clothes. It will put you in a work state of mind. Julie Smith, who has been telecommuting for years, likes to take it a step further. "I get up, shower, and I put on work clothes as if I was going to an office," she says. "That helps me set the tone and the mood. Sitting around in my sweats doesn't work for me at all."

  I prefer jeans myself unless I have a meeting with corporate types, but I can relate to the concept. Otherwise, if you're telecommuting regularly, you could end up living in your pajamas. That's how the downward spiral begins. The next thing you know, you're that smelly, unkempt guy wandering the neighborhood in a Cheeto-stained Bon Jovi T-shirt.

- **Be productive.** Working from home is *not* an excuse to slack off. If you start missing deadlines and blowing off conference calls, you will soon find yourself back in your cubicle under the watchful eye of your boss. Even if your productivity is through the roof, you'll want to avoid flaunting the joys of your out-of-office arrangement. Do not tell your co-workers about that awesome marathon of *The Real World* on MTV. Don't blog about your excessive amounts of free time. Avoid mentioning any midday napping. Yes, they're just jealous. You're more efficient than they are, and maybe you should be allowed an occasional nap as long as you get your work done. But arousing jealousy can be dangerous. It can lead to more work, more supervision, or bad mojo. As far as your boss and co-workers are concerned, you are always working and you're always busy.

- **Keep it separated.** You will have to make a real, conscious effort to keep your work separated from your home life. When your office is right down the hall, it can be much harder to disconnect from your job at the end of the day. You may find yourself spending far more time working than you ever did in the office. Try to set a daily quitting time and stick to it unless there are special circumstances. On the flip side, beware of letting your personal life interfere with your business responsibilities—or even appear to interfere. Appearances are important in the corporate world. If your two-year-old, your Nana, or your cockatoo is constantly interrupting your conference calls, people will notice and they will take you less seriously. The mute button on your phone is there for a reason, people. Use it. You need to maintain the illusion of complete and loving focus on your boss's every syllable.

FUN THINGS TO DO WHILE TELECOMMUTING

- Wait for the cable repairman.
- Take calls from recruiters.
- Wear inappropriate clothing.
- Use inappropriate language.
- Bask in actual sunlight.

Part-Time

Traditionally, part-time work was mostly for teenagers and entry-level workers in fields such as retail and food services. It was difficult to find interesting managerial or professional work on a part-time schedule, but that has been changing. Many working parents and other professionals are now choosing to work part-time, either temporarily or permanently, and companies are coming around to see the value of offering part-time arrangements to keep valued employees. The Bureau of Labor Statistics estimates that approximately 20 percent of workers classified as "professionals" worked part-time in 2004—and the demand is growing. A survey by the Families and Work Institute found that 24 percent of women and 13 percent of men who work full-time would rather work part-time. Meanwhile, 57 percent of older workers said they would prefer to remain in the workforce part-time. These Baby Boomers are rejecting traditional retirement in favor of continuing to work, but on a less demanding schedule.

Some people are looking for a long-term part-time arrangement that will accommodate other professional activities. A steady part-time job can be a great foundation for what's known as a portfolio career. People with portfolio careers have multiple income streams. They may balance a part-time job with running a small business or pursuing a less lucrative career in the arts or nonprofit sector. (See chapter 8 for more information about structuring a portfolio career.)

Others choose part-time work for personal reasons. They want time for family obligations, volunteer work, or treasured hobbies. They may be looking to scale back their schedules temporarily and intend to return to full-time work at a later date.

While the potential benefits of a part-time schedule are many, it's not the best choice for everyone. When you work part-time, you earn part-time money. You'll have to do the math to see if you can afford to pay your bills on a reduced income. Can you economize or cut out unnecessary expenses? Are you willing to make the sacrifices?

Make sure you also do your research on benefits for part-time employees. Many companies will require you to work a minimum number of hours per week to qualify for benefits. If benefits are offered to part-timers, be aware that you will probably be asked to contribute more than you did as a full-timer.

Once you've decided that part-time is the answer for you, you'll have to convince your boss. You are likely to have a much easier time negotiating a part-time schedule at your current company than you would finding a new part-time job elsewhere. You have goodwill equity (hopefully) with your manager and your company. If you've been doing your job well, there's a very good chance that they'd rather accommodate you than lose you.

That's not to say that moving to part-time is easy. This is often a more difficult sell than flextime or telecommuting because the change will have a bigger impact on your boss and your department. Who will take on the work you no longer have time for? At the same time, because salary and benefits changes will be required, your manager will have to get sign-off from Human Resources and possibly senior management.

Keep in mind that part-time arrangements aren't often advertised. Many of those I spoke with had to pitch the idea and work closely with their managers to figure out the details of the arrangement.

"At VistaPrint, it is really handled on a department-by-department basis because some jobs are more challenging to do part-time than others," says Manya Chait. She notes that there are a wide variety of options to suit different jobs and individuals. "Some of the engineers work four days a week or take every other Friday off during the summer," she says. "The company is absolutely willing to work with employees, and it is very individually focused."

You may have to get a little bit creative to find an arrangement that will satisfy both you and your company:

- **Job sharing.** With job sharing, two part-time employees share the responsibilities of one full-time position. The question is where to find that other person to take on half of your old responsibilities. You can sweeten this deal for your boss by doing a little legwork first. Reach out to your network and see if anyone knows a likely candidate. If at all possible, present your boss with a few viable options when you make your pitch. At a minimum, offer to take charge of recruiting, interviewing, and training in order to make the process as painless as possible for your manager.

- **Delegating.** Is there a promising junior person in your department who would love a chance to take on additional responsibilities? Think about ways that you could carve up your current job and give away nonessential parts of it to others in your group.
- **Hiring.** You might be able to hire a less experienced person to take on the least challenging aspects of your job. The final arrangement could even save your company money if the new hire earns less than the salary you're giving up.

Naturally, there are risks involved in going part-time. Some people worry that they'll delegate too much and get squeezed out by others in the department. And don't think that you can rest on your laurels once you've negotiated a part-time schedule. It will be more important than ever to continue to demonstrate your value.

Another risk is that your manager and co-workers will not respect your part-time schedule, and that it will eventually expand to become a full-time job for less money. You will have to set clear boundaries and be firm at times. Monitor the hours that you work and keep the lines of communication with your manager open.

One of the primary reasons that many hesitate to pursue part-time work arrangements is the fear that it could damage their careers. Some professionals are afraid to even ask about part-time work because they think it might brand them as uncommitted or somehow unable to hack a "real" job.

Unfortunately, that may be true in some corporate cultures. In many cases, though, these fears are overblown. As more and more professionals successfully move to part-time schedules and demonstrate how they can work, familiarity will continue to breed understanding.

Don't make assumptions. If you're serious about the idea, approach your boss in a professional way and see how she responds. The worst she can do is say no. She is unlikely to hold the very act of asking against you forever.

If you're concerned that you'll be seen in a different light and be considered less seriously for future promotions (and assuming you care), you can do damage control by assuring management that you are still 100 percent committed to the firm and will be simply delighted to continue in a full-time capacity if that's what the company needs. Then start looking for another job.

According to research by the Great Place to Work Institute, working part-time is not a résumé killer anymore. "It may still affect your career in that you may slow down your progress while you're working less, but that is not necessarily seen as such a bad thing anymore," says Amy Lyman. "It may take you five years to get to the next promotion instead of two years, but that's a trade-off many are willing to make."

Sabbaticals and Leaves of Absence

Sometimes it's just not enough to scale back. You need a complete break from work to recharge your batteries or deal with other responsibilities.

The Family and Medical Leave Act (FMLA) guarantees parents twelve weeks of unpaid leave to care for a newly born or adopted child, an ailing family member, or a personal illness. You qualify if you are employed by a firm with at least fifty employees and have worked at least 1,250 hours in the previous year.

Some companies also allow employees to take paid sabbaticals. A sabbatical is any extended leave from your job. Traditionally, teachers and college professors have taken sabbatical years in order to learn new skills or travel.

Now more and more corporate professionals are taking sabbaticals for a wide variety of reasons:

- **Personal responsibilities.** When a twelve-week FMLA leave isn't enough, some people take a sabbatical to devote more time to family or personal duties or focus on recovering from an illness or injury.
- **Personal passions.** Some take time off to follow a personal dream—writing a novel, recording a demo, training to scale Mount Everest, or getting a sideline business up and running.
- **Volunteering.** The search for meaning sometimes leads individuals to take a career break and devote time to building schools in Africa, protecting the rain forest in Brazil, or rallying for a local cause that needs them.
- **Going back to school.** It can be hard to balance a full-time job and a demanding graduate program or training curriculum. Those who can swing it often take leaves of absence to finish their MBAs, their PhDs, or their certificates in the fine art of puppetry.
- **Recharging your batteries.** Sometimes the goal of a sabbatical is to step away from a hectic, overworked lifestyle and regain your physical and mental health. A break can provide a new perspective and an opportunity to plan the next stage in your career adventure.

Some forward-thinking companies actually encourage sabbaticals for their employees, and a few will even pay your salary while you're away (see box on the next page). Firms have learned that offering sabbaticals can be a great way to keep their most talented people from burning out or moving on.

The latest numbers from the Society of Human Resources Management show that about 11 percent of large corporations offer paid sabbaticals; an additional 29 percent offer unpaid. Five years ago, only 15 percent of all companies (large and small) offered unpaid sabbaticals.

In most cases, even if your company goes for the idea, you probably won't be paid. However, your job (or an equivalent one—be sure to read the fine print) will be waiting for you when you return.

COMPANIES WITH COOL SABBATICAL PROGRAMS

- **American Express.** Employees who have worked at American Express for ten years can apply for a paid sabbatical of between one and six months. The company asks that you spend some time working for a nonprofit or school of your choice while on leave. After twenty years of service, employees have been granted longer sabbaticals of up to one year.
- **Intel.** At Intel, eligible employees qualify to take eight-week sabbaticals after every seven years of full-time service. Sounds like a great cure for the seven-year itch.
- **PricewaterhouseCoopers.** PricewaterhouseCoopers offers two types of sabbaticals—one for employees seeking personal growth and one for those interested in social service projects. You'll collect 20 to 40 percent of your regular salary and maintain most of your benefits while you're away. In order to take a sabbatical of three to six months, employees must agree to stay on at the firm for at least a year after they come back.
- **Xerox.** Each year, Xerox awards paid Social Service Leaves of up to one year to a select group of employees, who use the time to volunteer full-time in their communities. Recent participants included an engineer who spent six months building a database for the local fire department, and a purchasing manager who became a full-time instructor at a Girl Scout summer day camp. Xerox has granted Social Service Leaves to 469 employees since the program began in 1971.

Be prepared to negotiate on details such as the length of the sabbatical and when you'll take it. Make it clear that you will do everything you can to prevent business disruptions. Provide plenty of notice and avoid scheduling a sabbatical during a particularly busy period (but keep in mind that there will never be a perfect time in the eyes of your boss). If it's practical, offer to be reachable for questions or emergencies or even to handle a few key tasks while you're away.

Naturally, you are taking some risks by walking away from your job for an extended period of time. You will be completely out of the work loop, and you never know what you'll miss—promotion opportunities, exciting projects, birthday cake.

You might lose some of the career momentum you've gained. Corporate managers don't have very good long-term memories and are very much about what you've done for them lately.

You may also have some trouble returning from your sabbatical to the daily grind. Some people come back to the office refreshed and reenergized. Others find it harder to reengage.

The Step-by-Step Plan

While most companies say they offer flexible work arrangements, many make it hard to put them into practice.

So how do you negotiate a flexible work schedule if your company still values face time and long hours? You have to approach it as if you're making a sales presentation. Make it easy for your boss to say yes by clearly outlining what you want, developing a detailed plan for making it work, and clearly articulating the benefits to the company.

Don't be afraid to get creative. If working from home full-time or moving to a three-day workweek isn't feasible, think of compromises.

Step 1. Figure Out What You Want

Why do you need more flexibility at work? Are you looking for a few extra hours a week for your family or two months off to volunteer in Asia? Maybe you're not sure exactly what you want, but you know that something has to give.

What is your primary goal—to reduce stress, increase balance, or make time for a specific interest or responsibility? Is your need for flexibility temporary or long-term? Where are you willing to compromise?

Your personal motives are none of your company's business, but sorting them out will help you determine your best options.

Step 2. Research Your Company's Current Policies

Many companies have official flexible work policies, some more generous than others. Review your employee manual and understand the options available to you and any implications for health coverage and other benefits. If you can't find the information you need in the handbook, contact someone in Human Resources for additional details. If at all possible, speak with another employee who has actually used the arrangement you're most interested in. This is a good way to get a sense of any obstacles you might encounter.

Step 3. Understand the Company Culture

Unfortunately, some companies talk a good game about work–life balance but don't back up their written policies. If you fear that taking advantage of flexible work policies will label you as less committed and jeopardize your career, talk to people in the organization who have successfully negotiated flexible schedules to better understand the potential pros and cons.

Step 4. Increase Your Value

The most valued employees get the most consideration when it comes to flexible work arrangements. Are you an asset to the firm? Does your boss understand everything you do and how hard you would be to replace? While you're putting together your plan, think about how you can better demonstrate your worth to the company to strengthen your case.

Step 5. Create Your Business Case

Make an honest assessment of how your company and your boss will benefit from the arrangement you're proposing. Spend some time thinking about what option—or combination of options—would work best for both you and your company. Think creatively about potential solutions that will give you the flexibility you need and keep your employer happy.

Will it save the firm money, time, or headaches? Will the arrangement increase your productivity?

THE GREEN ARGUMENT

Help save the planet by letting your employees work from home! Nine out of ten of us drive to work and the average commute is up to 25 minutes in each direction. That's a lot of time wasted and a lot of gasoline becoming CO_2 emissions. Employees who work at home also have reduced absenteeism and save their companies money in real estate costs.

Source: *Live Earth Global Warming Survival Handbook*

Step 6. Put Your Proposal in Writing

Organize your thoughts by putting them down on paper. Spend time anticipating objections and thinking about all of the angles—

including the WIIFM (*What's in it for me?*) for your boss. For example, perhaps telecommuting would allow you to start the workday earlier or to spend more time on important paperwork. Then put a detailed pitch in writing. This is a business proposal, and your document must clearly explain the value of the arrangement for your company. Your boss will take you more seriously if you show that you've thought this idea through and are willing to invest in making it work. A written proposal also makes it easier for your boss to get buy-in from his superiors.

Step 7. Sell the Idea

Schedule a meeting with your manager to present your proposal and discuss the details. Start the conversation by making it clear that you are committed to the firm and are not planning to walk out the door tomorrow. Avoid issuing ultimatums or getting defensive. Spell out your request and respond to concerns and questions.

Step 8. Be Prepared to Negotiate

Listen to your boss's concerns and be open to possible compromises. For example, if your manager has doubts, suggest a trial period of three to six months. Set dates for the trial and then do everything you can to demonstrate the brilliance of your proposed arrangement. Let your boss know that you are ready, willing, and able to address any problems that come up.

Step 9. Have a Long-Term Plan

Think about how you will respond to different outcomes. If your proposal is rejected, what does that mean? Can you be content continuing as you have been, or will you start looking for another position? If your plan is accepted, what preparation work needs to be done before you can get started?

   If your proposal is accepted, set some dates for reevaluating the arrangement as you go along. If it's a temporary arrangement, think about how you will phase back into a full-time schedule.

Step 10. Prepare for the Challenges

While flexible work offers many benefits, it can also be challenging. Honestly evaluate the pros and cons. What are the potential downsides, and what sacrifices are you willing to make in exchange for flexibility?

Get the Space You Need

What if, despite your best efforts, your company won't provide the flexibility you're looking for? If the practical approach fails, you may have to take more radical steps.

You can always make a move to a company with better work–life balance policies. Reach out to your network first, as it will be easier to negotiate a flexible arrangement with a manager who already knows your value.

You can also just go ahead and take the leap without a corporate net. Make your financial plan, quit your job, and take your own sabbatical.

Michelle T. hated her job in commercial banking and fantasized about taking a year off to windsurf in Hawaii. "I needed a little break to figure out my future because I was highly unhappy in what I was doing," she says.

She tried to recharge her batteries on a Hawaiian vacation, but fell deeper in love with the idea of taking a year off. "Everyone said it was just vacation hangover and that I would get over it, but I couldn't."

Michelle researched the cost of living in Maui and started saving as much as she could from her paychecks. "I wanted a certain amount in the bank before I moved," she explains. "My plan was to have several months of living expenses, and supplement my income with waitressing if necessary." As it happened, Michelle's company laid her off before she could quit.

At the time, however, it was fairly inexpensive to live in Maui. Michelle was able to extend her time off and spend three years pursuing her windsurfing passion while waiting tables on the side.

Later, she found herself longing for more intellectually challenging work and moved to the Bay Area, where she joined a technology firm; eventually, she went back to school to get her teaching certification. Today she's back in Maui and loving her work as a first-grade teacher.

It took flexibility and resourcefulness for Michelle T. to take the break she needed, but she feels it was well worth the skimping, saving, and hard work.

TAKE A CAREER BREAK

Have you ever dreamed about ditching your job for a year to tour Europe, learn Japanese in Kyoto, or teach English to kids in Nairobi? The "career break"—a sort of gap year for grown-ups—is an idea that is catching on in the United Kingdom and Canada and may soon be coming to the United States.

The gap year has traditionally been an acceptable option only for those between the ages of seventeen and twenty-three. Millions around the world take a year off to travel and/or find themselves before, during, or after college.

In the last few years, though, many older professionals have also been drawn to the idea of taking time off for an adventure. More than 75 percent of British professionals surveyed said they would consider taking a midcareer break to travel the world. Canadian travel agencies have also seen an increase in interest in career breaks.

Career breaks average three to six months, but often last for a year or more. Some people take company-endorsed sabbaticals and put their jobs on hold, while others resign with the understanding that they will find their next opportunity when they return.

Many in their early thirties are choosing to take career breaks to get the wanderlust out of their systems before settling down to start a family. Professionals in their fifties are also increasingly attracted to time away after their kids have moved out and the college bills are paid.

Types of Career Breaks

- **Fun and adventure.** Take a break from your high-pressure work routine and see the world. Climb Ayers Rock at dawn or hike to Machu Picchu. Step outside your familiar circle of friends to meet new people and explore new cultures.
- **Improve the world.** Use your time away to make a difference in the world by teaching in a developing country, building homes for needy families, or campaigning to save endangered species.
- **Improve yourself.** For people looking to get out of a career rut, a break can provide the chance to learn a new language or gain valuable career-enhancing experience by working abroad. Live with a family in Tibet and immerse yourself in the culture or sign on to shadow someone in your dream job.

SEVEN

Swim in a Smaller Pond

In a start-up company, you basically throw out all assumptions every three weeks.

—William Lyon Phelps, journalist and professor

Never doubt that a small group of thoughtful, committed citizens can change the world; indeed, it's the only thing that ever does.

—Margaret Mead, anthropologist

If the bureaucracy and rules at a big corporation make you crazy, your best escape route may be to a small company or start-up. Employee satisfaction is often higher at small companies because people have more autonomy and feel as if their contributions matter. While you may be a "human resource" at a large firm, you are always a key member of the team at a small business.

After almost fifteen years in Corporate America, Tania Mulry left a senior product development position at a major financial services firm on the East Coast to join the management team of a small technology start-up in California.

Even though Tania had found great success and stability in her corporate career, something was missing. She thought about starting her own business, but felt the risk would be too great. She had a big house, a husband, and three kids. "I had mouths to feed and college educations to save for," she says. "My family relied on my income."

Instead, Tania took a senior management position with an equity stake in a promising start-up venture. It was the perfect solution. Her new job at mobile technology start-up Teleflip pays a salary similar to her old one, along with the ownership upside. Teleflip even paid for Tania's family to relocate to California, a move they'd been thinking about making before the position came along.

Most important, the new position allowed Tania to jump into a more challenging career that offered an opportunity to help build a business.

Tania is just one of thousands of corporate superstars who have defected to join small and start-up firms. They go for many reasons—for excitement, for bigger responsibilities, for flexibility, and for future riches.

Although big corporations tend to pay higher salaries, employees at smaller companies are generally happier. According to research by Gallup, engagement is highest at companies with fewer than fifty people and lowest at those with one thousand to five thousand employees.

That higher engagement translates into better productivity. In fact, many innovative large firms have established policies to limit the size of project teams in order to boost results.

Start-Ups 2.0

For a while there, *start-up* was a dirty word. After the tech meltdown that led to the extinction of so many high-profile dot-coms, most of us retreated to the seeming stability of established companies.

Back in the late 1990s, it was a different story. Workers left big corporations in droves to join the dot-com revolution. We were lured by stock options, company foosball tables, and the ability to take our dogs to work. Most of all, though, we were seduced by the opportunity to build something, to see what we could really do.

I went from being managed by committee in a corporate environment to having sole responsibility for multimillion-dollar client accounts at my dot-com job. That was my first major career change. I left a good job at an established financial services firm to join a small Web development and online marketing agency. Within eighteen months, that small agency had become an international company with six-hundred-plus employees and *Fortune* 500 clients.

It was fun while it lasted. Everything was moving so quickly, the opportunities for the smart and the ambitious were unlimited. I think I learned more in those two years than I did in my subsequent five back in Corporate America.

Then the bubble burst and everybody got laid off. Good jobs were scarce and everybody suddenly wanted to work at a nice, "safe" conglomerate again. Like Michael Corleone, we had tried to get out, but they pulled us back in.

It was a tough transition back to cubicle land. But the economy was in the crapper and we felt lucky to have jobs at all. Even the largest, most outwardly stable companies were laying people off left and right. Times were tight; employee satisfaction was the last thing on anyone's mind.

Luckily, those days are over. Small companies are back, baby, and now they're actually being managed by grown-ups (mostly). Small businesses generate 75 percent of new jobs in this country and account for 50 percent of the American workforce.

For disgruntled corporate employees, the time may once again be right to make a move.

DARING TALES OF CORPORATE ESCAPE

From Spreadsheets to ABCs

Name: Alex Kay

Previous occupation: Investment banker

Current occupation: President and COO of Word World,
a children's entertainment production company

For more than a decade, Alex Kay was perfectly content with his
job as an investment banker. Then, after the stock market crash of
2000, Alex found himself among the ranks of the downsized when
the big firm he worked for was purchased by an even bigger one:

He decided to take some time off before looking for another
Wall Street job. Then September 11 happened.

"That was a big wake-up call for me," Alex remembers. "It made
everybody start questioning the real meaning of life and what they
were doing, and it made it easier to start looking at alternatives."

The idea of leaving investment banking was a daunting one.
"Those golden handcuffs are very real," he says. "You kind of build
your life around having a certain salary."

While he contemplated his next move, Alex paid the bills by
working on deals for a small boutique firm. That's where he was introduced to the founder of Word World, who was trying to raise
funding for the company.

Alex was intrigued by the concept behind Word World, an innovative approach to teaching literacy skills through kids' entertainment, and spent three months doing due diligence and working on
a business plan.

"I never considered for a moment that I would someday be
working for the company, but the more I learned, the more excited
I got about Word World and the idea of leaving banking for good,"
he recalls.

Eventually, Alex joined Word World as the company's third employee. Today, as the firm's executive vice president and producer,

he runs all day-to-day operations, managing fifty employees and a production studio.

The company currently produces a television series for PBS featuring the animated characters of Word World, which include a dog cleverly drawn from the letters *D-O-G*, a sheep in the shape of *S-H-E-E-P*, and their friends. "What we are trying to do is teach children between the ages of three and five to understand the concept of how letters fit together to form words that represent real-life objects," says Alex. The characters are also licensed for children's books and toys sold at Target and other retailers. At the same time, Word World is working on additional children's entertainment properties with purpose. The government recently awarded the firm's principals grant funding to develop two more literacy projects. "I love the notion that it's not just a business, but also a way to do good by doing well," says Alex.

Although Alex loves working at Word World, there are some additional pressures that come with the job. "In the corporate world, if I didn't do a deal, it didn't really affect the guy in the next office's paycheck," says Alex. "Here I am responsible for fifty people."

Every day is a challenge because the business is evolving so quickly, but the effort is worth it. "I am very proud of what we're doing at Word World. I just love it," he says. "The reward is so much more than monetary."

Alex Kay's Best Career Change Advice

"I think people tend to look at the downside and think about what they'll have to give up. But the upside is the ability to actually add value on a daily basis.

"Of course, you want to be smart about it, but it is so worth the risk. If you can just let go, you will find there is a lot more out there."

Small Can Be Beautiful

It turns out that size really does matter. A 2005 study by workforce consultants Age Wave/The Concours Group revealed that employees of small companies were more than twice as satisfied as those in large corporations.

"Why work for a large company when you can have so much more fun, so much more responsibility, and so much more potential for upside working at a start-up?" asks serial entrepreneur and Bloglines founder Mark Fletcher.

And start-ups are not the only small businesses. There are also plenty of established companies out there that keep their operations lean and mean.

While some may prefer the structure and predictability of a larger firm, others have discovered that small companies offer many advantages.

Scratch Your Entrepreneurial Itch

Joining a small enterprise is a chance to flex your entrepreneurial muscles without the risk of starting your own firm. You can get in on the ground floor and help build a company while still collecting a salary.

Gwen C. was ready for a change after many years at a large management consulting firm. She wanted to do more innovative work, but didn't think she was cut out to be her own boss. Instead, she took a management position with a small boutique consulting firm. She chose that job over a much more lucrative offer from a larger company.

"I was willing to take a hit financially for the learning and the environment," she explains. "I knew that getting that entrepreneurial experience was worth more than any dollar amount."

Working for a start-up can provide valuable lessons for any entrepreneur-in-training. You'll get hands-on experience in running a business and learn pretty quickly whether you have what it takes to start your own firm someday.

After working for several start-ups in Silicon Valley, Mark

Fletcher became a successful entrepreneur several times over. His start-up background gave him the knowledge and network he needed to strike out on his own.

Fletcher's first start-up, ONElist, was purchased by Yahoo! in a multimillion-dollar deal in 2001. Bloglines, a more recent Fletcher venture, was bought by IAC/InterActive Corporation in another lucrative transaction in 2005.

Get a Piece of the Action

In many cases, a job at a start-up comes with a literal ownership stake in the business. Because many of these companies are cash-poor, they can't always match the salary you were making in cubicleville. To sweeten the deal, most offer stock options and a chance to earn some serious dough if the firm does well.

Clearly, this is only a plus if you feel strongly that the company has the potential to succeed. During the dot-com implosion, we all learned that stock option deals aren't always worth the paper that they're printed on. However, options have also made plenty of people millionaires. If you truly believe that you're getting in on the ground floor of something great, taking a pay cut for an ownership stake could be a savvy investment.

"My choices were to stay where I was and suffer or to take a chance on something that could be huge," says Tania Mulry of her decision to move to a start-up.

Work can be much more rewarding when you have a real stake in the outcome. When you own part of the company, your hard work has a very clear purpose. If the company succeeds, you succeed. Your future rewards are tied directly to the business results, not to your manager's opinion.

Michael Sands, who left his COO position at a major consumer products group to launch the small snack food company Lesser-Evil, believes that workers are much more engaged when they own a piece of the company. "To me, the most important thing was for all employees to have stock and share in the value that we were creating," he says. "I want to make sure that everyone gets a financial return on their effort, not just the major owners."

Seize Career Opportunities

Many corporate refugees flee to small companies for the chance to start making management decisions instead of just management presentations. The opportunity to take on more responsibility can be a major draw for ambitious types who feel stifled in middle management.

At a small company, there is no hierarchy and very little time for politics. You'll have plenty of openings to step up and show what you can do.

"Every day I face a new challenge and every day I learn something new," says Alex Kay. "When you have stagnated in these large corporations for a long time, it's great to know that your mind still works and that you can actually make decisions."

If you're looking for hands-on experience, a smaller company is the place to get it. Because there are limited resources and more of an all-hands-on-deck atmosphere, you can get exposure to every aspect of the business.

Alex Kay has been involved in raising funding for the company, hiring staff, negotiating licensing agreements, manufacturing the company's products, overseeing the production studio, and much more. "What I have learned in the last three and a half years is just incredible."

This practical know-how can increase your marketability significantly and prepare you for a much bigger job.

BEST SMALL-COMPANY PERKS

A recent Salary.com survey of small-business employees identified the following nonfinancial reasons why people stayed in their jobs:

- Work–life balance—46.2%
- Commute—38.1%
- Loyalty—34.8%
- Their boss—31.4%
- Relationships with co-workers—29.5%

Have More Fun at Work

There's nothing quite like the thrill of being part of a successful start-up. Your days are full of new and exciting experiences, and there is enormous pride in knowing that you're helping to build a company from scratch.

The work itself can also be much more interesting. At a big company, you spend a lot of time following rules and getting permission. At a smaller company, there's more room for creativity and experimentation. That explains why most of the world's greatest innovations have come from small organizations.

"I like to move fast, and I was in a very slow-moving company that did not really want me to do the innovative things they said they wanted me to do," says Tania Mulry. "They found a way to bureaucratize every innovative idea out of existence."

After moving to a start-up environment, Tania enjoyed the freedom to let her creativity flow. "It is so nice to see your ideas come to life and be appreciated by customers and co-workers," she notes. "There is a great feeling of ownership in the outcome that doesn't exist in larger companies."

DARING TALES OF CORPORATE ESCAPE

Art, Toys, and Management Consulting

Name: Ben Cikanek

Previous occupation: Management consultant

Current occupation: Executive director of operations at Kidrobot

Ben Cikanek doesn't seem like the corporate type. He works sur-rounded by toys in his office at Kidrobot, the world's premier cre-ator and retailer of limited-edition art toys and apparel. Kidrobot products are collaborations with famous artists and have a serious cult following. New releases of limited-edition Kidrobot toys have been known to cause near riots in the company's stores in New York, Los Angeles, and San Francisco.

But Ben wasn't always on the cutting edge. "I think my reason for studying business was partially because my mom always imag-ined me as a professional," he remembers. During college, Ben scored an interview for a high-paying summer job with one of the Big 5 accounting firms.

"They had these summer jobs and were throwing money around," he says. The firm wooed him with dinners at expensive restaurants and limousine rides. Ben thought he had the job in the bag and was surprised when he didn't get it.

"I called them and asked them to reconsider because I had no other options for the summer and had just assumed they were go-ing to hire me," he says. "Which is kind of hilarious in retrospect, but made sense in my twenty-year-old mind."

Shockingly, the company actually returned his call and offered him the job. "That just reconfirmed my philosophy in life that a no is never actually a no."

Ben had a good experience that summer and landed an offer for a full-time job after graduation. "At the time I was applying to film schools, and I thought I would do the job for a few months and then get the hell out."

When he didn't get into the prestigious film programs he'd applied for, Ben had to rethink his strategy. "At that point, I was out of school and working for this big accounting firm, making piles of money that I didn't know what to do with as a kid of that age," he says. "But I was completely miserable and exhausted from flying back and forth every single week between Denver and Chicago."

He soon reached a decision. "I pretty much completely hated my life and was about to quit my job and just figure something else out entirely," he remembers. Then he discovered the company's Accelerated Solutions Environment (ASE).

"ASE was a little spin-off suborganization at the firm that did this incredible creative problem-solving work for clients," he explains. "They seemed like they were having a lot of fun, so I would just go back every day and try to convince them to let me work for them."

Eventually, he won them over and was offered a job. He loved the work, but didn't love the idea of the traditional consulting career path. "I wasn't cut out to go from management consultant to senior consultant to manager to partner," he says. "So I structured a contractor relationship with the ASE so that I could work two hundred days a year and have time for my outside interests."

He used that time to go to film school, study at the Improv in Chicago, and write and produce plays. "I had this very big creative life outside of my work."

When Paul Budnitz, the founder of Kidrobot, asked to meet about a job opportunity, Ben happily agreed: "Paul was very interesting to me because he was written up in *Wired* magazine as the first human being ever to edit a feature-length film on a home computer."

Paul sat down and handed Ben a study of Kidrobot's Dunny figure, a vinyl action figure that has been reimagined by dozens of artists over the years. The Dunny series is one of Kidrobot's most popular product lines. "Today we sell millions of dollars' worth every year," Ben says.

But at the time, Ben told Paul that he had no interest in leaving his comfortable part-time consulting gig. "I told him I didn't want the job and I didn't want a boss and he said, 'You're perfect!' " Ben remembers. "And the truth of the matter was that I was getting pretty damn sick of doing consulting work for those big companies." He ended up accepting the position as the director of operations for Kidrobot.

It didn't hurt that the job came with a healthy potential upside. "I have the kind of deal that says when Kidrobot succeeds, I get to enjoy the benefits of that success," Ben says. "As just a flat salary job, it probably wouldn't have been as appealing to me."

That deal was a pretty good move on Ben's part. For 2008, Kidrobot is on track to generate ten times the revenue the company earned in 2004. Future plans include expanding the Kidrobot clothing line (currently sold in Kidrobot outlets and at Barneys New York), opening approximately twenty new stores, and much more.

"It's hard to remember the person I was two years ago," says Ben. "The breadth of what I have been exposed to and the energy here have really changed me."

He loves the feeling that he is helping to build a company. "I think everybody has that sensibility because the autonomy that Paul gave me, I have in turn granted to everyone else here," he says.

Despite his busy work schedule, Ben also still makes time for theater projects. He is the artistic director for a theater company in New York called Kids with Guns. "We just had our latest production reviewed by *The New York Times*."

He can't imagine ever going back to a corporate gig. "Everyone that I know is miserable in their corporate job," he says. "I think the reason people don't quit is because you build up a lifestyle around your job, and no matter how much you make, even if it's half a million dollars a year, you are going to figure out how to spend it."

Ben Cikanek's Advice on Escaping Corporate America

"You've got to pay the bills, but if you are willing to work your ass off you can do two things at once. And once that second thing takes off enough for you to jump ship, then you do it."

Ditch the Bureaucracy

Corporate bureaucracy is a lot like water torture. Mildly annoying at first, it can slowly but surely destroy your productivity, your job satisfaction, and even your sanity.

In my unscientific online survey of more than 150 corporate professionals, I asked respondents to name the three worst things about working in Corporate America. "Too much bureaucracy" was the number one answer, beating out such seemingly more serious challenges as "lack of work–life balance" and "overwork/burnout."

At small companies, there is simply no time for bureaucracy. Tania Mulry was amazed when she discovered how quickly things get done at a start-up. "Decisions were being made right there in the room that would have taken three to four months to make in Corporate America," she says.

Embrace Flexibility

Smaller companies often offer more flexibility. You will work just as hard—if not harder—but you will probably have more control over your hours and your work location. Sometimes this is because these firms can't pay as well and want to attract top talent. Often it's just because you are more likely to be known and respected as an individual when you work on a small team. As long as you get your work done well, no one will be looking over your shoulder or scolding you for taking a long lunch.

Be a Real Team Player

By necessity, there is more collaboration at a small company. There are fewer people to do the work, and most employees are expected to pitch in wherever they're needed. Those who crave variety and challenge thrive in this kind of environment. You may help name a new product one day and pack boxes the next.

There is also a real sense of community, a *we're all in this together* attitude that is in stark contrast with the *pass the buck* mentality at many corporations. As a result, you get to know your co-workers pretty well. That's usually a good thing if you've chosen your small company well.

"No offense against corporate places, but they were not always the most interesting," says futurist Andy Hines of Social Technologies, a small consulting firm, of his experience working at larger firms. "A lot of the attraction of my current company was the ability to work for people who are really interesting. Who else would work as a professional futurist? You have to be a little nuts and I like that."

Ben Cikanek, in charge of hiring for Kidrobot, puts a lot of thought into who he brings on board. "There is an understanding that we're going to spend the better part of our lives in this place for a while, so it better be a hell of a lot of fun and we'd better really enjoy who we are sitting next to."

At a small company, you'll also work much more closely with senior management. That means it's harder to hide any screwups, but you also have a much better chance of having your ideas heard and your contributions noticed.

The Small Challenges

Working for a small company isn't for everyone. There are those who measure their value by the size of their staff, even though everyone knows it's in the way that you use it. Ahem.

And there are certainly drawbacks to working at a smaller firm, especially for those who are used to a big corporation:

- **Lower salaries.** Smaller companies tend to pay lower salaries than larger firms, though that's not always the case. Tania Mulry made a lateral move in terms of salary when she jumped. However, if your primary concern is money in the bank, you should think long and hard about leaving corporate for a start-up.

- **Less structure.** With limited infrastructure in place, you will have to be comfortable making decisions on your own with little guidance. Large companies tend to have established processes for just about everything. At small companies, you often have to make it up as you go along. While this can be a great opportunity for some, it can be terrifying for others.

- **Less support.** You may have to give up your assistant, your help desk, and other comforts of the bureaucracy. Some people are bothered by taking on tedious administrative tasks that they used to delegate.

  "I end up doing much more detail work than I was used to as an executive with a larger team," says Tania Mulry. "I've had to become more self-reliant."

- **More turbulent.** Small companies are more nimble, but they are also more easily rocked by market forces. Many start-ups don't make it, so be sure to do your due diligence on any firm that makes you an offer.

  If the management team seems flaky or funding is running out fast, you would be wise to wait for a better offer.

- **Dependence on leaders.** The leader sets the tone for a small company and often determines success or failure. A great leader makes for a great firm. If he's weak or gets in over his head, though, the whole firm suffers.

- **Less prestige.** Giganticorp, Inc., is probably going to sound more impressive at a cocktail party than 3 Guys Startup. Just think how silly the first employees of Google probably felt when people asked them what they did.

  Listing a big company on your résumé gives you instant credibility that you'll have to earn as an employee of a smaller business.

- **Working in close quarters.** At a small firm, you will be spending a *lot* of time with your co-workers. If some of those co-workers are crazy, mean, or incompetent, it will be hard to avoid them.

Sometimes bad employees can flourish in a small-company environment. There aren't as many formal processes in place to deal with performance and behavior issues.

The Step-by-Step Guide

The best thing about this particular corporate escape route is that you don't have to quit your job until you have an attractive offer in hand. Of course, many of the best opportunities are not listed on the job boards or in the classifieds, so you might need some help getting started.

Step 1. Define Your Preferences

- Are you looking for a dynamic start-up or a more established small firm?
- What kind of business model intrigues you? What industries are you most interested in?
- What type of role are you seeking?
- What are the trade-offs that you're willing to make?

Step 2. Find Opportunities

The easiest way to find good jobs is through your network. Smaller firms tend to locate candidates through personal referrals. They don't have the time or money to spend on a long formal recruiting process. They want to bring in someone they can trust quickly. The good news is that small businesses also make hiring decisions very quickly, and you won't have to put up with endless rounds of interviews and approvals.

To find the right gig for you, your best bet is to get out and mingle at events and functions that attract entrepreneurs and start-up professionals. It doesn't hurt to keep an eye on the job boards, especially nontraditional ones such as JobKite.com, which specializes in jobs at small companies.

Step 3. Get the Job

Your corporate background can be viewed as both an advantage and a handicap. To put your best foot forward, play up the valuable experience you've gained and the best practices you can share.

You may have to address concerns that you are too stuck in your corporate ways to be able to thrive in a fast-paced environment with little infrastructure. Highlight any start-up or entrepreneurial experience in your past, and make it clear that you're ready to get your hands dirty.

Step 4. Evaluate the Job and the Company

Before you accept an offer, it's very important that you do your due diligence and understand your risk. How stable is the firm? How much funding has been secured? Don't be afraid to ask the tough questions (just wait until you have an offer on the table before you get too nosy).

Make a point of meeting as many people as you can during the interview process. If you take the job, you will be working very closely with the whole team, and you want to be sure that there's a good fit.

When it's time to negotiate the job offer, be up-front about what you need to make the move. Be open to compromise and willing to think creatively. If the salary is less than ideal, could you be swayed by more equity, a bigger title, or a flexible work arrangement?

Step 5. Quit Your Corporate Job

Once you've accepted an offer, it's time for the fun part. Give your boss your two weeks' notice and start packing up your desk. Try to resist the urge to gloat too much.

DARING TALES OF CORPORATE ESCAPE

From Corporate to Start-Up

Name: Tania Mulry

Previous occupation: Vice president of product development at a large financial services firm

Current occupation: Senior vice president of product development at Teleflip, a technology start-up

"I don't know how I ended up in the corporate world," says Tania Mulry. "I guess I was always a bit of a generalist. I did everything kind of equally well and had no burning passion to pursue a particular career."

After college graduation, Tania ended up taking a job in investment banking and worked for four companies in three years, surviving reorganizations, acquisitions, and a near bankruptcy,

She got tired of the turmoil and went looking for more stability. "I was ready to find a place where I could stay for several years, work really hard, and be appreciated." She wanted to buy a house, have kids, and set up a stable life.

She found what she was looking for in her next position. "I spent ten years at one of the world's most solid and stable companies." Along the way, she was promoted several times, had three kids, and kept right on moving up the ladder.

"Then, after my third maternity leave, I was inexplicably demoted," she recalls. Despite outstanding performance reviews and great relationships within the company, she was transferred into a group run by a manager who didn't know her and seemed to resent her presence.

"It was extremely unpleasant. I tried for a year and a half to make it work," she says. She tried to transfer to another department and took on extra work to demonstrate her value, but wasn't able to get her previous seniority level reinstated.

"I realized that I was not going to change the situation," she says. "If they couldn't tell from their HR records that I was someone worth keeping and treating well, then it was probably not the company for me to stay with."

When she looked at her other career options, Tania knew she didn't want to go to another big company. "I just could not face starting over and learning to navigate a whole new bureaucracy."

She thought about starting her own business, but didn't have an idea that inspired her. Besides, her family depended on her income.

"The best plan seemed to be to go to work for a smaller business where I could take some kind of equity in the company," she recalls. "But I had no idea how to find those opportunities."

She started networking as much as possible, making an effort to speak at conferences and to improve her visibility in the industry so that she could meet venture capitalists.

"At one industry conference, I sat down to have a beer with a consultant I had worked closely with in the past," she says. "He had just become the chief marketing officer for a start-up in Santa Monica, and I told him I was thinking about a change. Within a week, I was on a plane to go meet with the rest of senior management about a job."

They basically designed a job for her and gave her about sixteen business hours to make a decision about coming aboard. Luckily, Tania had already discussed the possibility with her husband, and they had decided they'd be willing to move for the right opportunity.

"I didn't end up having to give up much in terms of income, but I did have to move my family across the country to a more expensive place," Tania says. "We figured we could get along in a smaller house for a while and we could give up owning three cars because I would be able to walk to the office."

Once the decision was made, things started to come together. "My husband's company transferred him to the Santa Monica area and it was actually a more lucrative opportunity for him as well.

"I don't think I would go back to big company life," Tania concludes. "In my current job, there is a great feeling of ownership in the outcome that doesn't exist in larger companies."

EIGHT

Go Solo

If money is your hope for independence, you will never have it. The only real security that a man will have in this world is a reserve of knowledge, experience, and ability.

—Henry Ford

I'm a loner, Dottie. A rebel.

—Pee-wee Herman

If you want a job that inspires you to leap out of the bed in the morning, you might just have to create it yourself.

Today it's easier than ever before to start your own business. Twenty years ago, becoming an entrepreneur meant shelling out for office space and expensive equipment (like typewriters, fax machines, and giant copiers). Now the same technological advances that keep you yoked to your BlackBerry and laptop have made it possible for people to start thriving companies from their kitchen tables.

In fact, research shows that 75 percent of businesses are run by self-employed individuals with no employees. Millions of successful enterprises consist of little more than an entrepreneur, a computer, and an Internet connection.

The Solopreneur Movement

A solopreneur is simply someone running a one-person business. That includes freelancers, consultants, interim executives, one-person product and service businesses, and many others.

I have decided to use the term *solopreneur* despite its whiff of manufactured cutesiness (I was unable to find the precise origin of the word, but I suspect it was coined by the same people who brought us *mompreneur, infopreneur,* and *seniorpreneur*).

The label fits these solo workers because they really are entrepreneurs, even if they aren't running the future Microsofts or Googles of the world. In fact, despite their size, many are earning serious revenues, launching innovative new products, and getting rave reviews in the pages of national publications.

Today the Small Business Administration estimates that there are at least twenty million solo business ventures that generate total annual receipts of $1 trillion. Two million people become self-employed each year, and many start their businesses with less than $5,000 in start-up capital. While some of these solopreneurs are perfectly happy to remain as one-person operations, others are in the early stages of growth and will become much bigger.

Although solo ventures have no direct employees, solopreneurs often partner with other freelancers and small businesses to compete with much larger firms. Many run their businesses according to the Hollywood model. In other words: *What would Jerry Bruckheimer do?* For every new film project, Jerry assembles a team of the best independent professionals he can find—including writers, actors, stunt people, best boys, and caterers. In the same way, a solopreneur can put together an A-team for every client project without paying the overhead of salaries and office space.

The Solopreneur Universe

The solopreneur universe is vast and complex. Many of the categories overlap, but they all have one thing in common: They are businesses of one.

- **Freelancers.** A freelancer is a specialist who pursues a profession independently and not as the employee of an organization. Freelancers traditionally perform specific tasks for clients—for example, they design presentations, write articles, or develop code for websites. Freelancers can work on-site at a company or from a remote location.

- **Consultants.** Consultants are outside experts who provide advice and/or high-level or complex services. They tend to have significant experience in their area of expertise—and charge accordingly. Many consultants work on a project basis, while others are engaged long-term at a client organization and function much like full-time employees.

- **Interim executives.** Companies hire interim executives to work on-site on a temporary basis—to fill in for an executive on leave, to manage a special project, or to solve a short-term problem. Interim executives are generally placed by agencies and move from project to project. Many experienced professionals have chosen this career path because it provides variety and allows for time off between assignments.

- **Solo service businesses.** In a solo service business, an entrepreneur partners with other solopreneurs and small businesses to provide a range of services without the overhead of hiring employees. Richard Fouts, for example, serves as a one-stop shop for his clients' marketing projects. He has a network of designers, writers, and other specialists that he brings in to assist him on an as-needed basis. Richard takes responsibility for managing his vendors and ensuring client satisfaction. The client gets one bill, and Richard handles paying his service providers.

- **Solo product businesses.** Solo product businesses range from independent crafters who sell their creations on eBay to one-person companies that produce goods sold in major department stores. eBay has been a major factor in the growth of solo product businesses. Nicole Arslanian McCarthy represents the other end of the spectrum. She is currently the sole employee of Talene Reilly, which produces a line of handbags that are sold at Nordstrom and have been featured in *O Magazine*. Nicole partners with vendors, freelancers, and consultants to help her manufacture, distribute, and market her products.

DARING TALES OF CORPORATE ESCAPE

Inspiration in Terminal B

Name: Nicole Arslanian McCarthy
Former occupation: Financial services manager
Current occupation: Founder and president of Talene Reilly, producer of stylish and functional laptop bags

Nicole Arslanian McCarthy had an epiphany one day as she ran through the airport to catch a flight to her next corporate meeting.

"I saw my reflection in a window with my briefcase and my hand-bag and my laptop bag and my adorable shoes," she says. "I was going for the pulled-together look of a professional woman on the go, but I looked like a dumpy mess because I had bags hanging all over me."

Not only that, she couldn't even get to her cell phone or take a sip of her coffee without everything sliding off her shoulders. "That's when I had my *aha* moment," she says. "I realized that what I needed was a chic laptop bag that was a cute handbag on the outside and all organized business on the inside."

She did some research and found that none of the big companies was selling what she wanted. "They were either fashion or function, never both," she says. "The people who were supposed to be making this product weren't doing it, so I decided to see what I could do."

Nicole started to investigate fabrics and manufacturers. "I was still working at my corporate job and doing all of this as a hobby at night and on the weekends," she says.

When she created a prototype bag and started carrying it to the office, she caused a bit of a sensation. "I was working with all of these women who traveled all of the time and didn't want to be stuck with a tedious nylon laptop bag and their handbag," she says. "They got the concept very quickly."

She started selling bags to colleagues, then hired a designer to help her build a website to sell her bags online. "Eventually, I realized that I couldn't juggle both the demands of a growing handbag company and my corporate job," she says. At the time, she didn't really dislike her job, but she'd always wanted to start her own business someday and felt her opportunity had arrived.

About eighteen months after she first had her brainstorm, Nicole was preparing to walk into her boss's office and give notice. She knew she would regret it if she didn't give her idea a chance by focusing on it full-time.

"Out of everything that I've encountered in launching a small business—including raising capital, lining up distribution, and everything else—nothing to me will be ever be as scary as making the decision to leave that cushy environment," she says.

Nicole had no real experience in manufacturing or in retailing. "The only thing I had was that I was smart and I had created something that people were really receptive to," she says.

To keep overhead low, Nicole opted not to hire any employees, but to function as a solopreneur and outsource the functions that made sense.

Now three and a half years old, Nicole's company, Talene Reilly, has seen revenues double year over year. Her products have also been embraced by the press and featured in publications, including the *New York Times, O Magazine, Daily Candy,* and *InStyle.*

The press attention has helped Nicole get her handbags into department stores including Neiman Marcus, which is a challenging hurdle for new designers.

Nicole looks forward to seeing what the future brings for her and Talene Reilly. She has never regretted her choice to leave Corporate America to pursue her dream.

"I love my work and I really feel like I can shape my destiny now," she says. "To have that feeling of being so empowered is something that I think a lot of people never get to experience in their lifetime."

Nicole Arslanian McCarthy's Advice for Corporate Escape Artists

"At the end of the day, the question is: Do you really believe in it? If you really think that you can make it happen, then you have to take the plunge because otherwise you may regret it forever."

Trends Converging

Solo doesn't necessarily mean small potatoes anymore. Trends in technology have made it possible to do a lot with very little as an entrepreneur. The computer equipment and software required to run a business are now affordable for the average Joe. The Internet allows solopreneurs to cheaply and easily sell to and communicate with millions of potential customers around the world. The 'Net also enables collaboration with and outsourcing to other small businesses, eliminating the need to hire employees.

These technology developments coincide with a number of important social trends. Corporate loyalty and job security are dead, employees are searching for more meaning in their work, and labor shortages are looming on the horizon.

In the past, potential entrepreneurs often stayed put in corporate careers for the sake of job security. But the world has changed, and there is a growing sense that it might be better to be insecure doing what you want than to feel the same way while working for a large company.

At the same time, the clamor for work–life balance has become deafening, and not enough companies are stepping up to offer viable solutions. For working parents and other corporate professionals seeking more time for a life, solopreneurship can be a very attractive option.

Most of these people are not looking to work less, at least not on a long-term basis. They are simply seeking more control over when and how they work. According to the Women's Leadership Council, many of the working mothers who opt out of their jobs are not rejecting work, but simply rejecting Corporate America and choosing instead to start their own businesses. Women-owned businesses have been started at twice the rate of other small businesses over the last ten years.

New opportunities have also opened up as large companies have gotten leaner and meaner in recent years, slashing departments to meet quarterly estimates. That's how some successful solopreneurs ended up working for themselves in the first place.

THANK YOU FOR DOWNSIZING ME

A large number of ex-corporate entrepreneurs are those who were laid off, went solo out of necessity, and never looked back.

Many of the corporate escape artists whom I interviewed said they probably never would have had the nerve to become solopreneurs if they hadn't been unceremoniously downsized. The idea just looked too scary from their vantage point in the corporate world.

Once they were unemployed, however, they were forced to freelance or consult temporarily to make ends meet while they hunted for new corporate jobs. By the time the job market improved, they had discovered that they could make a better or happier living working for themselves.

If they could make the leap from corporate to solopreneur with absolutely no planning, imagine how successful you could be with a little bit of preparation.

This trend toward corporate outsourcing is expected to continue. The World Future Society estimates that the fastest-growing field between now and 2012 will be professional and business services. Yes, some of that work will go overseas, but a lot of it will also go to domestic providers.

I hired a lot of freelancers and solopreneurs during my own time in Corporate America, and they were almost all local. While corporations are increasingly outsourcing certain types of work to countries with cheap labor, there is still a booming market for US service providers.

When it comes to knowledge work, companies often prefer to hire someone with specialized experience in their own market. Today's solopreneurs can offer corporations the best of both worlds—local, specialized skills at rates that are generally lower than those of larger US companies with more expensive overhead.

DARING TALES OF CORPORATE ESCAPE

Blogging for Dollars

Name: Perez Hilton

Previous occupation: Reporter

Current occupation: Gossip blogger and TV personality

Celebrity blogger Perez Hilton (né Mario Lavandeira) has become a bit of a celebrity himself—hitting the reality TV and talk-show circuits in his Day-Glo hair color of the week and matching hoodies to hold forth on the latest star meltdowns. As the man behind one of the world's most popular gossip blogs, Perez works around the clock to dig up the latest celebrity scandals for his millions of readers. His blog is a favorite guilty pleasure for plenty of bored corporate workers around the globe and set a record not long ago of 8.8 million page views in a single day. That traffic has led to pretty healthy advertising revenue for what was until recently a one-man media empire based out of a Los Angeles coffee shop.

But before he became a blog superstar, Perez spent several years in boring office jobs just like most of us. "I was never cut out for the corporate world," he remembers. "I have never been the nine-to-five cubicle kind of guy."

One of his most corporate jobs was actually for a large nonprofit organization. "I was working for this gay nonprofit, which should not have been that corporate, but it was," Perez says.

In an attempt to make the environment more fun, he decorated his cubicle to reflect his personality. "I've always loved celebrity, pop culture, and entertainment," he says. "So I covered every square inch of my cube with pictures of celebrities that I had ripped out of magazines."

His cubicle became a piece of installation art. "It got to a point where all of my co-workers would come by every day and look at the latest additions." Unfortunately, his managers didn't find it quite so amusing. "I got in trouble for doing that and being who I was," Perez says.

Later, he ended up at what should have been his dream job—working as a reporter for a celebrity weekly owned by a major media conglomerate. Unfortunately, the position wasn't as glamorous as he'd hoped. "I hated it there," he says. "It was toxic to me."

By then, he had launched his blog, which was originally called PageSixSixSix.com, in his spare time and it had started to attract some attention—in fact, the blog attracted some lawyers for the *New York Post*, home of the "Page Six" gossip column. Perez eventually opted to rename himself and his blog, taking the name Perez Hilton as an homage to gossip goddess Paris Hilton.

After he started to earn some advertising income from the blog,

Perez began to think about quitting his day job and focusing on the blog full-time. His co-workers all told him it was a bad idea. Even his mother advised him to hang in there.

"I remember telling my mother how miserable and unhappy I was," he says. "She told me, 'You know, son, that's why they call it work.' "

Eventually, his bosses made his decision for him. "I finally left the corporate world when I got fired, which was a blessing in disguise because I probably would have stayed otherwise," he says. "I was able to collect severance and unemployment, which gave me several months to get my head in order and my life back on track in the right direction."

Perez threw all of his considerable energy and genius for self-promotion into turning his blog into a viable business. "I work harder now than I ever did before," he says. "I put in seventeen to eighteen hours a day, but I love what I do."

That hard work quickly paid off as his traffic and notoriety grew dramatically. It didn't hurt that Britney, Lindsay, Paris, and Nicole kept making headlines with divorces, jail sentences, rivalries, and meltdowns. "After about three or four months, I was earning just enough to live on," he remembers. Today he prefers not to disclose specific revenue numbers, but reports, "I make enough income to be happy."

In fact, he recently hired his sister Barbara as his assistant and moved his base of operations from his favorite coffee shop to a home office in a new apartment.

Next up is his own series of reality specials for VH1 called *What Perez Says*. "I plan to keep doing this job forever and ever," he says. "I love it."

Perez Hilton's Career Advice

"Life is too short to be a slave to your job. Find a way to have fun at work."

The Corporate Advantage

If your dream is to be your own boss, then you're in luck. Your time in Corporate America will give you a huge advantage. You have developed business skills, made contacts, and built a résumé that will serve you well as a solopreneur and help legitimize you in the eyes of potential investors and clients.

"I am so grateful that I spent those ten years in Corporate America," says Marie Elena Rigo, a feng shui consultant and interior designer. "I learned about marketing, selling, accounting, budgeting, and so many other skills you need if you are going to run your own business."

At the same time, having an admired brand on your résumé can be invaluable when you're striking out on your own. Especially if you're running a service business, potential clients love to see that you've worked for a large company. If you were good enough to be hired by a *Fortune* 500 firm, especially if you had an impressive title, they figure you probably know what you're doing. And they're probably right. Large companies can afford to hire the best, and they obviously thought you fit the bill. You can't coast on a corporate résumé forever, but it's a great way to get your foot in the door.

During your time in Corporate America, you also had the chance to make contacts that can become valuable sources of business. My first consulting clients were referred by people I knew during my corporate career. Even today, I find most of my best clients through these connections.

The Corporate Disadvantage

You've built a great foundation for solopreneur success during your time in Corporate America, but you've probably also developed some habits that will be hard to break.

You have been trained to think like an employee to get ahead. Unfortunately, strategies that were applauded in Corporate America can lead to disaster as a solopreneur.

In the corporate world, there is an overemphasis on process. Most of us hate the bureaucracy, but we've also grown accustomed to always knowing the next step.

That's not going to work when you're running your own business. You will be doing a lot of things for the very first time, which can be both exciting and terrifying. You'll likely be able to adapt some of the processes you learned in Corporate America to provide some structure. Just remember not to get bogged down in it.

Solo businesses work because they're nimble enough to turn on a dime to take advantage of a business opportunity or pounce on a new lead. You have to be able to make decisions quickly and get things done without direction, feedback, or approval.

That can be extremely uncomfortable when you're not used to it, but don't worry. You are perfectly capable of making decisions all by yourself. If you've gotten out of the habit, you'll soon get back into it by necessity.

A more painful adjustment will be learning how to get by without the helpful corporate infrastructure. You'll have to book your own car, make your own copies, and clean up your own company bathroom (although at least you won't have to share it with foul-smelling colleagues).

The good news is that you'll be able to contract out some of the work you don't want or can't do to other solopreneurs and microbusinesses. But it's not quite the same. A virtual assistant will never be able to bring you a good cup of coffee.

When you work for a large company, you get pretty accustomed to big budgets and wasted time. As a solopreneur, you can't afford either. When you manage your own bottom line, you will swiftly learn how to prioritize both time and money more effectively.

You will do some penny pinching, and it may hurt to give up all those full-color printouts and catered meetings. It can also be a bit painful to realize just how much every minute counts. In your corporate gig, you got paid even if you spent the whole day pretending to work. On your own, you will quickly learn which tasks drive the business forward and which tasks do not. On the other hand, you will be pleasantly surprised to discover how much more time there is for productive work when you give up staff meetings.

DARING TALES OF CORPORATE ESCAPE

The Accidental Entrepreneur

Name: Richard Fouts

Former occupation: Technology executive

Current occupation: Founder and CEO of Comunicado, a solo communications consulting firm

"I'm the accidental entrepreneur," says Richard. "I got laid off after the Internet bubble burst, then 9/11 happened one month later."

As a former executive for Hewlett-Packard and Cambridge Technology Partners, Richard wasn't used to having trouble finding work. "Try as I might, I just couldn't get a job in high-tech marketing," he says. "So I hired myself."

Richard quit job hunting and launched his consulting business, but the first year was tough going. He thought he might be better off going back to a corporate job after all, though his heart wasn't in it when he started interviewing again. "When the hiring manager took thirty minutes just to explain the organization, I would get sick to my stomach," he remembers.

Richard scheduled lunch with mentor Jean Sun-Shaw, a professional development coach and fellow entrepreneur who had escaped from Corporate America, and asked her advice. "She told me that if I had a contribution to make, I owed it to the world to make it," he recalls. "She advised me to shut down my job-hunting activities and devote all of my energy to my company."

He decided to follow her advice and give it another shot. "Instead of looking at it as freelancing, I decided to come up with a company and a vision for my services," he says. "I had trouble leaving the VP title behind, so I just took a CEO title."

Five years later, Richard has more clients than he can handle and has resolved never to interview again.

Richard Fouts's Best Career Advice

"If the corporation isn't giving you the environment you need to fulfill the full contribution you know you can make, think about an alternative."

☕ Do You Have What It Takes?

Why go solopreneur? It's the fastest route to working for yourself, but it certainly isn't easy. While some shortsighted fools may sneer that it's not a "real business" if it's only one person, the truth is that solopreneurs work hard and have to be able to keep an awful lot of balls in the air. Not everybody is cut out for it.

Here are some common myths about the solopreneur life, along with the truths behind the lies.

- **Working for yourself is a life of leisure.** You might be able to work in your jammies, but that doesn't mean you'll be sleeping much, especially in the beginning. Luckily, it's much more pleasant to work your butt off when you're building your own business on your own terms. You'll also have a lot more flexibility regarding when and how you work. There's no clock to punch, no face time to put in. If you need to take Friday off and work on Sunday night, that's your decision—as long as you deliver for your clients or customers.
- **You won't have to answer to anybody.** Sure, your boss is his-

tory and you're running the show, but that doesn't mean you have complete autonomy. You still have to answer to your clients. Some will make unreasonable demands, some may bounce their checks, and some may be downright annoying. None will have any appreciation for the fact that you have other clients to think about, nor should they. You'll have to make each of them feel like your one and only priority. The good news is that you have a choice in which clients you take on. As Richard Fouts puts it, you earn the right to employ the "no-asshole rule." As you grow more successful, it becomes much easier to say no to potential nightmare clients, even those that pay a lot of moolah.

- **People will envy you.** Some of your old colleagues and new acquaintances may not be as impressed with your new career as you are. There are unenlightened people who still believe that *freelancing* and *consulting* are code words for "unemployed and can't find work." Certainly, there is a long tradition of the laid-off and/or jobless picking up freelance work to make a few bucks during the job hunt. Many successful solopreneurs started out that way. However, a large percentage of today's independent workers are doing it because they want to. Don't waste your time trying to convince anyone. Those who think working for a corporation is the only valid career choice are never going to understand you anyway.

- **You can't make real money as a solopreneur.** You could very easily make more money as a solopreneur than you did in your corporate job. Some consultants make hundreds of dollars an hour. Other solopreneurs make thousands while they sleep each night, selling products online or through other channels.

☕ Going Solo by Moonlight

Many solo businesses require very little start-up money and can be launched while you're still collecting your day-job paycheck, allowing you to minimize financial risk.

The secret to a successful transition from corporate malcontent to solopreneur is through strategic moonlighting. You don't have to jump without a net.

There's a lot that you can do while you're employed. You can plan your business and even start generating revenue before you submit that resignation letter.

In fact, there are solopreneur ventures that can be run on the side long-term. Some people find that having a side business—even a small one—provides a valuable creative or entrepreneurial outlet. You may deal more gracefully with an unexciting day job if you can look forward to interesting work after hours.

Many of the solopreneurs whom I spoke with were able to get their businesses up and running while still working at their day jobs. I'm not recommending that you blow off your regular duties and build your business on the company dime. To make moonlighting work, you will have to continue to do your job well. See chapter 4 for more guidance on effective moonlighting.

Obviously, it's no picnic to run a business and work a full-time job. You're going to have less time for fun, socializing, and sleep. Make sure that it's worth it to you.

You may decide that you aren't willing or able to quit your day job. In that case, at least you'll know that you gave your dream a shot. Maybe you'll choose to continue to pursue your solopreneur business as a hobby or a greatly scaled-back once-in-a-while proposition. Or maybe you'll give it up altogether.

On the other hand, if you moonlight successfully for a while, you can build a healthy income stream before you stop collecting a salary. For those practical types among us, it's worth spending a few weeks or months doing double duty to reduce the financial risk.

If you're already working a backbreaking schedule or having difficulty juggling work and home lives, launching a business in your spare time may seem like an impossible proposition. If so, you might prefer to focus on building enough of a financial cushion to make the leap without spending a lot of time incubating your business on the side.

You Can Always Go Back

For many of us who left the corporate madhouse, there was great comfort in the mantra, *I can always go back.*

Working on your own can be scary. Exciting, but scary. In the darkest sleepless hours, we toss and turn wondering, *What if I fail? Will I be doomed to a life of poverty and painful regret?*

The best thing about starting a business after a few years in Corporate America is that you have already earned skills and experience that nobody can ever take away from you.

So what if you fail? Or what if you discover that solopreneurship isn't your calling after all? Sure, it would suck. But you can probably always get a job similar to the one you're thinking about quitting.

As this book goes to print, we're in the midst of a pretty healthy job market. And if you read chapter 2, you know that labor experts are actually predicting a serious labor shortage by the year 2010 as the Baby Boomers leave their demanding corporate jobs to retire or pursue scaled-back careers.

That means there will likely be plenty of demand for smart, experienced knowledge workers who keep their skills up to date. In fact, spending a few years running your own business or working with a variety of clients as a freelancer will probably position you better for the desirable corporate jobs of the future.

Even if you're able to hang on to the same job for several years, staying put can make you less attractive to future employers in today's job market. Until very recently, hiring managers would raise an eyebrow at an applicant who had "moved around too much." Today moving around is really the only way to develop, learn, and grow. Companies want to hire people with initiative and a well-rounded skill set. Fair or not, the assumption today is that there must be something wrong with anyone who has stayed in the same position for several years. You are expected to move around—whether within the same company or outside.

In fact, most companies welcome people with entrepreneurial experience. That's good news if you're worried that quitting to pursue a freelance career or business idea means never working in Corporate America again. You may not want to go back once you've had a taste of freedom, but you'll always have the option as long as you know how to spin your résumé. You can highlight the many, many skills that you learned and perfected by working for yourself—sales, marketing, finance, laptop maintenance, and many others.

Whatever you do, don't let the fear of forever tarnishing your résumé hold you back from pursuing your solopreneur dream. I have interviewed many people who've gone back and forth between entrepreneurial and corporate opportunities.

Karl Schmieder went from corporate to freelance to corporate to entrepreneur to corporate to entrepreneur . . . and he's not done yet. Karl launched his branding consulting business, Messaging Lab, with a partner in 2001. He devoted himself full-time to the business for three years and worked on projects for clients including Yahoo! and Condé Nast. Although his business was a partnership and not technically a solopreneur venture, Karl and his partner each worked out of their own home offices and conducted most business virtually.

The business even gave Karl the flexibility to move with his wife and kids to Panama for a year to be closer to extended family. After a year in Central America, Karl was ready for a change and accepted an opportunity to move back to New York for a job in corporate PR. Both he and his partner returned to corporate jobs, but they kept Messaging Lab going on the side.

Then, in late 2006, Messaging Lab landed a big client and Karl decided the time was right to leave his day job and focus on the business full-time again.

As you can see, he has always been able to work Corporate America instead of letting Corporate America work him. You can do the same.

DARING TALES OF CORPORATE ESCAPE

A Health Crisis Inspires a New Career Direction

Name: Andrea Beaman

Former occupation: Administrative assistant

Current occupation: Natural nutritionist, chef, TV personality

Andrea Beaman had a corporate day job that many would envy. She was an executive assistant to a big shot at MTV. That meant attending a lot of cool parties with rock stars and flying around the country with her boss. Andrea didn't mind her job, but there was something missing.

Her perspective changed after she was diagnosed with thyroid disease. She immersed herself in the study of nutrition to find a way to heal herself. After radically changing her diet, Andrea regained her energy and conquered her thyroid problem. Then she took a look around and decided that it was time to make some career changes as well. She realized that her true calling was in teaching people about the dramatic benefits of healthy eating.

"At my old job, I felt completely empty at the end of the day," Andrea says. "I felt like I did nothing of any consequence in the world. I had no passion."

She was afraid to trade in a secure position for a new career she knew little about, but a little voice kept nagging her that the time had come. Eventually, Andrea summoned up the courage to make the leap.

"The more I focused my energy on what I loved, the more opportunities opened up," Andrea says.

She studied nutrition and built a thriving business as a nutritionist, self-published author, and healthy chef. Then she was chosen as a contestant for the first season of the hit Bravo reality show *Top Chef* and discovered the power of television to spread the word about nutrition. Today she hosts *Wise Up!*, a show about healthy living that is broadcast on the Veria cable network.

There were some lean months and some sleepless nights along the way. But Andrea persevered and is now living the life she's always dreamed about. She has shared her healthy eating philosophies with millions of TV viewers and spends her days doing what she loves.

Andrea Beaman's Best Career (and Life) Advice

"Find something that you love to do and then go toward it with wild abandon—and always be open."

The Step-by-Step Plan

Step 1. Find Your Niche

The possibilities for solopreneurs are practically endless. Chances are that there's a way to build a business around what you love to do. Naturally, you'll have an easier time if you can boast a successful track record in your area of interest. If you already have ten years of experience as a graphic designer for Giant Company, Inc., you'll be able to make a pretty seamless transition to operating a graphic design firm serving similar companies.

It's also possible to go solo in an area that's completely unrelated to your corporate career. Rich Gee went from technology marketing manager to executive coach. Nicole Arslanian McCarthy went from middle manager at a financial services company to handbag designer. Leaping to a totally new industry will take a bit longer and might involve some additional training and creativity. Keep reading for more information on how to do it.

If you did the work in chapter 3, you should have a pretty good sense of what career paths appeal to you at this stage in your life. You may have a fully formed picture of exactly what you want to do or more of a vague sense of an industry or area of specialization.

If you're still not sure, try these exercises. Give yourself permission to brainstorm freely and jot down any ideas that come to mind. Don't dismiss anything out of hand. During the brainstorming phase, there is no such thing as a bad idea.

Once you're done brainstorming, you'll do some further research and analysis to see which ideas may have potential.

Solopreneur Brainstorming

- **What professional skills could you sell on a freelance or consultant basis?** The simplest and most direct route to solopreneurship is to start selling your current skills and expertise on the open market as a freelancer or a consultant. Designers, writers, programmers, and other professionals have been following this model for years. It can take many forms.

  Some occupations lend themselves to the solopreneur service model more readily than others, but there are free agent opportunities in just about every field. Stephanie Fried was a corporate marketing executive who became an interim marketing manager, hiring herself out to companies for temporary engagements to consult on important projects or fill in for executives on temporary leave. Marcia Reynolds was a training manager who started a freelance business developing training programs for big corporations.

- **Could you help others learn to do what you do? Do you know a lot about a particular subject?** Could you become a teacher, a trainer, or a coach in your area(s) of expertise? Could you write and sell e-books, training guides, or other information products online and/or at your classes? Rich Gee was good at motivating people as a corporate manager; so he used his skills to launch an executive coaching and public speaking business. Tevis Gale turned her yoga expertise into a business devoted to helping corporate employees find balance.

- **Do you know how to solve a common problem for people or companies?** What would people be willing to pay you to fix? Could you become an efficiency expert, a personal shopper, a wedding planner? Could you design a better mousetrap, a craftier coaster, or more effective software? Think creatively. Your idea doesn't have to be related to your current job. Andrea Beaman became passionate about nutrition after healthy eating helped her recover from a serious illness. She followed her enthusiasm into a career as a health counselor who helps others learn the benefits of a proper diet.

- **Do you have a great idea for a product?** Have you ever been struck with an ingenious product idea? Something that solves a problem (see above) or fills a need?

  Cathy Detloff started her business because she couldn't find an appropriate condolence gift for a friend who had recently lost a family member to cancer. Her company, Just Because Originals, sells blankets and pillows that are named and personalized in honor of the gift recipient or the loved one; she also donates a percentage of each sale to a worthy charity in the loved one's name.

- **Do you have a hobby or passion that could become a busi-**

ness? Do you have a passion for fashion? Maybe you could become an image consultant or personal shopper. Do you love to entertain? Maybe you could be an event planner. Perez Hilton's obsession with celebrity gossip turned into a blog empire.

Research the Market

So you think you have a good idea. Now how do you know if you can make a living at it? It's all well and good to follow your bliss, but never forget that you are launching a business. And if you really want to escape from Corporate America, your business will eventually have to earn enough to pay your bills. That means getting a real, clear-eyed sense of the market potential.

Who will buy the products or services you want to sell? How much will they pay? How will you reach potential customers? Who are your competitors? How are you different?

Even if you're only looking for a side business to make a few extra bucks and brighten up your drab corporate days, you should learn as much as possible about your potential market.

- **Check out the competition.** See what you can find out about other businesses in the sector. Look up competitor's websites and check out how they present their products and services; who their clients, distributors, and partners are; and what their pricing looks like.

    This is easier if you're selling tangible products. You can often look up exact prices and order samples to examine. For service businesses, it's a bit trickier. You can usually find some information on competitor's websites, though it's harder to pin down rates. Some consultants and freelancers post such information, but most do not. You can always e-mail or call to inquire.

- **Reach out to your network.** Do you already know potential customers? If you're starting a solopreneur business that's related to your current occupation or hobby, chances are good that someone you know has bought what you want to sell and can tell you the going rates.

These contacts are worth their weight in gold. They may even be able to share competitors' sales materials, proposals, catalogs, or other valuable information.

You will want to be selective about whom you approach and how much information you reveal. You're not ready to advertise your plans quite yet, especially around the office. A little white lie can be very effective here. Tell people you're evaluating vendors for a work project or as a favor for a friend or colleague.

- **Connect with a professional organization.** Professional organizations can often provide the latest and most trustworthy market information. They frequently conduct member surveys and closely track trends in the industry. You can find relevant trade groups by searching online or by looking in the *Encyclopedia of Organizations,* which should be available at your local library. See what information is on the organization's website and/or call the office to see if there is additional research that they can provide. If the group has a message board, dig around for discussions about market demand, rates, and business trends. You can also post a question and try to get feedback from other members.

Step 2. Take Action, Any Action

Once you have a sense of what you want your solo business to look like, it's time to dive right in. Don't worry. We'll get to the business plan in a minute. I'm a big believer in planning, and there will be plenty of it to do before you quit your day job.

However, I also know that it's easy to get bogged down and

intimidated by the idea of creating the perfect plan. Many great business ideas die that way.

The best way to start turning an idea into a business is to do something. Take your business idea for a test drive. Don't quit your job. Don't buy a new laptop. Not yet, anyway.

Yes, you can make time. You can start as small or as big as you'd like and work at your own pace. Too many people put off taking action until they've done all the research, written up the business plan, and eliminated all potential obstacles. *News flash:* You will never have the perfect plan. Starting a business is a process.

If you wait until the timing is ideal and you know everything you need to know, you may never get started. You have to jump on your idea now while you're excited about it. Take a step—any step—toward what you want. Don't file the idea away with all those other notions gathering dust in your closet.

Stop thinking about it and start doing it—in whatever way you can. Find out if you're cut out for the solopreneur life before you invest more time and effort in it. Maybe you'll discover you want to shift directions slightly or completely once you have some hands-on experience. Maybe you'll identify a major obstacle that needs to be dealt with. Or maybe your business will take off more quickly than you ever dreamed it could.

Taking Action: Service Business

Get a client, any client, while you're still in your day job. Start with a small, defined project if you can. You can go after a "real client" or you can volunteer your services for a friend, a charity or community organization, or a local small business.

Yes, you should try to get paid if you can. However, since you'll be a bit limited by the fact that you still have a day job to manage and no track record as a business, you may have to be a bit flexible at first.

If you can make some cash right off the bat, that's a [ ] sign, but don't worry if you can't or if you're not yet com[ ] selling or haggling about rates. Everybody has to start somew[ ] You will be more than fairly compensated by the confidence a[ ] experience you'll gain and by your very first client testimonial.

Ellen B. dreamed of becoming an image consultant, though she had no professional experience in the field. She started out by offering her services for free to a few friends, then began bartering image consulting for services she needed (Web design, yoga classes). Pretty soon, she had her first paying customers thanks to the word of mouth she generated by working for free. And she accomplished all of this while juggling a demanding corporate day job.

My own brother is another great example. Jeremy Skillings was a market research manager who wanted to be a search engine optimization consultant, but he didn't know where to start. He offered his services for free to a relative's business and delivered stellar results. With a glowing testimonial in hand and great work experience to point to, he soon gained "real" clients.

So don't be shy. Get out there and get started. Learn as much as you can from this experience. What was easy and what was hard? Do you need to work on your client management skills or your time management? Do you enjoy working for yourself?

Taking Action: Product Business

Get busy designing your first product or prototype. Take your idea beyond brainstorming and make it tangible. What materials will you use? Will you need any help? Could you hire a designer/ seamstress/programmer/printer to help you bring it to life?

Nicole McCarthy's concept for a stylish laptop bag was just a good idea until she designed samples to show her co-workers. Soon after, she was selling her products faster than she could make them.

There will be kinks to be worked out as you go along. This is how

e willing to invest your time and energy in

ct businesses are more challenging to get

ervice counterparts. However, products

oney over time because your pay is not

literally make money in your sleep.

u must be passionate and committed to

it's going to have a fighting chance. It's not

ough to identify a market opportunity. Just because there's a demand for porcelain monkey figurines doesn't mean you're the right person to produce and sell them.

Step 3. Write Your Business Plan

Yes, you really do need a business plan. That doesn't mean you have to spend months on a forty-page PowerPoint presentation with 3-D charts, but a well-crafted business plan is crucial for setting objectives and focusing your efforts.

Many businesses miss major opportunities because they don't do enough up-front planning and research. Besides, if you treat this endeavor like a hobby or a casual experiment, it may never become anything more than that.

Once you've dipped your foot in the water (see step 2, page 197), you may be tempted to just move full speed ahead and deal with a business plan later. Hold on.

This isn't the time to wing it and hope for the best. It's great to take action and get positive momentum going, however, before you make significant investments in your business (with your money, your time, or your effort) and certainly before you quit your job, you'd be smart to put together a solid business plan.

The process of working through your plan will help you define your goals and identify any major obstacles or requirements that should be addressed early on.

Coming from the corporate world, you probably have some experience with planning, documenting, and prioritizing. Now, finally, you have a chance to use those skills to make some money for you, not just the company shareholders and the guys upstairs with the sickeningly huge bonuses.

Over the course of my career, I have worked on dozens of business and marketing plans for both small and large companies. The most effective business plan for a solopreneur will be a bit different from the traditional model in business school textbooks (for more about traditional business plans, see chapter 9).

The most important difference is that the business plan for You, Inc., should take into account your personal goals and priorities. After all, you are your business. Most likely, you're interested in becoming an entrepreneur for personal as well as economic reasons. You want your business to be successful on both fronts, so why not include both in the process?

This business plan isn't for anyone's eyes but yours right now. If you are ever asked to present a business plan to a potential investor, you can turn your solopreneur plan into a document for securing funding by following the advice in chapter 9.

KEY ELEMENTS OF A SOLOPRENEUR BUSINESS PLAN

- **Mission statement.** What is the driving purpose of your solopreneur business?
- **Business description.** What products or services are you offering?
- **Market analysis.** Who are your customers? What demand will you meet? What will you charge?
- **Competitive analysis.** Who are your competitors? What are their strengths and weaknesses? How will your business compete?
- **Marketing strategy.** How will you connect with and sell to your target market?
- **Financial plan.** What are your start-up costs? What is your projected cash flow?

Step 4. Write Your Mission Statement

The best way to get started with your solopreneur plan is by defining your mission statement. Here is where you have to get very specific about what you're trying to achieve by going solo.

Business Mission

Your business mission statement should communicate exactly what your company does, why it's different, and how you provide value. Limit it to three sentences—the shorter and more focused the better.

Take a look at some sample business mission statements:

- **Diva Designs** creates innovative websites for corporate clients in the fashion and entertainment industries.
- **Healthy Strategies** helps people improve their health and fitness through nutrition planning, training, and coaching services.
- **Morrison Management Consulting** assists corporate clients with optimizing their hiring and training processes to improve employee performance and retention.

Personal Mission

Your personal mission statement is all about what you want out of the business. Of course, you want to be successful and make money. But you can make money in your corporate gig. What are your other top goals?

The whole point of escaping from Corporate America is to be happier and more fulfilled. What does that mean for you? If your primary desire is to earn six figures, you may make different choices from someone whose main goal is to have more flexibility even if that means making less money.

If your personal mission is to quit your corporate job as soon as reasonably possible, your focus should be on getting those revenue streams flowing ASAP. That means you may opt to be less choosy about what kind of work you take on. For example, your dream may be to run a fashion PR firm, but you can grin and bear assignments to write press releases for Widgets, LLC, for a while if it pays well. You may also be okay with putting flexibility and balance on hold and working like a fiend until you get established.

If you don't define what's important to you now, you can easily get off track. Keep in mind that you will likely have to make some sacrifices at the beginning. The key is to decide where you're willing to sacrifice and where you're not.

My original personal mission was to earn a defined amount each month as a consultant and have the flexibility to spend more time on my writing. I was okay with making some sacrifices in the beginning to get to my goal.

I was willing to take on some less-than-ideal projects so that I could start building experience and momentum. I wasn't willing to give up my freedom by taking a full-time, on-site consulting gig at a big company. I turned down more than one attractive offer. If my primary goal had been to make as much money as possible as a consultant, I would have said yes in a heartbeat.

I said no because it would have felt like going backward for me. It took a lot for me to be able to leave Corporate America, and I feared that I could be easily sucked back in. At the same time, working on-site full-time for one company would have left little time for writing or for finding future clients that would keep my business going after the assignment ended.

Once I got established as a consultant, I was able to say no to more assignments that didn't make business sense anymore. I could turn down projects that paid less than I was worth, projects that sounded unbearably tedious, and projects offered by clients with attitude problems. I can be more selective now because I've worked hard to find repeat clients and develop referral networks. I don't have to worry so much about making enough to get by and can focus more on seeking out the projects that excite me.

Here are some examples of personal mission statements:

- Sign on at least two long-term clients so I can quit my job in one year.
- Have the flexibility to spend time on my music every day.
- Earn at least $75K per year and still have time to pick up my kids at school every day.

PURSUE A PORTFOLIO CAREER

What if you want to, or need to, pursue multiple careers at the same time? Have no fear. Many solopreneurs balance several part-time pursuits that add up to one perfectly customized full-time dream career.

The experts call it a "portfolio career," which just means cultivating a portfolio of income sources. This approach has a number of benefits for those who can handle a little juggling. You can balance one beloved but nonlucrative career with another that provides more financial stability. Or you may turn to a portfolio career for variety, excitement, or fulfillment.

On a practical level, a portfolio career means you always have a Plan B. If one of your career paths gets bumpy, you can focus on the other to pay your bills.

In her book *One Person/Multiple Careers: A New Model for Work/Life Success*, Marci Alboher calls this approach "the slash effect." In other words, you can be an actress/bookkeeper/corporate trainer or an artist/designer/yoga instructor. Marci herself is an author/speaker/coach.

Sometimes portfolio careers develop over time as people discover additional talents and interests. Often, portfolio careers are consciously designed to support multiple career dreams.

Many of the solopreneurs whom I interviewed have portfolio careers. Most say that they tend to switch between careers as opportunities arise.

- Marie Elena Rigo is primarily a feng shui consultant, but she also offers interior design services to help clients implement her recommendations for their homes. On top of that, she has several coaching clients and is evaluating offers to host a feng shui TV show.
- Andrea Beaman is a holistic health counselor who also gives cooking lessons to individuals and groups, writes books about nutrition, and hosts a cable TV show.
- David Kucher is a writer, editor, dramaturg, teacher, and real estate investor.
- Marcia Reynolds is a training consultant, a public speaking coach, and a public speaker in her own right.

A portfolio career could make sense for you if you're having trouble deciding which of several interests to pursue. It's also a good choice if you're concerned that your primary solopreneur business won't earn as much as you'd like. For example, if you're trying to launch yourself in a new area without a lot of experience, you could take on part-time work in a more familiar field to help pay the bills while you're getting established.

There are challenges involved in balancing multiple careers. You'll have to be flexible, be resourceful, and get very good at managing your time and priorities. The payoff is that you can create the perfect custom career for yourself and never, ever be bored at work again.

Step 5. Build Your Support Team

Because you'll be running this business all by yourself, it is particularly important for you to assemble a quality network of people you can turn to for advice, assistance, and support.

Your professional advisers should include an accountant and a lawyer. You may not have to put these two on speed dial, but it can be helpful to consult with experts on matters such as incorporating your business, setting up your books, understanding your tax liabilities, and lining up any necessary licenses.

There is a lot of free information out there for those who favor a do-it-yourself approach. Still, my recommendation is to at least schedule consultations with a small-business accountant and a lawyer. Legal and tax mistakes can end up costing you much, much more than you'll save by cutting corners.

Step 6. You're in Business

Congratulations on your first official day as a solopreneur. Your immediate priority will be to land some paying clients and start generating revenue.

- **Work your network.** Let the people in your network know that you're open for business. Make it easy for them to refer clients by making clear exactly what you do and what kinds of projects are up your alley. Hand out extra business cards and encourage your friends to share them.
- **Partner up with other solopreneurs.** Other solopreneurs can be great sources of referrals. Busy consultants and freelancers often outsource or pass along work.
- **Work with an agency or interim staffing firm.** Investigate whether any staffing firms in your area handle the types of freelance or consulting projects you want. This is a good, fast way to start picking up work because you can leverage the agency's existing relationships.
- **Explore online job sources.** At online freelance marketplaces such as Guru (www.guru.com), eLance (www.eLance.com), and SoloGig (www.sologig.com), you can bid on or apply for projects. You can also find prospects through online social networks like LinkedIn and Facebook.

A FEW WORDS ABOUT TAXES

First, a disclaimer. I am not an accountant, and that's why I hired a professional to help me with tax planning when I started my business. I highly recommend that you do the same. The up-front investment can save you money, time, and plenty of headaches.

When you work for a corporation, your check comes with all the relevant taxes already deducted. As a solopreneur, you will have to deduct federal, state and local income taxes, as well as both the employee and employer portions of Social Security contributions, yourself. The IRS also requires you to pay quarterly estimated taxes on your business earnings.

The good news is that when you're self-employed, you can deduct expenses that are "ordinary and necessary" for your work. Potential deductions include home office equipment, client entertainment costs, insurance, magazine subscriptions, phone bills, and many other expenses.

Please see the Escape Tool Kit section in the back of this book for links to more information about the joys of solopreneur taxes.

Step 7. Quit Your Day Job

Are you ready to quit your day job? How do you know when it's time? The decision regarding when to give notice is often a financial one. Many make their move once they have regular client work coming in and enough savings to get them through any dry spells.

Before you leave, don't miss the opportunity to try to turn your employer into a client. When you sit down with your manager to tell her that you're leaving to go solo, mention that you'd be interested in continuing to work with her on a freelance basis.

And don't forget to let all of your co-workers know that you're available. You just never know where a good referral could come from.

DARING TALES OF CORPORATE ESCAPE

The Search for Meaning

Name: Marie Elena Rigo

Former occupation: PR and marketing executive

Current occupation: Feng shui consultant, interior designer, and life coach

"Most people assume that it is too big of a risk to leave, but I think if people experienced the freedom and satisfaction that come with running your own business, they would feel differently," says Marie Elena Rigo.

Marie Elena worked hard to build a successful career in corporate public relations and marketing. At first, it was fun, but the intensity soon started to take a toll on her health. "I was sick all of the time," she remembers.

But she was too driven to let that slow her down. She had set a goal to become a vice president earning a salary of at least $100,000 before she was thirty.

By the time she was twenty-nine, she had achieved that goal and was ready for the next challenge. She accepted a bigger job, but soon realized it was more than she'd bargained for.

"I had to travel back and forth between London and New York once a month, and it was exhausting," she says. "Then the tech boom turned into the tech bust and they told me that I had to start cutting heads."

Around that time, she and her fiancé moved into a new apartment and hired a feng shui consultant. Marie Elena was intrigued when the consultant told her about a master's program in spiritual psychology at the University of Santa Monica. "My ears perked up, my heart sort of leapt, and I just thought, *Oh, I wanna go there.*"

At first, she dismissed the idea as impractical. But she couldn't let it go. "I felt that if I could go back and forth to London once a month for work, I could certainly manage to go to California for classes one weekend a month. It was the same amount of time by plane, pretty much."

She started attending the program in October. "All of a sudden, I was surrounded by like-minded people and studying fascinating subjects that really resonated with me," she says. "I realized that I couldn't go back to being that corporate person anymore."

When she heard that her company was restructuring and laying people off again, she was able to negotiate with the CEO to take a package. "Because I was a senior person working for a London-based company, I had a contract that entitled me to a minimum of three months' salary if I left," she says. "At the time it was a little scary, but now I can really appreciate how it gave me the freedom to start looking for a job that would be more fulfilling."

Marie Elena had also saved about $60,000, which had previously been earmarked for a real estate investment but would now provide the cushion she needed to create her new life.

She broke up with her fiancé and moved to California to focus on building a new career as a life coach and a feng shui consultant. She continued to take her classes and began to take on a few clients.

"My business officially launched in August of 2004," she says. "But I was really crafting it for six months to a year prior to that." Soon she expanded to offer interior design services to help her clients implement the feng shui changes she recommended.

"I cannot see myself ever going back to that kind of a job," Marie Elena says. "I just feel like this is what I am supposed to be doing. "

Although she faces challenges every day, Marie Elena still feels she's better off relying on herself than on a corporate employer. "Having your own business is probably the most secure thing that you can do because no one is going to watch out for your best interests better than you are."

Marie Elena Rigo's Top Advice for Career Changers

"There is a perception that risk is negative. To me, risk means getting out of your comfort zone, and that allows you to grow. If you feel the call to do something different, do it. It's actually more of a risk to stay where you are than to move forward in the direction of your dreams."

NINE

Build a Business

There is only one way to make a great deal of money; and that is in a business of your own.

—J. Paul Getty, oil tycoon and once the richest man in America

The entrepreneur always searches for change, responds to it, and exploits it as an opportunity.

—Peter Drucker, author and business management guru

Some business ideas are too big to bring to life with just one person and a laptop. If your entrepreneurial vision includes making millions, appearing on the cover of *BusinessWeek,* or changing the world, you will need a grander plan than the one outlined in the previous chapter.

Leaving corporate to launch any venture that requires attaining outside funding and hiring employees involves a greater degree of difficulty—whether you're opening a neighborhood bistro or the next YouTube.

There is no one way to start a new business. And, let's face it, it would be impossible for me to squeeze everything you need to know about entrepreneurship into one chapter. Volumes have been written about this subject by experts much wiser than I.

My focus will be on what you need to know to start planning your transition from corporate employee to power entrepreneur. You don't have to quit your job to get started. In fact, you don't have to quit your job until after you have funding if you don't want to.

Because the best way to learn is often from the experiences of those who have succeeded before you, I am devoting a lot of space to the stories of the incredible entrepreneurs who were kind enough to speak with me about their successes and challenges and offer their best advice. You've probably seen some of their names in *Fortune* magazine, while others keep lower profiles. They represent different industries, different geographies, and different business models, but they all have one thing in common. They all had the courage to leave the security of Corporate America to take a risk and follow their passions.

DARING TALES OF CORPORATE ESCAPE

The Big Idea

> **Name:** Marc Benioff
> **Former occupation:** Senior executive at Oracle
> **Current occupation:** Founder and CEO of Salesforce.com

You have likely read about Marc Benioff and the extraordinary success of his company, Salesforce.com, in the business magazines. The firm is a leading provider of customer relationship management applications and services and it posted nearly $500 million in revenue for fiscal year 2007.

In 1999, Benioff walked away from a senior position at Oracle to start Salesforce.com with just three employees and a lot of passion. He took the time to share his story and his advice for making the move from employee to entrepreneur.

How did you make the decision to leave Oracle to start Sales force.com?

In May 1996, I took a sabbatical after ten years of working at Oracle. I went to India and the Big Island of Hawaii. I had enough time by myself to think about something that interested me very much—what the future would look like.

What I became most excited about was what was happening on the Internet. I kept asking myself a simple question: What if complicated enterprise software could be delivered on a website that was as easy to use as Amazon.com or Yahoo!?

In 1999, I founded Salesforce.com with three fantastic developers and a mission to deliver sales force automation software as a service on the Web.

While I was committed to this new way of delivering software, I was also inspired to create a new way of doing business that integrated giving back to the community into its business model.

What were your biggest challenges in walking away from such a successful corporate career to start your own business?

The truth is, I never planned on working at a big corporation. I had always been an entrepreneur; I started Liberty Software when I was fifteen and I ran it out of my dorm room when I was in college. Right before graduation, two of my professors at USC, Tom O'Malia and Mac Davis, gave me some sage advice: The best entrepreneurs would be the ones who got real-world experience before pursuing their dreams. Surprisingly, they said that corporate experience would ideally be in a position of sales. Or, as they called it, "carrying a bag."

I took their advice and, although I was initially repulsed by the idea of selling as a career, I stomached it and found out that it was actually more fun than writing code. What was supposed to be a brief real-world experience turned into thirteen years at Oracle.

While it wasn't easy to leave a great job and the golden handcuffs of a lucrative salary and ever-flowing stock options, I really believed in Salesforce.com. That made the challenge of leaving something stable and predictable more than worth it.

What advice would you give to someone who feels frustrated in a corporate job that doesn't inspire or challenge them?

If someone feels frustrated or uninspired, that likely means that it's time to move on to something new—be it a new position, new corporation, or to start a new venture. Andy Warhol famously said, "They say that time changes things, but you have to change them yourself." I believe that. Someone who is unhappy in his or her job isn't stuck, they just have to be brave enough to make a change. And there is a whole world out there that is in great need of more people who are passionate about what they do. Passion sparks the most creativity and drives the biggest successes.

The Entrepreneurial Dream

Merriam-Webster's Dictionary defines *entrepreneur* as "one who organizes, manages, and assumes the risks of a business or enterprise." The word comes from the Old French for "undertake."

That's a pretty broad definition—and entrepreneurship has come to represent a pretty broad range of options these days. Today entrepreneurial ventures include everything from one-woman eBay weekend businesses to multimillion-dollar, venture-capital-backed start-ups.

Entrepreneurship has always been an American dream. History's most inspiring self-made successes rose from nothing and Americans love the idea of pulling yourself up by your bootstraps and manifesting your own destiny.

CORPORATE-TO-ENTREPRENEUR HALL OF FAME

Did you know that many of the most legendary entrepreneurs of all time started out as corporate employees?

- **Henry Ford** was the son of farmers and toiled in an engineering job before striking out on his own to form Ford Motor Company.
- **Walt Disney** was an illustrator for an advertising agency before he and his brother Roy started a business in their uncle's garage that eventually became the Walt Disney Company.
- **Ray Kroc** was a salesman for the Multi-Mixer Corporation when he bought a California hamburger restaurant from the MacDonald Brothers and turned it into a multibillion-dollar international chain.
- **Mary Kay Ash** was a sales director for Stanley Home Products for twenty years before she retired and used her life savings of $5,000 to get Mary Kay Cosmetics going in 1963.
- **Steve Jobs** and **Steve Wozniak** spent time as engineers at Atari before they created Apple Computer.
- **Jeff Bezos** quit his job as a senior vice president on Wall Street when he came up with the revolutionary idea for Amazon.com.
- **Michael Bloomberg** was a senior manager at Salomon Brothers until he was squeezed out after the company was acquired in 1981. The unemployed Bloomberg went on to make his fortune by starting Bloomberg LP, the financial information company, and later used his billions to finance a successful run for mayor of New York City.
- **Martha Stewart** had a successful career as a stockbroker before she turned a catering business into a media empire.

In a recent survey, 77 percent of respondents said that their dream job would be to run their own business. People are drawn to the idea of taking control of their careers and making their own rules. Many who leave corporate jobs to start new companies do so because they see it as the only way to reach their full potential and do the level of work that they're capable of doing.

At the same time, building a business offers the possibility for enormous financial returns. When you work for someone else, the amount you earn is decided by your corporate overlords. When you run the show, your compensation is tied directly to your performance—and the sky is the limit.

A study by the Harrison Group found that 70 percent of today's big family fortunes are less than thirteen years old, and the majority of them were amassed by entrepreneurs.

The dream is now within much easier reach than it used to be. Technological advances have removed barriers to entry. Cheap software and computer equipment allow a few to do the work of many. The Internet has opened up distribution channels and created new ways to operate. Today a small start-up can compete with a huge multinational.

DARING TALES OF CORPORATE ESCAPE

Beer Is a Wonderful Thing

Name: Jim Koch

Previous occupation: Management consultant

Current occupation: Founder and chairman, the Boston Beer Company

As founder and chairman of the Boston Beer Company and the man who introduced Samuel Adams beer to the world, Jim Koch has a job that many would envy. On the day that I spoke with him, he was preparing to fly to Denver for the Great American Beer Festival (an annual event that serves approximately eighteen thousand gallons of beer to forty-one thousand attendees) before continuing on to Germany on a hops selection trip.

With duties like these, it's no wonder that Jim is enthusiastic about his job. "Beer is a wonderful thing," says Jim. "It has been in my family a long time."

For five generations, men in the Koch family were brewmasters. But for a while, it seemed that the tradition would end with Jim's father. The industry had consolidated from a field of more than eight hundred breweries when Jim's father graduated from brewmaster school in 1948 to fewer than forty by the early 1980s. The three big American breweries dominated the business and there weren't many jobs for brewmasters.

So Jim put his love of beer aside and enrolled in a joint JD/MBA program at Harvard. Halfway through, he took three years off to work as an Outward Bound instructor and expand his horizons, but eventually returned to complete his degrees. Upon graduation, he accepted a position with the Boston Consulting Group.

"It was a great opportunity to learn business strategy and to work with great client companies," he remembers. After almost seven years, though, the thrill started to fade.

"I decided I didn't want to be a consultant for the rest of my life," he said. "And if I didn't want to be a consultant for the rest of my life, why should I be a consultant tomorrow?"

What he really wanted to do was quit his high-paying consulting job to start his own brewery. "I saw a need for really high-quality, fresh American beer," he says. Using one of his great-great grandfather's recipes, Jim brewed his first batch of Samuel Adams Boston Lager in his kitchen in 1984 and became convinced that there would be a market for it.

But he was in his mid-thirties with a wife and two young kids. "The perceived risk of leaving my job was very high," he says. On the other hand, Jim was convinced that it was a bigger risk to stay at a job that wasn't fulfilling and to waste his life.

"I started the company with two people and financed it with $100,000 of my own money and $150,000 that I raised from friends and family," he remembers. "People will give you $5,000 or $10,000 to start a beer company. One guy I knew invested $3,000 and said he could justify it based on free beer alone."

Jim's initial goals for the company were modest. "The plan was to be a small brewery and make a middle-class living. I wasn't seeking a path to great wealth. I just wanted to build a company, support my family, and be happy."

But just six weeks after Samuel Adams made its debut in Boston, it was selected "The Best Beer in America" in the Great American Beer Festival's Consumer Preference Poll.

"Once we were selected, I realized that this could actually be huge," remembers Jim. He was right. Samuel Adams helped to start a craft-brewing revolution in the United States.

Today, Boston Beer Company is America's largest microbrewery and a publicly traded firm with almost four hundred employees. Jim has also built a company that people love to work for. What's his secret for employee engagement? "Well, all employees get two free cases of beer each month, so that's a nice start," he says.

Even more important, Jim has always felt strongly about hiring the right people for the right jobs. "Happy people make better companies. If someone enjoys what they're doing, they'll do it well."

That theory has certainly proven true in Jim's own life. "After twenty-three years, I still love what I do," he says.

LEARN FROM THOSE WHO HAVE DONE IT

Here are just some of the businesses launched by the corporate escapees I interviewed for this book:

- Bloglines, the blog and newsfeed aggregator service.
- Boston Beer Company, the brewer of Samuel Adams beer.
- Build-A-Bear Workshop, the national toy retailer.
- Cranium, the award-winning game company.
- EDImports, an importer of handcrafted home and gift products from emerging countries.
- Futurethink, a boutique innovation consulting firm.
- Grand Central Solutions, an Atlanta-based technology firm.
- GuidePoint Health, a health insurance brokerage for small businesses.
- Iatria Spa and Health Centers, a chain of three spas in North Carolina.
- The Institute for Integrative Nutrition, a professional training institute for health counselors.

- LeadQual, an Internet marketing and sales solutions firm.
- LesserEvil, a healthy snack food manufacturer.
- Multiply, an online social networking community.
- Pure Food and Wine, an award-winning raw food restaurant in New York City.
- Salesforce.com, a leader in customer relationship management software and services.
- SheSpeaks, a market research firm specializing in the opinions of female consumers.
- Tom and Sally's Handmade Chocolates, a Vermont gourmet chocolatier and candy maker.
- Urban Junket, makers of Italian leather handbags.
- Zagat Survey, publishers of America's most famous restaurant guides and other products.
- Zenbu Media, the company behind *Relix* magazine, Relix Records, and the Green Apple Music Festival.

DARING TALES OF CORPORATE ESCAPE

From Hobby to Big Business

Name: Tim Zagat

Previous occupation: Attorney

Current occupation: Co-founder, co-chair, and CEO of Zagat Survey

Zagat Survey, the company behind the famous restaurant guides, started out as a fun idea at a dinner party. Tim Zagat was a partner at the law firm Pomerantz, Levy & Block and his wife, Nina, was an attorney at the distinguished Wall Street firm Shearson & Sterling.

"We were at a dinner party one night, discussing the fact that the restaurant critics were not very reliable," Tim remembers. "I had done some political survey work and, because I was having my tenth glass of wine at the time, I said, 'Why don't we do a restaurant survey of our friends?' "

He felt certain that a survey of a large group of people who dined out frequently would be more helpful than the subjective opinion of one restaurant reviewer. After all, his friends were mostly lawyers and other professionals who dined in New York City restaurants as a way of life.

"Some people know more about food and cooking than others, but who says their taste is your taste?" Tim notes. "And who says a professional critic knows any more about décor and service than you do?"

The Zagats and their friends had a good time conducting the survey and decided to share it with others in their circles. "We did it for the first year on a single eight-and-a-half-by-fourteen sheet of paper and people loved it," Tim remembers. Recipients started making copies and passing the survey along to friends and acquaintances.

"We gave away ten thousand free copies the first year with two hundred people voting," Tim recalls. "By the third year, with a thousand people voting, it was getting pretty expensive to do all of the tabulating on paper. My wife suggested that we start selling the survey so that we could at least make our hobby tax-deductible."

In the first year that the Zagats charged for the guide, they broke even. In the second year, they made some money. "In the third year, we made quite a lot of money," says Tim.

One of the company's big breaks was receiving an order for five thousand custom books from financial printing company R. R. Donnelly. The order represented half the total number of books the Zagats had sold the previous year.

Then R. R. Donnelly gave out copies of the custom book to its clients, who were all top executives of big companies. "Before long, I got a call from Citibank about ordering ten thousand custom copies," Tim remembers.

The Zagats didn't have the same success with approaching publishers about a book deal. "We went to every publisher in the world, practically, and we were turned down uniformly," says Tim. "And who knew that that was going to turn out to be one of the best things that ever happened to us?"

Even with an uncle in the publishing business, Tim couldn't catch a break. "My uncle had owned Atheneum Publishers, which used to publish the New York Times Guides, and he's the only one who told me why he was turning me down," says Tim. "He said they didn't like local books and that even the New York Times Guides only sold about forty thousand copies."

Luckily, Tim didn't let this expert and well-meaning advice discourage him. "Four years later, I went back to my uncle and told him that we had sold seventy-five thousand copies in the first month alone. We dedicated the book to him that year."

All along, Tim and Nina kept their day jobs as attorneys while building their restaurant survey business in their spare time. "I never left practicing law until the hobby became more profitable than my law practice—and I was pretty well paid in law," Tim reports.

Today Zagat Survey has 125 full-time employees and between 300,000 and 350,000 reviewers. They now cover many cities and many subjects beyond restaurants—including nightlife, hotels, theater, and shopping.

"I think too many people let themselves do things that they hate on a daily basis," says Tim. "I happened to like law practice most of the time, but there were also times that weren't so great. I have been doing this now for twenty-eight years and I still love it."

Tim Zagat's Career Advice

"In life, you're much better off doing something you love than something that you're not enthusiastic about. First of all, you'll be better at it if you like it. Second, you'll work harder and you won't feel like it's work at all."

Do You Have What It Takes?

The decision to start a business should not be taken lightly. "I really think starting a business is like having a child," says Sally Fegley, co-founder of Tom and Sally's Handmade Chocolates. "The child is your creation, and you're happy when the child does well and sad when the child doesn't do well. You can't stop thinking about the child and the child never gives you a day off."

Hating your day job isn't a good enough reason to dive in. Not everybody is cut out to run a business.

However, if you're drawn to entrepreneurship or have a great idea for a business that keeps you up at night, you owe it to yourself to investigate your options.

One school of thought holds that entrepreneurs are born, not made. I disagree. It's true that several of the entrepreneurs that I interviewed spoke of always having an urge to incorporate and open their first businesses at fourteen or fifteen years of age. Many others, however, didn't discover their calling until later in life when an idea or opportunity pushed them out of their comfort zones.

DARING TALES OF CORPORATE ESCAPE

It's Good to Be Grand Poo-Bah

Name: Richard Tait

Former occupation: Microsoft executive

Current occupation: Founder and Grand Poo-Bah, Cranium (yeah, that's his real title)

After a ten-year career at Microsoft and honors including Microsoft Employee of the Year, Richard Tait was ready to try something new.

"I had done thirteen start-ups within Microsoft and I wanted to prove to myself that I could start something outside of the company just like I had done inside," he says. "The hard part was that I didn't know what I wanted to do next."

Richard and his friend and former Microsoft colleague Whit Alexander would get together to brainstorm possible Internet business ideas, but couldn't come up with anything that inspired them.

"That was probably the darkest period of my life so far—that time of self-doubt," he recalls. "I would be in the basement in my jammies and the only reason I would get dressed was because my wife was coming home from work."

It didn't help matters that he was finding it more difficult than anticipated to adjust to life outside Microsoft. "In today's society, so much of your credibility comes from the organization that you are associated with," he says.

After years of being "Richard Tait from Microsoft," it felt strange to just be Richard. "You feel so naked when you don't have that corporate armor surrounding you."

But all that doubt and uncertainty disappeared after a flash of inspiration during a game night with his wife and another couple. Richard was struck with the idea that there should be a game that let everyone have a chance to shine. The Cranium concept was born.

Whit Alexander thought he was nuts at first. A board game hardly seemed like a hot prospect during the Internet boom. Plus, neither of them had any experience in the market.

But Richard eventually won Whit over with his enthusiasm. "Designing the game was not difficult at all for us because we applied the same product development methodologies that we had used to develop software at Microsoft," he says.

Unfortunately, distribution proved to be more difficult. "We approached the major retailers, and none of them wanted to stock the game," he says. It turned out that they had missed Toy Fair, the industry event where all the buying decisions were made, because they hadn't known it existed.

This was an obstacle that seemed impossible to overcome. "We had twenty-seven thousand games in trucks on their way to Seattle and we had no idea where to put them," Richard remembers.

Then came another moment of inspiration. "We decided to take our games to the places where our customers were shopping instead of to the places where games were traditionally sold," he says. They targeted Amazon, Barnes & Noble, and Starbucks.

Cranium eventually became the first game to be sold by all three of those retailers, but it took some creativity to get in the door. At a pitch meeting, a Barnes & Noble official told Richard that its stores didn't sell games, but Richard wasn't about to give up so easily. He recruited two women at the hallway watercooler to join the buyer and himself for an impromptu game of Cranium. "Fifteen minutes later, we were set to sell Cranium in 110 Barnes & Noble stores."

Today Cranium products are sold in forty thousand stores; there are fifty-four million active players (Craniacs) around the world. Cranium is also the only company that has won the Toy Industry Association's Game of the Year award three years in a row.

As for Richard, he no longer has any hesitation when introducing himself to strangers without his Microsoft title. "When I say that I work for Cranium, the response is always unbelievable," he says. "The most common response I hear is, 'That must be so cool! I love those games.' "

Richard Tait's Advice for Those Stuck in Unsatisfying Jobs

"If you are not passionate about what you do, then find something that you can be passionate about. There's nothing more depressing than dedicating your days to something that doesn't fulfill you."

The Corporate Advantage

As mentioned in the previous chapter, the business experience that you've gained in Corporate America will likely serve you well in running your own company—whether it's a solo venture or a bigger business. Any background in managing projects, people, and budgets will be extremely valuable. You've also made contacts that will help make the transition easier—potential investors, advisers, partners, clients, and employees.

"There are all kinds of things that you learn from working in a big company that are incredibly useful when you start your own business, so I do not regret for a moment that I was not one of those people who started a business right out of college," says

Aliza Freud, founder and CEO of SheSpeaks, a market research firm. "I think that the skills that I gained when I was working at a big company really helped to make me a better entrepreneur."

Your background, accomplishments, and big-company pedigree may also boost your credibility with investors. And interestingly enough, your past successes can help you with another key ingredient for success on your own—confidence. Recent studies have shown that the most successful entrepreneurs tend to be overly confident.

The Corporate Disadvantage

On the other hand, some people have trouble making the adjustment. You'll have more responsibility, less structure, and fewer resources at your disposal. You will wear many hats, and you may find yourself performing tasks that you consider beneath you.

Most frightening of all, you will be flying blind in many ways. You will be confronted with tasks you don't know how to do and problems you don't know how to solve. Those used to corporate rules and structure may find it overwhelming.

"Whoever said that it's lonely at the top was right," says Ralph Jovine, founder and CEO of the Atlanta-based technology firm Grand Central Solutions. "The days of running to your boss to complain about something and get advice are over. It's up to you to get everyone to rally around the cause and to create an environment in which your team can be successful."

The biggest adjustment may be the financial one. You will probably earn less than you do at your current job (at least at first). In fact, it may be several months before you can afford to pay yourself a salary.

☕ Don't Quit Your Day Job

If you've been paying attention, you won't be surprised to read that I recommend holding on to your corporate day job and your steady paycheck for as long as you can. It takes time to build a business, and you will want your financial cushion to be as fluffy as possible.

Use the moonlighting approach and do your research, planning, and preparation while you're still employed. Some of my corporate escape artists didn't give notice until they had already secured enough funding to start taking a salary.

☕ What Kind of Business Is Right for You?

The key to success is choosing a product or service that you're passionate about. While most of the entrepreneurs whom I interviewed chose to build their businesses from scratch, there are also a number of other options for aspiring business owners.

The best choice for you will depend on your area of interest, your financial resources, and your lifestyle needs.

Buying a Business

When you purchase an existing company, the benefits include immediate cash flow and an established brand and customer base. You may also get valuable employees and equipment as part of the deal.

You will be able to evaluate financial statements and get a good sense of the sales history and any potential problems before you commit. Look for opportunities where your ideas or experience can take an already solid company to the next level.

Just be sure that you look carefully for any signs of trouble. "We thought about buying a business, but our joke at the time was, 'Why should we buy somebody else's problems?' " says Sally Fegley.

You can find businesses for sale listed in industry publications and online. You can also work through a professional business broker. See the Escape Tool Kit in the back of this book for some specific places to start browsing.

DARING TALES OF CORPORATE ESCAPE

The Corporate Rock Star

Name: Steve Bernstein

Former occupation: Senior banking executive

Current occupation: CEO of Zenbu Media, the company behind *Relix* magazine, Relix Records, the Green Apple Music Festival, and other music publications and projects

Steve Bernstein was a managing director at one of the world's largest banks when he bought *Relix*, a small music magazine that started out as a hand-stapled newsletter for Grateful Dead fans.

It may have seemed like a strange move to some, but Steve had always been passionate about music, and he had reached a point in his corporate career where he knew he was going to need an exit strategy.

Early on, *Relix* magazine was just a small sideline. Steve had no intention of leaving his high-powered bank job anytime soon. He had been with the same company for twenty-plus years, and the future looked bright.

But when Steve lost his brother on September 11, he knew his world would never be the same. "One of the lessons I took away was that you only have one shot, so you have to live your life to its fullest," he says.

He stuck it out in banking for a little while longer, but eventually decided he needed a change. "Years ago, I had promised myself that I would leave if I didn't feel like I was growing and was only there for the money."

When he told his managers that he was ready to retire, they tried to convince him to stay and take on a new role in Japan, but Steve had made up his mind. "It was right in the middle of the division firing a thousand people, two hundred in the area that I ran," he remembers. "I was supposed to give them my list of people to be laid off, and I added my name to the bottom of the list."

After leaving his corporate job, Steve decided to pour all of his considerable energy and business experience into that little music magazine he had purchased six years previously.

His company, Zenbu Media, is now much more than a Grateful Dead fanzine. The company runs four magazines dedicated to musical genres from world beats to heavy metal, a custom publishing business, eight websites, an events division that produces the country's largest Earth Day festival, and a record label.

Steve now spends his days doing work he loves and sees the benefits in every aspect of his life. "If I'd stayed and continued to play the game, I would be wealthier but miserable," he says.

Franchising

Buying a franchise of an established company can be a shortcut to entrepreneurship. You get name recognition, established processes for running the business, and the support of a larger company behind you. You may also have an easier time securing funding because you're dealing with a proven business model.

However, if you're leaving Corporate America to get away from rules and procedures, a franchise may not be the right choice for you. Some franchises offer little room for creativity or innovation.

A franchise also offers limited upside potential. Make sure you do the math to determine whether potential franchise opportunities provide attractive enough cash flow to make it worth your while.

Multilevel or Network Marketing

You have probably seen the cheesy come-ons for multilevel marketing (MLM) programs on late-night TV or in your bulk e-mail folder. You typically join an MLM program as a distributor and earn commissions on your own sales as well as those of people you recruit to join your sales team.

Many legitimate products are sold through multilevel marketing. However, there are also a lot of scams out there, so it's important to carefully evaluate these opportunities.

Multilevel marketing can offer a flexible, part-time opportunity to build a business if you find a product that you believe in. You can sell and recruit after your regular office hours.

However, these programs can also require significant up-front investment in inventory. And to be successful, you will have to be comfortable selling to and recruiting your friends, neighbors, and random passersby.

DARING TALES OF CORPORATE ESCAPE

The Sweet Taste of Success

Name: Sally Fegley

Former occupation: Corporate real estate executive

Current occupation: Co-owner of Tom and Sally's Handmade Chocolates

When the rat race become too much for them, Sally Fegley and her husband, Tom, turned to chocolate. They quit their well-paid positions in corporate real estate in Manhattan to go make chocolate in Vermont. Seventeen years later, they're still going strong.

The idea for Tom and Sally's Handmade Chocolates was born

when Tom got transferred to another city and Sally's company was involved in a hostile takeover. "We were making a lot of money and we were successful but it was very stressful," Sally says.

They decided to start their own business so they would have more control over their lives. At first, they weren't sure what the business would be or where it would be located; they just knew they wanted to do something they enjoyed. "Why take such a huge risk and not get something out of it?" Sally asks.

When they started researching ideas, they realized that there was an opportunity in the high-end chocolates market in the United States. Vermont seemed like a perfect location because of the cold climate and proximity to major retail markets. "We decided that it would be hard to find a more pleasant life than making chocolates in Vermont."

With their goal in sight, the Fegleys immediately put a transition plan into place. Both held on to their corporate jobs, which for Tom meant commuting from New York to Atlanta every week. "We thought it was important to do as much as we could possibly do while we were still employed so that we could go from paycheck to opening our store as quickly as possible," explains Sally.

The two spent months researching chocolate in both New York City and Atlanta. They went to every sweet shop and apprenticed on weekends learning how to make chocolates. Every weekend and lunch hour were spent on preparation and research.

"On the day we quit, we had a lot of knowledge, a bit of experience, and some idea of what we were getting into," says Sally. "You are never 100 percent ready, but I think we were as ready as we possibly could have been before we made the leap."

To prepare financially, they saved as much as they could and financed the purchase of their new house in Vermont with the proceeds from selling their home in New York. "We were confident in our skill and in our ability to get jobs again if we did not succeed, so we went ahead and took the plunge," says Sally.

That was seventeen years ago, and the Fegleys haven't looked back. "I really feel that we had not fully lived until we did this because it is so consuming and challenging,"

There have also been plenty of setbacks and lots of hard work along the way. "We really do live by our wits," says Sally. With ten employees and seasonal help during their busiest times of year, Sally and Tom still have to wear many hats. They have to keep up with the markets, with what colors and ingredients are hot, with manufacturing costs, and with distribution strategies. "We have to know everything," says Sally. "And sometimes we still clean our own restrooms in the store."

But for Sally, the rewards of running their own business more than make up for the headaches. "The freedom of having one's own business is really exhilarating," she says. "You cannot be so free and creative in a corporate environment."

Sally Fegley's Advice for Aspiring Entrepreneurs

"Don't do it unless you can put your whole heart into it. You really have to have the passion. You hear these fairy-tale stories about people who started businesses and got rich in a year or two, but that is the exception and not the rule."

The Step-by-Step Planning Guide

Step 1. Do Your Homework

The best way to minimize your risk is by doing your homework upfront. Take the time to research your market and refine your business idea.

- Who is your target market?
- What are they willing to pay for your product or service?
- How will you be different from your competitors?
- What kind of investment will be required to get your business up and running?
- Do you have the skills and experience to run the company?

See the Escape Tool Kit at the back of this book for reference sources to use as you conduct your research.

COMMON REASONS THAT BUSINESSES FAIL
- Not enough capital.
- Lack of market research.
- Pricing is too high or too low.
- Improper management.
- Failure to budget properly.

Step 2. Get Help

Don't be afraid to reach out for advice and support.

Find a Mentor

Is there someone in your network who has the expertise you need? If not, try reaching out to your university alumni network or a professional organization or networking group.

Another great way to connect with a mentor is through SCORE, the nonprofit organization affiliated with the Small Business Administration and dedicated to providing counseling to entrepreneurs and small business owners. The SCORE network includes more than ten thousand volunteer mentors, primarily retired business owners, in offices across the country.

I have had the pleasure of working as a volunteer counselor for SCORE's New York City chapter and can personally vouch for the value of the service the organization provides. The counselors represent a wide range of industry and functional expertise. You can meet with your mentor in person or conduct your sessions via e-mail.

SCORE also conducts workshops and provides business plan templates and other resources. Visit www.score.org for more information.

Join the Community

Investigate networking groups for entrepreneurs in your area. It's a great way to meet other business owners and learn from their experience.

"I decided to talk to as many people as I possibly could," says Aliza Freud, who left her job as a senior financial services executive to start the marketing research firm SheSpeaks. "I got very involved with a club for entrepreneurs. I was the only corporate person sitting there in those meetings, but it was so helpful for me to listen to the problems that these entrepreneurs were having with their businesses."

Aliza took her networking a step further in order to gain some hands-on experience. "I donated my time to a few start-up companies," she says. "In fact, I was eventually offered senior management jobs at two different small companies, but I had come to the conclusion that I really wanted to run my own business and not someone else's."

"Start putting yourself in the environment you want to be in and talking to as many people who do what you want to do as you can," Aliza advises. "It really does make a difference. I found that people are extremely generous with their time, if you are interested enough in them to want to sit down and talk about what they do."

You'll find groups catering to different types of entrepreneurs—from Ladies Who Launch for women business owners to Startup ping.com for those starting Internet businesses.

Online communities make it easy to network without wearing a dorky name tag. You can browse through message board topics, post questions, and jump right into the discussion.

Assemble Your Advisory Team

Once you get serious about where you're headed, it's time to put a support team in place. You will ultimately need an accountant, a lawyer, and an insurance agent to help you through the process of structuring your business.

You may want to line these experts up now to consult on the development of your business plan (see step 3). This is not the time to cut corners. These advisers will be invaluable in helping you avoid financial and legal disasters down the road.

DARING TALES OF CORPORATE ESCAPE

The Business of Relaxation

Name: Erika Mangrum

Former occupation: Human resources director

Current Occupation: Owner, Iatria Spa and Health Centers

After twelve years of working in Corporate America, Erika Mangrum was "a walking stress ball."

"I was so driven for the next thing, the next promotion, the next opportunity that I did ridiculous things to myself and to my health," says Erika. "I thought that if astronauts could go without sleep, so could I." She set her clock back one hour each night and weaned herself off sleep until she was down to three hours. The goal was to make more time for her punishing work schedule and driving back and forth to attend business school classes in another state.

"One night I drifted off while I was on the road and woke up literally seconds before I hit a guardrail," she recalls. "I almost drove over the side of the mountain and I ended up getting really, really sick after that."

She decided to go to a spa to get a massage and try to relax. While she was there, it occurred to her that the spa business would make a great subject for her upcoming business school project. "When I did the research and saw that the levels of interest in complementary medicine and relaxation were so great, I started thinking about how I could build a business around it."

She tried to forget about the idea, but found herself drawn to spas whenever she traveled. "I would go in, talk to the owner, and do a little bit more research," she says. "The next thing I knew, I had a business plan."

Erika presented her plan to a couple of different banks, but ultimately decided to follow the recommendation of a business adviser who suggested she borrow from her 401(k) and pay herself back with interest.

She quit her corporate job in March 1999 and opened the first Iatria Spa and Health Center in Raleigh in September. "I remember all of the preparations that we made for opening day, all of the marketing," she recalls. "We were all set for people to come streaming through the doors."

Instead, they had a grand total of three people visit on opening day. "I remember trying to stay positive for the staff and then I went home that night and just burst into tears thinking, *What have I done?*"

Luckily, business soon picked up, and Erika's husband was able to quit his job to help run the business full-time. "It was a good thing, because we found out later that year that I was pregnant," says Erika. Over the next few years, Iatria went on to open three more spa locations and now has eighty employees. The firm was recently included in the 2007 Inc. 5,000 Fastest-Growing Private Companies.

Erika is much happier now than she ever was as a hard-charging corporate executive. "I really feel like I am making a difference in the quality of people's lives now," she says. "It's hard to do that when you're just a little cog in the corporate machine."

Erika Mangrum's Best Advice for Aspiring Entrepreneurs

"Find a very good accountant, attorney, and insurance agent. Don't look for the best deal, because those three people are critical to the long-term success of the business and having the right processes and procedures in play."

Step 3. Write a Great Business Plan

You will need a compelling business plan to raise funding. No ifs, ands, or buts. Even if you're planning to bootstrap your company or rely on friends and family for capital, working through the process of writing a business plan will help you clarify your objectives and identify obstacles and opportunities. Put it in writing.

Volumes have been written about the art of the business plan. Below is a list of the key components. If you're overwhelmed by the detail, stop and take a deep breath. There are templates and software programs out there that can guide you through the process with minimal pain. You can also hire a financial expert if the financial plan section makes you dizzy. You can even hire a writer with experience with these documents to help you polish or punch up the plan for maximum effect. Please see the Escape Tool Kit at the end of this book for more information and tools for getting your brilliant ideas down on paper.

Basic Business Plan Components

- Executive summary.
- Description of the business.
- Market analysis.
- Competition.
- Marketing plan.
- Management team.
- Operating plan.
- Pricing.
- Financial plan.

Put together a solid draft of your business plan, then reach out to get some feedback from your mentors or from more-seasoned entrepreneurs in your networking group. You can also contact SCORE to get an honest review of your business plan from a SCORE counselor.

Step 4. Raise Money

Once you have an irresistible business plan in hand, you're ready to line up the capital you need.

Estimate How Much You'll Need

First, calculate how much it will cost you to launch and sustain your business (you should have already crunched those numbers while developing your business plan in step 3). Then think about how much you can contribute. Investors like to see that you're committed enough to put some of your own money into the deal.

Evaluate Your Funding Options

- **Friends and family.** Do you have friends or family members who might be willing to invest in your business idea? Do you feel comfortable asking them to risk their money? This can be one of the quickest and least expensive ways to finance your business. If you proceed with funding from family and friends, consider using a service such as Virgin Money (formerly CircleLending) to keep everything businesslike (www .virginmoneyus.com).
- **Banks.** Your local bank offers a range of business loans and lines of credit. The Small Business Administration also guarantees business loans to entrepreneurs who qualify. You will need good credit and collateral to be considered by most lenders.
- **Angel investors.** Angels are individuals and groups that invest in early-stage start-ups. Visit the Angel Capital Association website (www.angelcapitalassociation.org) to find angel investors and research their preferences.
- **Venture capital firms.** Venture capitalists are professional investors that typically finance new and rapidly growing companies. Learn more about the industry at the National Venture Capital Association site (www.nvca.org).

Make Your Pitch

Investors will want to see a solid business plan and financial projections, your bio, and your personal credit history. You may also be asked to make a formal presentation. Take the time to prepare your speaking points and responses to any anticipated questions or objections.

Do Your Due Diligence

Read the fine print and research the pros and cons of proceeding with any given lender. Take the time to understand the loan expectations and ensure that any funding arrangement is in the best interests of your business.

Step 5. Full Speed Ahead

Once your financing is in place, the real work begins. Are you ready to quit your job and start building your empire?

As an entrepreneur, your days are about to get a lot more challenging and exciting. By this point, you know what you're up against and you've done your homework. Now it's time to put all of your plans into action.

Check the Escape Tool Kit in the back of the book for additional resources to support you in getting your business up and running.

HOW MUCH SHOULD YOU PAY YOURSELF?

Make sure you include a line item for your salary in your business plan's financial projections. Your salary estimates should be based on a reasonable range for the work that you'll be doing and how much your company can afford to pay you. Many entrepreneurs opt to take reduced salaries and pump as much money back into the business as possible.

That's fine if you have savings, but even entrepreneurs need to eat. Just make sure you can afford to live on what you're paying yourself.

DARING TALES OF CORPORATE ESCAPE

From Corporate President to Chief Executive Bear

Name: Maxine Clark

Former occupation: President, Payless ShoeSource®

Current occupation: Founder and Chief Executive Bear of Build-A-Bear Workshop®

Maxine Clark earned an enviable salary in her role as president of Payless ShoeSource, one of the country's top footwear retailers, but it wasn't enough. "My psychic bank account was empty," she says. "I wanted to do something creative with children."

The idea behind the phenomenally popular Build-A-Bear Workshop retail chain came during a shopping trip with a ten-year-old friend. "My inspiration to start this company was really a culmination of my years of retail experience combined with the goal to bring the fun back to shopping the way I remembered it when I was a child."

It wasn't easy to walk away from a high-powered career to start her own business, but Maxine did leave with some advantages. "After twenty-plus years of experience with the May Department Stores, I had the experience, know-how, contacts, and financial wherewithal to develop the business plan and the model for Build-A-Bear Workshop," she says. "I have vast experience in product development, sourcing, and marketing, and these were exactly the skills I needed to get started."

Maxine set out to create a new kind of company from the very beginning. "I wanted it to be all of the things I liked from my past jobs and from other companies that I had long studied and admired," she says. "It was—and is—exciting for me each day to share this vision and watch the concept grow with the amazing team we have."

Today Build-A-Bear Workshop operates more than three hundred stores in the United States, Canada, the United Kingdom, Ireland, and France. The company posted total revenue of $437 million in fiscal year 2006. Maxine even shared her business advice with the world in her book *The Bear Necessities of Business*, and donated 100 percent of the book's proceeds to the Build-A-Bear Workshop Bear Hugs Foundation.

Maxine Clark's Advice for Entrepreneurs

"People need to allow themselves first to dream big and then to believe in their dreams. Start by believing that you can truly achieve whatever you set your mind to, then write a formal business plan that details the dream—this will always be a working document but will serve to not only convince you to do it but to convince others to support you. Real success starts with a dream and a lot of determination."

TEN

Follow Your Creative Dreams

> All children are artists. The problem is how to remain an artist once one grows up.
>
> **—Pablo Picasso**
>
> Happiness is not in the mere possession of money; it lies in the joy of achievement, in the thrill of creative effort.
>
> **—Franklin Roosevelt**

Sarah F. always wanted to be a writer. But somewhere along the way, somebody convinced her that writing wasn't a very practical career choice. Sarah got caught up in other people's doubts and fears. She didn't want to live on ramen noodles and sleep on the street. So she grew up to be a public relations executive for a multinational food products conglomerate.

And then there's Laura, the musician who went into investment banking. And Georgia, the filmmaker who became a management consultant. Maybe you can relate to their stories.

The Creative Dream Versus the Corporate Reality

When you're little, everyone thinks it's cute that you want to grow up to be an artist or a singer or a movie star. Unfortunately, as little artists get older and less adorable, most are steered away from silly creative dreams and toward more practical career prospects. Or at least gently nudged into developing a "fallback plan."

Most parents mean well. After all, many of them grew up with the idea that success is a corner office and a split-level ranch house in the suburbs. Nobody wants their little bundles of joy to end up on the welfare line or, worse yet, sleeping in their childhood bedrooms forever.

People drift away from childhood fantasies. You can't major in Fairy Princess, and few entry-level jobs exist for astronauts these days.

For others, however, the creative urge never goes away—no matter how many promotions they earn or mortgage payments they make. They snivel in their cubicles, wishing they could change their lives.

The good news is that it's possible to make the transition from corporate suit to artist. The change just takes creativity, hard work, and guts. Laura the musician/investment banker got a record deal and went on tour with Elvis Costello. And Georgia the filmmaker/management consultant apprenticed with Martin Scorsese, got financing for her first feature-length film, and went on to win a top prize at a major film festival.

◻️ This Is Not My Beautiful Life

"One day I looked around at my life and thought, *What the hell happened to me?*" says Roger P., an actor/insurance agent. He's not alone. A lot of artists take "temporary" jobs to pay the bills while they figure out what they really want to do with their lives. Then, because they're smart and talented, they sometimes find themselves climbing the corporate ladder almost by accident. Pretty soon, they look around and are horrified to find they're entrenched in a career that doesn't make them happy, but is too comfortable to walk away from.

Writers end up in corporate marketing jobs. Visual artists

become graphic designers. Actors become salespeople. Musicians and filmmakers flock to day jobs that will make them enough money to pay the rent.

A corporate day job can work well for some artists. But only for those who can keep the two worlds separate and rabidly protect their creative time. Living a double life becomes increasingly difficult as you gain more responsibility and status in your day job.

The money and benefits are only part of the corporate attraction. Being validated and appreciated feels good—even if it's in a job that you don't find particularly fulfilling. This is especially true for people who are struggling to make it in a creative field, facing rejection and competition at every turn.

Unfortunately, most corporations are not good homes for creative personalities. With the typical corporate focus on productivity and following established processes, little room for creative expression or truly new ideas remains. Sarah F. tried in vain to apply her creative mind to her day job. But every new idea she proposed was rejected flat-out or died in the approval process. The endless bureaucracy was almost comical. "I got to the point where I knew I had to get out before my brain atrophied," says Sarah.

☕ Your Money or Your Life

So why do people like Sarah stay in jobs they hate? For many, it's mostly for the paycheck and the benefits. The "starving artist" cliché persists for a reason. Only a lucky few earn comfortable livings from artistic pursuits. During the Renaissance, wealthy families such as the Medicis provided financial support to artists like Michelangelo. Otherwise, Michelangelo might have ended up hauling marble instead of carving it.

Today most artists scrape by and make sacrifices. It's a lot easier to make that choice when you're young and naïve. It's much harder for someone who has attained a measure of success in the corporate world to make a major life change. You've become accustomed to a certain standard of living, and you may also have responsibilities to consider—say, a spouse, children, or a mortgage. The idea of chucking it all to follow your artistic dreams can seem irresponsible or even ridiculous. Luckily, repressed corporate artists can rediscover their creative dreams without giving up solid food or moving into their parents' basements.

DARING TALES OF CORPORATE ESCAPE

Telecommuting from Elvis Costello Concerts

Name: Laura Cantrell

Former occupation: VP of administration at an investment bank

Current occupation: Musician and recording artist

When Laura Cantrell became an administrative assistant on Wall Street, it was strictly a "rent-money job" so that she could pursue her music and passionate (though nonpaying) love of radio on the side.

For a while, it was a great day job. After hours, she had time for her weekly radio show, gigs around New York City, and a bit of songwriting.

"I took my corporate bonus of $5,000 and used it to get into the studio and record for the first time," she recalls. That recording found its way into the hands of a friend of a friend in Scotland, who called to tell her he wanted to work with her to record an album.

"It took about a year to record more songs, put together photos for the cover, and all of that stuff," she says. Meanwhile, she got promoted at her day job and it got a bit harder to find time for her music.

"Luckily, it turned out that that goofy guy in Scotland had a real record company," she says. She was delighted when the album came out and sold pretty well in England.

Soon Laura was spending all her vacation time in England performing and promoting her record. At that point, things got a bit hairy. "My day job was a pretty heavy job by then," she says. "I was the business manager for the Equity Research Department for a large organization."

While her managers were supportive of her music in theory, that support didn't translate into much extra time off. Things came to a head when Laura received a thrilling offer to open for Elvis Costello on a national tour in fall 2002.

The tour just happened to be scheduled during one of the busiest times of year in her department, and she knew it would be difficult to get her bosses to let her leave. "I had to ask myself how much this opportunity meant to me and what I was willing to risk to do it," she says. "I didn't want to look back in twenty years and wonder what could have happened if I'd gone."

She went to her bosses to see if she could work out a solution. "I told them I would take a laptop and a phone on tour and do as much as I could from the road," she recalls. She was thrilled when they agreed and she didn't have to resign.

Although she appreciated the support, it was extremely difficult for Laura to work from motel rooms and tour buses between concerts. Worst of all, there was a major layoff scheduled for the day that she was returning to work.

"I had been playing in these theaters in Cleveland and Minneapolis and having the time of my life," she says. "Meanwhile, I'm also reviewing lists of names and trying to justify who should be laid off."

She felt a huge amount of stress about the situation and realized that there was no way she could continue to balance the job and her music career long-term. "I really thought that if I continued to try to split my brain between the two, there was going to be a train wreck either at work or on stage," she says. "It had gotten to the point where the stakes were too high."

Laura resigned from her job in March and went on tour in England to celebrate. This time she didn't have to take her laptop along. "It was great to go out and actually play for a living," she says.

Since she left her corporate job four years ago, Laura put out another album, was featured in the *Wall Street Journal* and *O Magazine,* and had a baby.

She is currently facing a new challenge—trying to balance full-time musicianship with full-time motherhood.

Laura Cantrell's Advice for Artists with Day Jobs

"Don't think that having to struggle means you aren't successful. Many artists over the ages have struggled with the idea of how to pay the rent."

Are You a Creative Soul Trapped in a Cubicle?

If you're a creative soul trapped in a cubicle, you may have learned to suppress your artistic passions or to channel them into more "appropriate" activities (like PowerPoint presentations).

For some people, that may be enough. It is possible to live a creative life without running off to write the Great American Novel. The most extraordinary breakthroughs in science and business have come from creative souls who found new ways of looking at the status quo.

But if you're feeling stuck in your corporate job, it might be helpful to think about why you never pursued your creative dreams. If you can understand how you got stuck, it will be a lot easier to figure out how to get un-stuck. Some common reasons for giving up on artistic dreams include:

- **Fear of failure.** Putting yourself out there is scary. What if you're not good enough? The only cure for fear of failure is to feel the fear and do it anyway. Failure is no fun, but every successful person goes through it. Stephen King's first three novels were rejected—repeatedly. Every failure and setback is an opportunity to improve.

- **Security.** Being poor is no fun. Even if there's no such thing as true job security anymore, corporate paychecks can help you keep a nice roof over your head and nice shoes on your feet. However, there's no reason you can't be an artist with nice shoes. You don't have to quit your job to explore your artistic side.

- **Not being ready.** Some lucky people have known their career destinies since they were babies. Others need time to figure out what they're good at and what they love to do. Many future artists require life experience to season their natural talent before they are capable of greatness.

  It's never too late to get started. Laura Ingalls Wilder didn't publish her first novel until well into her sixties. The great Raymond Chandler published his first short story at forty-five and his first novel at fifty-one after being fired from his job as an oil company executive.

- **Lack of time.** If only you had the time. This is one of the most common reasons that people don't pursue their creative dreams, and it's a legitimate one. But Jenn W. has two kids under two, a husband, a house, a full-time job, and a thriving career as a writer. How does she do it? She prioritizes, she gets up early, and she has the endurance of an Energizer Bunny.

- **Lack of support.** Becoming an artist is hard—especially when everybody else wants you to be an accountant. Maybe your parents pushed you into a "practical" career. Perhaps your significant other pressured you to start bringing home the bacon. If you support others financially, it's understandable that they may feel threatened by your talk of changing careers. When you're the breadwinner in the family, you can't make any major, sudden moves. Reassure your family or significant other that you will continue to meet your responsibilities while you explore your new career. If you still can't find support from those near and dear to you, reach out to others in the creative community. See the Escape Tool Kit at the end of this book for information on support networks and communities to explore.

🍵 True Calling or Fantasy?

Eventually, the time will come for the rubber to hit the road—or the paint to hit the canvas, or the fingers to hit the keyboard. Do you really want this creative dream or is it just a fantasy?

The artist's life is not all fun and games. It takes hard work, perseverance, and sacrifice. Most people who stick with their creative dreams do it because they love what they do enough to deal with the challenges.

In your corporate life, you put up with endless meetings and stupid bosses so you can take home a nice paycheck. Artists sacrifice material luxuries and open themselves up to criticism and rejection—all for the simple reason that they can't imagine being happy doing anything else.

The good news is that you can "try on" the artistic lifestyle without quitting your day job. Then, if you're ready to make a major life change, you can take the next step.

Quitting your day job doesn't have to be a far-fetched dream. Franz Kafka was a clerk in an insurance office for many years before he was recognized as a great writer. Paul Gauguin worked as a stockbroker before running off to Tahiti to become a famous painter. Kevin Costner was a marketing rep before quitting to pursue a career as an actor and Oscar-winning filmmaker.

The Step-by-Step Plan

Step 1. Just Do It

That's right. The first step is to actually sit down and draw, paint, write, compose, or do whatever tickles your creative fancy. On a regular basis. Even when you don't feel like it and when the muse isn't showing up.

Don't Be a Poseur

Some people call themselves artists but don't actually do anything but cultivate an edgy fashion sense and talk a good game. Like the guy who's been "working on a novel" for years (and may actually write a paragraph or two someday) or tells you he has a masterpiece "in his head," but is just too busy to sit down and "type it up." Don't play this game.

You won't know how good you are—or how good you can be—until you work at your creative endeavors consistently for a period of time. Even more importantly, you won't know if you actually like the artist's lifestyle—or if you just like the fantasy.

The romantic idea of the artist at work can seem pretty damn cool from your cubicle, but the reality often isn't so glamorous. Who knows? You may find yourself running back to your corporate job, but you won't have to wonder what might have been.

Make Time for Your Passion

Start by working on your creative projects during evenings and weekends. Schedule the appointments in your calendar. I know what you're going to say—you don't have time. You barely have time to do your laundry what with your fifty-hour workweek, your commute, and your attempt at a social life.

You have to make the time if your dream is important to you.

Even if it's only a few hours a week. After all, how much time do you waste in an average day—between the endless bureaucracy at work and the after-hours drinking and vegging to try to forget about the endless bureaucracy at work? Spending a little time each day on your passion should energize you and lift your mood.

For example, Andrew T. found that he would return to the office refreshed after a lunch hour spent taking photographs. "Somehow, those lunch breaks made dealing with the crap at work a little bit easier."

FINDING CREATIVE TIME IN A BUSY CORPORATE LIFE

- **Schedule a date with yourself at least one evening each week.** Force yourself to leave work at a reasonable hour and devote the entire evening to your art. Find a babysitter and tell your significant other you're booked.
- **Block out time on the weekends.** Set Saturday mornings or Sunday evenings, or some other predefined time period, as your creative time. Then stick to it.
- **Get up early** and work for an hour or two before you start your morning routine. Jenn W. rises before dawn and enjoys two hours of peaceful writing time each day before her two children awake.
- **Slip out of the office at lunch** and escape to a nearby park or coffee shop, where you can spend an hour on your creative project. This works more easily for writers and visual artists, of course. You may feel awkward sculpting or practicing your violin in the park or coffee shop. But you can at least jot down ideas for your next sculpture, or listen to a great violinist on your iPod. Find ways to work some creative activity into your day.
- **Book a regular meeting with yourself** in your work calendar. Then treat it like all of those other meetings your boss is constantly

inviting you to. Lock your office door or find a conference room or a quiet cubicle somewhere and do some creative work.

• **Start working nine to five.** Set your boundaries and stop staying late or coming in early unless it's strictly necessary. This often takes some cojones. If everybody else in the office stays late, marching out the door at five (and facing the judgmental stares) can be hard. But if you do your job well and put in extra hours when there's a real crunch time (like when the big boss arbitrarily decides he needs that presentation tomorrow), it's hard for anyone to reasonably complain.

• **Telecommute.** If you can arrange to work from home on a regular basis, you can free up the time you normally spend commuting. Heck, you can even free up the time you normally spend showering, shaving, and struggling into your panty hose. If you're lucky enough to telecommute, don't take advantage. Don't slack off—or at least don't be obvious about it—or you'll ruin it for everybody else.

• **Take advantage of downtime.** In even the busiest jobs, there is occasional downtime. The trick is to be prepared and take advantage of it. For example, business trips can be good opportunities. Away from your personal responsibilities (whether you like it or not), you can often find time on long flights and during layovers and solo evenings at strange hotels. You can also take advantage of downtime after a major project is completed and everybody else is celebrating with long lunches and half days.

Set Goals

Set small and attainable goals—say, finish one drawing or ten pages of your screenplay by a non-negotiable deadline—and achieve those objectives. This will allow you to build momentum and feel a sense of accomplishment. It'll also discourage you from slacking off. Your creative talents are like muscles. They need to be exercised regularly or they don't get stronger—they get flabby and soft and look terrible in a bathing suit.

Be protective of your work at first. When it's new, you're still a little green and more easily bruised by people's criticism or off-hand comments. Spend some time nurturing your talent and building your confidence before you share your work with the world. But don't wait too long. Art is meant to be experienced and won't do anyone any good gathering dust in a drawer or closet. Besides, feedback from others can help you take your work to a whole new level.

A class or workshop can be a great way to get feedback. Do your homework and find a teacher who knows his subject and how to communicate it to students (see the Escape Tool Kit at the end of this book for recommended classes in your area). A class can also be invaluable in providing structure and deadlines that force you to get things done. Some people are more likely to complete a project if there's a deadline and someone else is waiting for it. Taking a class with homework assignments was the only way that I was able to force myself to write consistently during my years in the corporate world. Sometimes I squeezed in writing time only so that I could hand in my assignment on time and not look stupid in class. It's a lot harder to blow off your writing when you have a whole classful of people to answer to.

Take a Creative Holiday

You might consider taking some vacation time and spending a week (or at least a day or two) as a full-time artist. This will give you a taste of what your life would be like if you could quit that annoying day job. You can devote entire days to your creative work—maybe even finish that painting or symphony or screen-play. And it's a great low-risk way to try out your desired lifestyle. You may love it. Or you may be bored stiff. You're better off knowing now, either way.

If you're not cut out to be a full-time artist at this stage of your life, that doesn't mean you should give up your creative pursuits entirely. Many people are better suited to being part-time artists. Your painting or writing can become a treasured hobby that adds fun and fulfillment to your life. It can be an essential piece of your life without becoming your whole career.

DARING TALES OF CORPORATE ESCAPE

Having More Fun at *The Office*

> **Name:** Paul Lieberstein
>
> **Previous occupation:** Corporate auditor
>
> **Current occupation:** Writer/producer/actor for NBC's *The Office*

Ever wonder how NBC's *The Office* can capture the day-to-day insanities and inanities of corporate life so vividly? It probably doesn't hurt that Paul Lieberstein, who is a writer and co-executive-producer for the show and also portrays beleaguered human resources manager Toby, did a brief stint in cubicle land as a corporate auditor.

Although Paul decided he wanted to be a writer in junior high, he found himself led astray by a well-meaning career counselor during his last year in college. "I said I was interested in being a writer, and there was a long pause while he just stared at me," Paul remembers. "After another pause, I said I was also interested in investment banking, and then he started to talk."

After graduation, Paul didn't land any job offers from investment banks, but a big accounting firm did come calling. "They had a new program where they threw unqualified people out into the auditing field," he remembers. "Who could resist that? Not me."

It seemed as good a career move as any at the time. "It wasn't until my sister started working as an assistant at *Saturday Night Live* and I started meeting her friends and her writer boyfriend who later became my brother-in-law [Greg Daniels—the executive producer of *The Office*] that I realized people could actually make a living writing for television."

In the meantime, Paul tried to make it work in the corporate world. "It was interesting at first," he says. "I guess I just mean the first ten minutes."

For his first assignment, he found himself trapped in a conference room with three annoying co-workers. "The woman in charge sat me down, put the 'C' books in front of me, and said I should just look through them to familiarize myself with the audit," he remembers. "I asked what I was looking for and she said to just look. I spent the whole day on the 'C' books and I still don't know what 'C' books are."

His other two colleagues weren't much better. One spent the day talking to herself out loud. "I tried to engage the tall man with the adding machine in conversation at one point, but never figured out what door I could open to make him speak," he says. "I think there was once a door and working there made the door shrink to a size so small that words like *no* were the only thing that could come out. I think this because while working there I felt my own door shrinking."

It wasn't a very good feeling. "It was the hours of silence, the perceived useless necessity of what we were doing, and the possibility that it would stay exactly that way for forty years of working," he says. "A life sentence is often only twenty-five years."

Paul's decision to quit his miserable job was sudden and dramatic. The next step in his logical career path at the time was business school, which required taking the GMAT test. "I studied for it, took a class, took the test, and then just sat there," Paul recalls. "I sat there with my completed test and thought that this was the start of a road I didn't want to go down. The test somehow seemed to be the key, so I voided my score—that was my decision moment and I quit shortly thereafter."

Once the decision was made, Paul was ready to leave and never look back. "I could only give one week's notice because two weeks seemed impossible."

He made time for one final act of rebellion. "On my last day I wore a shirt with stripes and a tie with stripes," he says. "People thought it was insulting."

Two days after he quit, Paul finished his first script. "It wasn't good, but I was so charged up that I wrote a few more, then started working with a writing partner. We got an agent together and the agent got us a job writing for a series."

Later, after splitting with his writing partner, Paul got his first job writing solo for the *Weird Science* series through a guy he played volleyball with. Paul went on to write for *King of the Hill* and other shows before landing his present gig on *The Office*.

"There were tough times along the way for sure, but I never considered going back to an office job," he says. "I thought about going back to school to teach. I even dusted off my old economics books once. They couldn't be more obsolete, but they still represent my only escape route if things turn dark again, so I keep them."

The future looks pretty bright for Paul at the moment. *The Office* is an Emmy winner and a bona fide hit. "I'm happy because I work with funny people and we sit around on couches and think up jokes and stories and I get to wear jeans," he says. "There's a lot to love about my job, but it's relative. In auditing, I met people who loved it, and a creative field would have been a disaster for them."

At least Paul has been able to use his unhappy experiences in Corporate America as fodder for his writing. "I suppose I've used a few details of my corporate days in my writing, but mostly I've just kept with me that general sense of soulless, infinite desperation that's part of the day-to-day operation of business," he says. "Toby certainly knows that."

Paul Lieberman's Career Advice

"Our work lives are too long. We can't sit in a job we don't like for fifty years, it makes no sense. Fifty years! If we hate our jobs, we have to leave them, that's our responsibility to ourselves."

When the Going Gets Tough

Some people can be perfectly happy enjoying their creative talents in their spare time. But for others, living a double life can become exhausting. If you're serious about your creative work, the struggle to balance both worlds can start to make you crazy.

The good news is that feeling this way probably means you're well on your way to succeeding as an artist. It may also mean you're ready to make some job changes to create more time for your creative pursuits.

Step 2. Work to Live (*Don't Quit Your Day Job*)

Day jobs get a bad rap. Most artists dream of a future in which they can quit their day jobs and focus full-time on their passions. That's a great goal. But the truth is that a good day job can give you the best of both worlds, providing financial security and plenty of flexibility for your art.

Picking the right day job is very important. A bad one can suck the life out of you and your creative endeavors. A good one doesn't require a lot of overtime or leave you too exhausted or demoralized to work on your passion.

Most mid- to senior-level corporate jobs don't work well as day jobs. They usually take up too much time and energy—too many late nights, too much effort pretending you care deeply about fourth-quarter results or your boss's golf game.

However, some savvy people know how to make corporate day jobs work well for them—through a little creativity and the guts to stick to their boundaries. How do they do it?

Punch Out at Five O'Clock

If five isn't realistic, make it five thirty or six. Just pick a reasonable quitting time and stick to it. Don't schedule meetings that will run past your predetermined quitting time. Don't make eye

---

Day Job: One's primary job, usually at daytime and enabling one to pursue a secondary activity from which one would eventually like to draw an income.

—American Heritage Dictionary

contact with the colleague who hovers around your cubicle at four fifty-five. This will take willpower. You may have to deal with some passive-aggressive, snarky comments from co-workers. "Half day today?" "I sure wish I could leave at five, but I'm soooooo busy." Ignore them. They probably have no lives.

Now, there will be days that call for making exceptions. Use your professional judgment—you need to keep doing your primary job well. Evaluate every request to put in overtime very carefully. Don't be a pushover. Only stay when it's truly necessary.

If your boss squawks, you could offer to come in a little earlier. Don't offer right away. After all, most companies' standard operating hours are nine to five. However, a lot of corporate day jobbers find that arriving earlier in the morning, though painful at first, can open up a lot of extra time in the evenings. Often early mornings can be less hectic—fewer co-workers around, fewer meetings and phone calls, more time to catch up on backlogged work. As a result, early risers can leave at five guilt-free and devote a stretch of several hours to their creative projects and/or personal lives.

If your boss and co-workers continue to give you grief about your hours, even though you're pulling your weight, a little white lie can work wonders. Tell them you have a class or that you have to pick up your kids at a certain time (this works best if you actually have kids). It's best to avoid lying—if you get caught, your credibility will take a serious hit. But this approach worked well for actor/insurance agent Roger P. "At first, I told my boss and co-workers that I had a class every Monday and Wednesday and I had to leave at five," he says. "After a while, they got used to the fact that I wasn't there late on those nights and I was able to drop the fib about a class."

Make Your Boss an Ally

Life in a cubicle is a lot easier when your boss is your closest ally. Establish a good working relationship with your manager and earn her trust. That means doing your job well and delivering on all your commitments. A boss who likes and trusts you is far less likely to raise an eyebrow when you leave at five or take an occasional personal day. If you've been working your butt off in your current job, you probably already have a strong relationship with your boss. Leverage it to make your work life saner.

Of course, some bosses are psychos, face-time junkies, or power-mad dictators. If your boss falls into one of these categories, it's probably time to start working on that résumé. Even if you consider your current gig a temporary day job while you establish your creative career, it's not worth the stress to stay in a job with an unreasonable or bullying boss.

Stop Climbing the Ladder

If you're serious about your artistic pursuits, you need to stop devoting excess energy to being a star at your corporate job. You can do your job well and earn your keep without being the top pupil. This is easy to say, but often difficult to do. Most people have strong work ethics. They want to excel and be recognized. This is admirable, but it's very difficult to be the number one player at work while you're nurturing a thriving second career in the arts. You can't compete with co-workers who are logging sixty-hour weeks and living for the next promotion.

You have to make a choice. It's tempting to give in to old habits when the boss comes by with a "high-profile project" that you know will require late hours and weekends. This is particularly true if you have a reputation as a go-to person. You will have to learn to cut back your hours, turn down projects, and take vacation time. You will likely get some strange looks and some critical comments. Resist the urge to cave.

When co-workers get plum assignments and praise, don't succomb to the reflexive surge of jealousy or competitiveness. Ask yourself what's more important—to be a star at work or to make time for the things that you love.

Stay Out of the Politics

This is easier said than done, but office politics can suck hours out of your day. Avoid the temptation to spend lunch hour speculating about the rumored reorg. Walk on by the coffee klatch gossiping about the latest office affair. Stop participating in the long and repetitive I-hate-this-place bitch sessions.

Sure, sometimes you need to vent your frustrations. As long as you choose a trusted confidant and limit your kvetch time, an occasional gripe-fest is fine. But try not to get swept up in the gossip and negativity. It wastes your time and usually puts you in a bad mood to boot.

Ask for Help

If your current workload makes the idea of leaving at five o'clock seem like an unattainable fantasy, consider asking for help. Make a case to your boss for hiring an additional person to take up some of the slack. Prepare a business case showing your excessive workload and outlining the business advantages of hiring more staff—greater efficiency, faster turnarounds, and so on.

Unfortunately, many corporations are so focused on the bottom line that they'd rather burn out their valued employees than pay for another warm body. If your request for more head count gets shot down, you do have other options. Propose transferring some of your projects to a co-worker who has more free time. Consider delegating work to an ambitious assistant or junior staff member. Often, these junior co-workers are looking for more challenging projects that will let them show their capabilities.

If all else fails, ask for an intern. Interns can be wonderful resources. Most companies waste their interns because they don't want to take the time to train them. The time spent to get an intern up to speed is well worth it, if it allows you to off-load some of your extra work. An intern will thank you for giving him something to do besides sit in a cubicle and stare into space.

Step 3. Get Creative

If you can't find a way to scale back or reengineer your current day job, a more drastic step may be in order. When your creative pursuits can no longer coexist with your current day job, the time has come to evaluate more drastic approaches. That may mean major life changes. The following are options to consider at this stage:

Go Part-Time

Many companies offer flextime and part-time job schedules. Part-time generally means working only a few days a week or a few hours a day, while flextime allows for customizing a forty-hour workweek (for example, working late four days a week and taking one day off). Look into your corporate policies and understand the requirements, as well as the impact that part-time or flextime would have on your salary or benefits.

Going part-time will likely mean less pay. Evaluate your financial situation and determine if you can afford to make the change. Then you'll have to sell the idea to your boss and to the Human Resources Department. Keep in mind that asking for a part-time or flextime schedule could label you as less committed to the organization, which could hamper you on the promotion track. This is usually an easy trade-off if you're serious about making an escape from Corporate America.

Take a Sabbatical

Many companies also have sabbatical programs, allowing employees to take off a few weeks, or even a few months, without sacrificing their jobs. Most of these sabbaticals are unpaid. However, some companies will actually pay long-term employees to take a break. Intel, for example, offers a paid eight-week sabbatical after seven years of service. Look into your company's sabbatical policies to understand your options and any financial ramifications. To score a sabbatical, you will likely have to make a business case to your boss and demonstrate your commitment to returning to work (refreshed and raring to go, of course) at the end of the allotted time. It's a small price to pay for several weeks away from your cubicle.

See chapter 6 for detailed advice on negotiating a sabbatical or a flextime or part-time work schedule.

DARING TALES OF CORPORATE ESCAPE

The Scenic Route from Consultant to Filmmaker

Name: Georgia Lee
Former occupation: Management consultant
Current occupation: Filmmaker

When Georgia Lee fell in love with movies in the film archives at Harvard, it never even crossed her mind to pursue film as a profession. She had been raised by her strict parents to understand that she had only three career options: doctor, lawyer, or businesswoman.

She chose Door Number Three and started a job at a top consulting firm right out of college. She remembers an epiphany on a first-class flight back from a client engagement in Paris at the age of twenty-one. "I guess I've made it," she remembers realizing. "I'll continue to work hard, I'll become a partner, I'll get married and have kids, the whole thing."

The thought made her a little bit queasy. "It wasn't what I wanted, and I knew it wouldn't make me happy."

She decided it was time to shake things up and took the summer off from work to enroll in a crash film course at New York University. "The secret to losing ten pounds fast is to not eat, not sleep, and just make films all the time," she jokes.

She could sit in the editing room all night and completely lose track of time. "I didn't have the courage to leave my job to pursue film full-time, so I went back to work in the fall, but I continued to make short films on the side," she says.

Her first short film was about Tiananmen Square and was inspired by the work of Martin Scorsese. She decided to send him a copy via his fan mail address.

"I was shocked when I got a call at work while I was up to my eyeballs in spreadsheets and learned that Scorsese wanted to meet me," she remembers. She visited the man himself on location in New York City and asked for his advice on becoming a great filmmaker. He said, "You make films."

Soon after, Georgia was thrilled when Scorsese invited her to apprentice on the set of *Gangs of New York* in Rome. It was an opportunity that she could not refuse.

"I took a sabbatical from my job and went to Rome to try to learn everything I could about film by osmosis," she says. It was five months of de facto film school working with Scorsese, set designer Dante Ferretti, and the best of the best.

By now, Georgia knew that her passion was for filmmaking, but she somehow let her parents convince her to enroll in Harvard Business School after she returned to New York.

"It's hard to explain how ingrained it was in me not to go against my parents' wishes," she says. She sat in rigorous business classes for a semester, feeling miserable and dreaming about the films she was making in her spare time.

Finally, she got up the nerve to take a leave of absence from business school to write/direct/co-produce the feature film *Red*

Doors. She had saved up some money during her consulting career to provide a bit of a financial cushion while she worked on the film.

Georgia and her co-producers cobbled together $200,000 from investors to make the movie, and Georgia lived in a friend and co-producer's kitchen to save money while they shot. It was a labor of love that paid off.

The film was accepted at the Tribeca Film Festival in spring 2006, where it won a top honor, and was released in theaters later that year.

"It took me many years to make the leap to what I really wanted to do," Georgia says. "I have a lot of friends who are still unhappy as lawyers, consultants, and bankers. They are all making great money, but they're entering their thirties and wondering what they're really doing with their lives."

Georgia Lee's Advice for Corporate Escapees

"If you really have a passion, then go do it. The way I did it was in baby steps. I didn't quit my day job and I followed parallel paths until I was dead sure what I wanted."

Get a Less Demanding Day Job

A less demanding day job can free up a lot more time and energy for your creative endeavors. You will probably have to take a pay cut, and maybe even swallow a little pride, but many artists say it's worth it.

Based on interviews with artists, here are some tips for making a less-demanding day job work for you:

- **Find something you like . . . but not too much.** Your day job shouldn't be mind-numbing drudgery. If you're going to dread going to work every day, you might as well stay in Corporate America. It won't all be fun and games, but it doesn't have to be misery. If you love books, check out jobs in libraries or bookstores. If you love people, consider a sales or service gig. If you enjoy the Zen of repetitive busywork, look into office temp work. Find a day job that pays the bills and keeps you sane, but avoid anything that will tempt you to put in overtime.

- **Keep your ego in check.** Most undemanding day jobs don't come with status or underlings. You will probably have to swallow a little pride if you're making an adjustment from corporate muckety-muck. You'll have to learn to separate your true identity from your job. You may have to deal with a few pitying looks from ex-colleagues who think you've lost your mind. You may even have to do some menial work. Weigh the pros and cons—is it really worth it?

- **Set your boundaries.** Go ahead, make friends. Have a beer with your co-workers. But set some boundaries from the start. This is your day job, not your career. Put in your hours and go home to focus on your real career goals.

- **You've got to keep it separated.** Your day job is just business. Your employer is subsidizing your creative endeavors. That's all. You can't let yourself get caught up in the politics or drama at the office. You can't take the job too personally or let it affect your self-esteem. It's not worth the time and energy.

- **Just say no to promotions.** If they offer to promote you, run! You took this day job to minimize the time and energy you expend at work. Don't let yourself get saddled with more responsibility that will keep you from your true calling. Weigh any promotion offer very carefully—if they're offering more money for similar work effort, great. Otherwise, just say no.

Go Freelance

When you're the boss, you get to set your own hours. Think about it. You probably have a lot of marketable skills that other companies will pay for. You may even be able to make more money as a free agent.

Keep in mind that going freelance is not for the shy or the risk-averse. You don't receive a guaranteed paycheck when you're a freelancer, and you usually have to pay for your own health insurance (although some freelance organizations do offer health plans). You're responsible for finding work, dealing with clients, billing and administrative work—the whole nine yards.

However, if you're able to build a thriving freelance business, you can make your own schedule and carve out plenty of time for your creative pursuits. If you're serious about going freelance, start by talking to other freelancers and researching the market to see how much you can make and how easy getting clients will be. You may want to save some money to help get you through the first slow months and/or try to line up some clients before you leave your full-time position. See chapter 8 for more information about starting a freelance business.

Get Laid Off

Keep your eyes open for an opportunity to get laid off and collect a generous severance package. These opportunities are rare. To finesse this tricky move, you will probably need a connection in the HR Department and a supportive boss. Nobody likes layoffs, but they've become standard operating procedure for most corporations these days.

When a "workforce reduction" or "reduction in staff" is on the horizon, rumors will start to fly. That's usually because senior managers and human resources lackeys are reviewing the lists of employees and deciding who will stay and who will go. If you can see the writing on the wall and know somebody you can trust on the inside, consider inquiring discreetly about whether they're accepting volunteers and what the severance arrangements would be. This kind of move is risky—but it can have a big upside.

Find a Sugar Daddy

Sugar daddy, sugar mommy. Gender isn't important. If you're lucky enough to have a supportive significant other with a steady job, you may be able to arrange a nice deal. Don't take advantage of your loved one's goodwill. If he or she agrees to be the sole bread-winner for a while, agree to some compromises to make it easier. Decide on an initial time frame and a date when you will reevalu-ate the situation and consider getting another job if things aren't going well. Volunteer to spend more time on household chores to make your sugar parent's life easier. Be appreciative and plan to return the favor and shoulder more of the financial responsibility in the future, once you get your creative career off the ground.

Taking the Leap

Only you can decide when you're ready to take the leap. If you're a creative soul stuck in a cubicle, you owe it to yourself to heed your true calling and stop suppressing your artistic talents. That doesn't have to mean quitting your day job. A lot of options are available for adding more creativity to your life and rediscovering that childhood dream.

A CORPORATE ESCAPE ARTIST PRODUCTION

Anthony Moody, producer, and Rob Malkani, writer/producer

For Tony Moody and Rob Malkani, the producer and writer/producer behind the feature film *Day Zero*, starring Elijah Wood and Chris Klein, it was a long and winding road from cubicle to cineplex. Their stories are proof positive that even the most dramatic career dreams are achievable.

Tony

Tony Moody began his career as a trader at a big Wall Street firm, regularly trading millions of shares of stock a day for institutional clients. "It was an incredible amount of stress, but it was not very creative or intellectually stimulating," he says.

After some soul-searching, Tony decided to leave his job to attend business school and explore other career options. During business school, he spent some time working at a dot-com start-up before he got bit by the film bug.

He began taking as many classes related to the business of media and entertainment as he could. Soon after, he hung out his shingle as a producer and started looking for scripts. His first film, the coming-of-age basketball story *Rock the Paint*, was a winner at the 2006 Montclair Film Festival and selected for the Creative Promise Award at the 2005 Tribeca Film Festival.

Rob

Rob Malkani, Moody's old college friend, started his career path at Harvard Law School. Upon graduation, he took a job as a corporate lawyer at a prestigious Wall Street firm, just as everyone expected him to do. Unfortunately, although Rob had enjoyed studying law, he found the practice to be extremely tedious.

After about a year, he knew that he had to make a change and began to investigate opportunities in investment banking. With his Harvard pedigree and Wall Street experience, Rob soon landed a position at a top investment bank. He loved the work at first, but the backbreaking hours began to take a toll after four years. He was earning a lot of money, but he was so busy that he literally never had a spare moment to speak with his mother for weeks at a time. It soon became clear that something had to give.

Luckily, Rob had been able to put aside enough money to pay his bills for a while, so he quit his prestigious job to take some time off and contemplate his next career move. With a bit of time on his hands at last, Rob signed up for an intensive filmmaking workshop at the New York Film Academy, where he discovered he had a talent for screenwriting and a fascination with the production side of the business.

Tony and Rob

After co-producing one film with other partners, Rob reconnected with his old friend Tony Moody and the two decided to collaborate as producers on the indie film *Turning Green*, starring Timothy Hutton.

After a great experience on that film, they opted to work together again on a script that Rob had written—*Day Zero*, which imagines a modern-day reinstatement of the draft. *Day Zero*, the third film produced by Moody's Indalo Productions, was a featured selection at the Tribeca Film Festival and released in theaters in January 2008.

Tony and Rob are currently collaborating on two more upcoming projects. Their noir film *Black Wings Has My Angel* will be co-produced by *Day Zero* star Elijah Wood. Tony will also be producing Malkani's directorial debut: the gritty thriller *147 Greenwich*, which Rob also wrote.

ELEVEN

Make a Difference

Deprived of meaningful work, men and women lose their reason for existence; they go stark, raving mad.

—**Fyodor Dostoyevsky**

I truly believe that individuals can make a difference in society. Since periods of change such as the present one come so rarely in human history, it is up to each of us to make the best use of our time to help create a happier world.

—**Dalai Lama**

Genevieve Piturro left a glamorous career in television to give away pajamas to needy kids. Ken Lesley was a senior engineer when he gave it all up to become a public school teacher.

Maybe you, too, have felt the pull toward the nonprofit sector or a helping profession like teaching. Many who are unhappy in Corporate America say they long for work with more meaning. They're sick of pushing papers and fantasize about using their skills to make the world a better place.

If you've thought about making the transition to teaching or nonprofit work, I have some good news. There are more opportunities out there than ever before. Consultants at the Bridgespan Group estimate that nonprofit organizations will have to attract and develop more than 640,000 new senior leaders—approximately 2.4 times the number currently employed—over the next ten years.

At the same time, there is a desperate need for qualified teachers in our country's public schools. Programs like The New Teacher Project recruit midcareer professionals to train for and launch careers as teachers.

🍵 The Rewards

Why would anybody give up the prestige and the fat salary of a corporate gig to take a job as a do-gooder? It's certainly not about the money. The biggest lure is the ability to do work that feels important. The people attracted to these jobs are people with passions—to educate kids, to cure diseases, to feed the hungry, to change lives and maybe even change the world.

They want to use their time and talents to make a difference, not just add pennies to a corporate bottom line. They want the fulfillment that comes with knowing they played a part in making a positive change. While some can get this satisfaction from volunteering, others need more.

The nonprofit sector can also offer attractive career opportunities. These organizations tend to be lean and mean, so employees often are given more autonomy. There are lots of opportunities to get involved in projects outside your area of focus and to expand your skills. You may even end up with the chance to run the show instead of taking orders.

Some corporate types are drawn to working in the nonprofit sector by the misperception that it will be easy and low-pressure. The truth is that you will probably work just as hard, if not harder. And because you will be more emotionally invested, it may be even more difficult to leave your work at the office at the end of the day.

However, many make-a-difference jobs do offer more flexibility than the typical corporate gig. There tends to be more respect for people's lives outside work in the nonprofit sector—and teachers, of course, get their summers off.

DARING TALES OF CORPORATE ESCAPE

Making a Difference with Pajamas

Name: Genevieve Piturro

Former occupation: Marketing manager

Current occupation: Founder, the Pajama Program

Five years ago, Genevieve Piturro was working as a corporate marketing manager when she came up with the idea of donating pajamas to needy kids. The Pajama Program, the nonprofit organization that grew out of that flash of inspiration, has now given away more than 130,000 pairs of brand-new PJs to kids in shelters and group homes. Genevieve even appeared on *The Oprah Winfrey Show* and inspired Oprah and her viewers to donate forty-five thousand pairs of pajamas to her cause.

Before she discovered her calling, Genevieve worked for several years in the television syndication business. The job was exciting at times, but Genevieve always felt like something was missing: "I didn't see a purpose to what I was doing and I had this nagging feeling that I was supposed to be doing something else."

For years, she had worked as a volunteer at homeless shelters in her spare time. One night, on the subway ride home from her volunteer gig, the image of pajamas popped into her head along with the words *Pajama Program*. She had no idea where her vision came from.

"I got off the subway and ran for a pay phone so that I could call my husband," she remembers. "I said, 'I got it! Pajama Program!' " She knew that nighttime was a scary time for kids in shelters and group homes. She thought a program that donated pajamas and books could help them sleep a little bit easier.

She tested out her hypothesis by buying pajamas and taking them with her to the shelters where she volunteered. "The reaction was just amazing," she said. "Many of these kids had never owned a pair of pajamas before in their lives."

Genevieve started asking friends and families to give her children's pajamas for every gift and holiday. Soon she connected with other donors and manufacturers who wanted to help. "Giant boxes of pajamas were being delivered to our little one-bedroom apartment," she remembers. "My husband and I would have our dinner on top of a box because there was no room at the table."

After a while, Genevieve decided to leave her full-time marketing job and take a part-time gig handling public relations for an Italian linens importer. She thought that a part-time schedule would leave her plenty of time to run Pajama Program on the side, but she didn't anticipate how quickly the idea would take off.

"My cell phone was ringing off the hook," she says. "I would always be hiding in the corner trying to take calls for Pajama Program and my boss got a bit impatient with me."

She could understand his frustration. "But at that point, my heart was in Pajama Program," she says. "I couldn't ignore a call from a shelter or from a manufacturer who wanted to donate six boxes of pajamas."

Her husband advised her to take a chance, quit her job, and focus on Pajama Program full-time. He worked in television production and had a fairly unpredictable income, so it wasn't an easy choice to make.

"Some months he'd make good money, and other months much less," she says. "We had to sacrifice ourselves financially to do it." They sold their co-op and used the proceeds to help supplement living expenses.

Genevieve ran the program full-time for three years before she started collecting a salary. Her husband backed her up with lots of support and by lending a hand with packing, picking up, and delivering pajamas. Now, that's commitment.

Today the Pajama Program has thirty-one chapters across the country and gives away both pajamas and books. The organization is staffed by Genevieve, two part-time employees, and lots of volunteers. In 2007, Genevieve was invited to appear on *Oprah* for a show about people who pursued their passions. Oprah and her audience surprised Genevieve by donating too many pajamas to fit in the studio.

"It is a totally different universe that I live in now," says Genevieve. "I love it, but I probably sleep less and worry more. I have a green folder full of pajama requests that never gets empty."

The best thing about her new life is the feeling that she is making a difference in kids' lives. "It changes your day-to-day feeling when you wake up in the morning," she says. "My dream is to be sitting in my rocking chair at ninety-five and have somebody come up to me and say, 'When I was ten, I got a pair of pajamas. Thank you.' "

Advice from Genevieve Piturro on Following Your Passion

"If you feel like you were born to do something, you have to do it and trust that you will find the support. It's worth it."

The Trade-Offs

First and foremost, you're probably going to have to take a pay cut. It's all well and good to help people, but is it worth tightening your belt?

In general, salaries in the nonprofit sector are significantly lower than those for similar jobs in Corporate America. How much lower? That all depends on the job and the organization. Groups with larger budgets tend to pay higher salaries. For example, based on a 2007 survey by PayScale, the average salary for a Web developer was $69,000 at a for-profit firm and $60,500 at a nonprofit.

Tighter budgets also mean fewer resources and smaller staffs. Forget about padded expense accounts and expensive consultants. You'll have to learn to do a lot with a little.

As a result, you may find yourself stuck with tasks that you aren't crazy about. Everybody plays multiple roles at a nonprofit organization. You pitch in where you're needed.

And the nonprofit sector is no vacation from corporate stress. You will work hard for less money, and you can very easily get burned out.

The pros and cons of a teaching career are along the same lines. I probably don't have to tell you that teachers are underpaid. They also tend to work long hours and go above and beyond the call of duty to get things done with limited resources.

📓 Are You Ready to Make a Difference?

In a bad corporate job, it's easy to feel like a cog in the big, impersonal moneymaking machine. Most people spend more hours at work than they do with their best friends. They want to feel like those hours are spent on something that matters.

Corporate professionals are often inspired to make the change to more altruistic work by a personal experience. Sometimes a personal loss or health scare will cause people to reevaluate what's important to them. Others discover a passion for a cause that drives them to totally rethink their careers. Still others are motivated by a change in personal circumstances—perhaps becoming a parent leads to a shift in priorities, or an older child's graduation from college means a parent can consider a career that pays less.

But how do you know if it's the right career path for you? If you worked through the exercises in chapter 3 and identified intriguing possibilities in these areas, you should at least investigate what it would take to make the move.

📓 Define Your Goals

The first step is to clarify what you're looking for. What are you really passionate about? If you're going to take a pay cut and make other sacrifices in exchange for more meaningful work, you'd better take the time to understand what's meaningful to you. Answering the following questions can help you to identify your best options.

What are you willing to sacrifice for the career of your dreams?

_____

_____

_____

_____

_____

_____

What are your deal breakers?

_____

_____

_____

_____

_____

What is the motivation for your career change?

_____

_____

_____

_____

_____

What issues are you most passionate about?

_____

_____

_____

_____

_____

What skills and talents do you most enjoy using?

_____

_____

_____

_____

_____

_____

Have you had volunteer experiences that were particularly re-warding?

_____

_____

_____

_____

_____

What is your ideal work environment?

_____

_____

_____

_____

_____

What kind of impact do you want to make? Could you achieve this through volunteer or pro bono work?

_____

_____

_____

_____

_____

Are you willing to take a pay cut? What is the minimum annual salary you need to make?

_____

_____

_____

_____

_____

What benefits do you expect from your new career that you aren't getting from your current one?

_____

_____

_____

_____

_____

What type of organizations appeal to you? Is there a specific group that you admire?

_____

_____

_____

_____

_____

How committed are you to making a change? What does your time frame look like?

_____

_____

_____

_____

🍵 Evaluate Your Options

There are many different pathways to a more meaningful career. Now that you have a better sense of what you're looking for, it will be much easier to decide which one is right for you. Best of all, you can plot your course and do much of the required prep work without quitting your corporate job.

🍵 Make a Difference Part-Time

You don't necessarily have to get a new job to make a difference. You may be surprised how much good you can do in your spare time without going through the effort of a career change.

Volunteer

The key is to find volunteer opportunities that provide the elements missing from your corporate job. That could be the ability to do work that matters, personal fulfillment, intellectual challenge, a chance to give back, or the opportunity to connect with like-minded people in your community.

The best volunteer gigs are long-term ones that allow you to use your talents. The satisfaction of helping out with a one-day bake sale for your local women's center will fade quickly. You want to get involved on an ongoing basis—maybe by volunteering to head up public relations for all future women's center events. This will give you a way to connect with the group and the people it serves and really see the results of your labors.

Volunteering can also be a great way to develop new skills, gain experience in a new area of interest, and build your professional network. If you're considering a career change of any kind, volunteering can make you more marketable and even open a door to a brand-new field.

But how do you find these great volunteer gigs? Websites like Network for Good (*www.networkforgood.org*) and Idealist.org feature listings of thousands of volunteer opportunities. If you still can't find something that grabs you, you can always create your own volunteer position. Approach an organization that you admire and ask if you can help out in the area that interests you.

If you are drawn to teaching, you can try it out by volunteering to teach classes for a nonprofit organization. Many charities seek people who can teach computer and job skills. Other organizations need help with tutoring or mentoring kids of all ages. You can also try volunteering at a local school or after-school program.

Your connection to Corporate America can make you particularly valuable to the organizations and causes that you care about. You may be able to approach your employer about becoming a corporate donor or a sponsor. Many corporations will even agree to match employee donations to approved charities.

At the very least, you have access to a whole cubicle farm of potential volunteers and individual donors. Naturally, you don't want to be obnoxious, but if Bob from Sales can hit you up to buy wrapping paper from his kid every year, then surely you can put up a flyer or two in the break room.

When you're doing volunteer work that energizes you, it can make even the dreariest of corporate jobs tolerable. Naturally, you will want to find the best possible corporate day job, preferably one that doesn't put you to sleep. However, you may find that you don't have to escape from Corporate America completely after all.

Then again, if you're not satisfied with the impact you can make as a volunteer, you may be ready to think about a bigger move.

Get on Board

If you're looking for more senior-level involvement in an organization, you may want to join a board of directors. As a member of the board, you will have input into the nonprofit's strategy and a direct role in the success of a worthy organization.

Through service on a nonprofit board, you can also learn about best practices in nonprofit management and the ins and outs of the industry. This leadership experience looks great on any résumé and can be excellent preparation for a switch to the nonprofit sector.

Keep in mind that nonprofits are looking for board members with extensive management experience and the ability to help with fund-raising. They may also be looking for particular types of operational backgrounds or expertise in specific areas such as marketing, curriculum development, or law.

If you are employed by a well-known corporation, that can help you get in. Having representatives from respected companies on the board can increase a nonprofit organization's credibility.

There are a number of board matching services that connect potential board members with nonprofit organizations. Board-NetUSA (*www.boardnetusa.org*) allows prospective board members to search for openings online.

A number of universities and continuing education institutions also offer Nonprofit Board Leadership Programs, which train professionals to serve on boards and often help match them with appropriate opportunities.

Make a Difference in a Corporate Job

One way to get the best of both the corporate and nonprofit worlds is by pursuing a career in corporate giving. Most large companies have departments that manage their charitable and community activities. Some big firms also have corporate foundations devoted to giving back to the community. Imagine the satisfaction of being able to influence where large amounts of corporate philanthropic money and support go.

A quick search on Monster.com found dozens of jobs related to corporate giving—including positions at companies from Playboy to Safeway to Washington Mutual.

The specific qualifications for these positions vary. Most require some background in the nonprofit sector combined with management and community relations experience. Your background can help you by demonstrating that you have the ability to manage within a corporate environment. You will likely also need a strong volunteering and/or nonprofit board service background to qualify. Some experience in public relations or community relations is usually helpful as well.

If you're interested in this path, scour the job listings for positions related to "corporate giving" or "corporate philanthropy." If your current employer has a corporate giving department or foundation, see if you can speak with people there about what they do. If not, ask within your network if anyone has a contact in a related job and see if you can pick their brains.

Make a Difference Through Teaching

Teaching is among the top ten most gratifying jobs, according to a recent survey by research company Greenfield Online. Teachers reported 69 percent job satisfaction (70 percent for special education teachers) despite their notoriously low pay.

If you gave up your dream of teaching to climb the corporate ladder, it's not too late. Public schools are looking for midcareer professionals who want to teach—and you don't even have to take time off to go back to school full-time.

Step 1. Explore Teaching

It's hard to know whether teaching is the right career for you until you spend some time in a classroom. Doing your research will also help you identify the types of teaching opportunities that most intrigue you. Are you passionate about a particular subject matter? Is there an age group that you feel the most rapport with?

The best way to get a true sense of what teaching is about is to connect with an experienced teacher. Do you have a friend or relative in the profession? Do you have a friend or relative with kids who can introduce you to a great educator?

As long as you ask nicely, most people are happy to answer questions about what they do. Invite a potential teacher mentor out for coffee and ask her questions about what it's really like. What are her greatest challenges? What have been her most rewarding achievements?

If all goes well during your chat, ask if you can come into the classroom to observe one day and see education in action. You could even volunteer to speak to the class about your profession or about an area of expertise relevant to their studies.

You can also try calling local schools directly to ask about visiting to observe a class. With luck, they'll say yes, but understand that most schools won't let just anybody come by and hang out with the kids, and some may require references and/or a face-to-face meeting before inviting you to visit.

Step 2. Find the Right Program for You

Perhaps the easiest route for someone making the transition from a corporate job to teaching is through an alternative certification program specifically designed for midcareer professionals.

Up until recently, it was almost impossible to become a teacher without taking time off to get your master's degree and teaching certification. These new alternative programs were established in response to the growing need for qualified teachers, especially in urban schools. They generally provide training to chosen candidates, place them in schools, and then support them in getting the continuing education credits they need for certification through part-time programs.

The New Teacher Project is one such organization, a national nonprofit devoted to increasing the number of outstanding teachers in the US public school system. "We are looking for people with outstanding achievements in other careers," says Ariela Rozman, vice president of the Teaching Fellows Program for The New Teacher Project.

The organization sponsors these programs in fifteen cities nationwide. "Over the past ten years, we have placed more than twenty-three thousand teachers in schools across the country," says Rozman. "We get about seven applicants for every vacancy."

If you're interested in learning more about alternative certification programs for teachers, please see the information in the Escape Tool Kit section at the end of this book.

DARING TALES OF CORPORATE ESCAPE

A Calling to Teach

Name: Kenneth Lesley

Former occupation: Engineer

Current occupation: Public school teacher

Kenneth Lesley earned his mechanical engineering degree at MIT and spent the next several years working as an engineer for large firms in the petroleum industry. At one point, he lived in Nigeria for a year and earned enormous sums for dangerous work that required handling radioactive materials and explosives.

Eventually, he made the switch to consulting and contracting work so that he could be flexible enough to relocate with his wife, a navy helicopter pilot, whenever she moved to a new base.

In 2001, they were living in Washington, DC, and Ken was working on a project designing databases for a government contractor. He wasn't happy at the job and felt burned out on the idea of consulting, so he decided to take some time off to figure out what to do next.

He soon got involved in mentoring his son's school robotics team and made friends with the faculty advisers. "They saw that I worked well with the kids and thought of me when an opportunity came up at another DC school to fill in for a math teacher who left in the middle of the school year."

Ken soon found himself teaching ninth-grade algebra. "I think I actually taught them something and that was with no educational background in teaching whatsoever." He learned a lot on the job and started to think he might have a future in teaching.

The following year, one of his daughter's teachers recruited him to fill in for another teacher who quit with only a few days' notice. "I covered that class for the rest of the year and it was nice because both my son and daughter attended the school and I was right there in the building with them if they needed anything," Ken recalls.

By that point, he was beginning to think that fate was pushing him toward a teaching career whether he liked it or not. He got a call that summer from one of his son's former teachers who had moved on to become assistant principal at McKinley Tech High School in DC. "She asked me if I would be interested in teaching there full-time, and I said I'd be more than happy to."

Ken then worked with The New Teacher Project through its DC Teaching Fellows Program to get some formal training before taking on the job. He has been teaching at McKinley ever since and coaching the school's robotics and soccer teams.

"The difference in pay is significant," Ken says. "But I believe that if you do what you have a passion for, the rest has a way of working itself out. The right answers will eventually reveal themselves."

Ken Lesley's Advice for Career Changers

"Make the money secondary. Make your happiness primary and then figure out how you can make the money work."

📔 Work for a Nonprofit Organization

For those drawn to working in the nonprofit sector, there is no shortage of opportunities. There are almost a million and a half nonprofit organizations in the United States, and many are hiring right now.

Step 1. Explore Your Options

What types of organizations most interest you? Do you want to work with children? Are you passionate about the arts? Think about what your ideal career in the nonprofit world would look like so that you can focus on the opportunities with the most potential.

If you're not sure where to start, browse through the listings on an online job board such as Idealist.org, which specializes in nonprofit jobs, and learn about different organizations and what types of positions they offer.

Step 2. Identify Transferable Skills

The easiest route from corporate to nonprofit is to find a job that's similar to the one you have now in terms of duties and experience. The environment will be different, but it's pretty likely that if you're an administrative assistant or media relations professional at a corporation, you'll be qualified to do the same job at a nonprofit.

If you're interested in making a bigger change, you may have to get creative or build up your skills first. For example, if you're in sales or marketing, you might be good at fund-raising, but you will probably have to get some hands-on experience before you'll be hired.

Find out what specific skills or experience you will need to make the transition and then get creative about gaining them. Try doing some pro bono or volunteer work or taking classes to strengthen your qualifications.

DARING TALES OF CORPORATE ESCAPE

Dancing Out of Corporate

Name: Cheryl Todmann

Former occupation: Marketing manager

Current occupation: Director of community relations, Brooklyn Bureau of Community Service

Cheryl Todmann spent several years working in marketing roles for major media companies before she discovered her true calling. "I left corporate for the nonprofit sector because I had a deep and constant soulful urging to take my marketing skills and use them to benefit my passion, which is dance," she says. "I didn't start dancing until I was thirty; however, I fell in love with every aspect of it: performing, marketing it, fund-raising for it."

Cheryl loved her corporate salary and benefits and the prestige of working for one of the world's best-known media brands. But, she was weary of the bureaucracy and confinement of corporate life and the racism and glass ceilings she had encountered over the years.

"It was a difficult decision to leave because we are trained by society and our parents to go to college, get a good corporate job, and make lots of money," says Cheryl. "We are not encouraged to cultivate independent and entrepreneurial means of income or to fulfill our passions."

Making the transition to a nonprofit job wasn't difficult for Cheryl. She quickly found a position as the director of marketing and development for the Creative Outlet Dance Theater of Brooklyn. "Most dance organizations need marketing assistance. The difficulty is that they often don't have the resources to pay for marketing consultants on a consistent basis because they lack infrastructure."

Later Cheryl was briefly tempted back to the corporate world by a senior marketing job at a top cable network. After a year and a half, she was itching to get back to the nonprofit world.

Today she's the director of community relations for the Brooklyn Bureau of Community Service, one of Brooklyn's largest and most respected community service agencies, and works part-time with dance organizations. "Working at the Brooklyn Bureau gives me the ability to create goodwill in the lives of underserved people," Cheryl says. "My part-time work with dance companies allows me to promote dance to various audiences, train, and take classes."

Cheryl appreciates the relaxed and flexible atmosphere at the Brooklyn Bureau of Community Service and the opportunities to take on new responsibilities. "At a nonprofit organization, you have the ability to create and expand your job and to learn other areas of the business because there is usually a lack of resources," she explains.

Of course, there are also drawbacks to working in the nonprofit sector. The same lack of resources that creates opportunities can also make it more challenging to get the job done. Salaries are lower, too, which means more of a hustle to make ends meet.

For Cheryl, the payoff has been worth the challenges. "I am much more relaxed, happy, and comfortable than when I worked in corporate," she says. "I feel fulfilled and complete when I am working in and around my calling."

Cheryl Todmann's Advice to Career Changers

"Follow your heart, the money will come. It may take some time, but it will come."

Step 3. Find a Nonprofit Job

Start your search by browsing through the listings at nonprofit job sites such as Idealist.org or Philanthropy.com. Networking is also a great way to hear about opportunities that aren't officially listed.

Before you apply for a position, make sure you customize your résumé to show your transferable skills to their best advantage and to highlight your volunteer experience. Use an "Objective" or "Summary" section at the top to make it clear that you are looking to make a move to the nonprofit sector. Otherwise, a hiring manager may glance at your résumé, see all the corporate experience, and dismiss you out of hand.

For an easier transition, you might want to investigate nonprofit organizations with for-profit components. Your corporate experience could be a great asset in a position related to the for-profit initiatives.

Step 4. Get Hired

Be aware that some nonprofit leaders are resistant to hiring corporate professionals. Common concerns are that you may require too much time to get up to speed, that you won't fit into the culture, and that they won't be able to afford you.

The interview is your chance to counter these assumptions and show that you're the right person for the job. Take the time to prepare responses to questions and potential objections.

Make a Difference Through Entrepreneurship

Today more and more entrepreneurs have discovered that they can change the world and establish a successful business at the same time. Some do this through partnering with or donating to nonprofit organizations. Others establish Fair Trade businesses that positively impact economically disadvantaged artisans and farmers around the world.

DARING TALES OF CORPORATE ESCAPE

Making a Difference Through Entrepreneurship

Name: Liz Wald

Former occupation: Technology consultant

Current occupation: Founder and CEO, EDImports

Economic Development Imports (EDImports) is not a charity. It is a business that happens to also make the world a better place by providing income-generating opportunities to women in developing countries in East and West Africa.

EDImports and its partner firm, One World Projects, import handmade products from artisans in Latin America, Asia, and Africa. Through the sale of these goods, the artisans support themselves and their families, build self-esteem, and help assure their communities of sustainable futures.

"We give people a fair wage and provide an alternative to working in a coal mine or living in the slums," says Liz Wald, founder of EDImports. "At the same time, we are a for-profit company that needs to make good products."

Liz started her career at Nike. "I loved working there. When you are a sports person and twenty-two years old, what could be better?" After a few years, she left Nike to go to business school and launch a career in consulting. She eventually connected with a group of other MBAs that had formed a small consulting firm and landed America Online as a client just as the whole concept of retail on the Internet was starting.

"At that time, America Online was still fairly small, and Compu-Serve was the big player," she remembers. "Eventually, the Internet craziness came along, and we sold our little consulting group during the height of the boom."

Their deal required them to stay at the acquiring company through the end of 2000. "Then I quit and took some time off to travel around the world," Liz says. "I was in India, I was in China, I was in Uzbekistan. I went rafting in Chile and skiing in Colorado, you name it."

She returned to New York on September 8, 2001, ready to look for her next job. Three days later, 9/11 took the whole world by surprise.

"I decided I didn't want to go back to some consulting job only to help a big company get another percentage point of market share," Liz says. While she tried to figure out what was next, she did some volunteering with a group working in Rwanda.

"I thought that I would love to start a business that could also do some good in the world," she recalls. She went to Africa in the fall of 2003 to do some research and came back with two new partners and two new product lines.

"The very first product that I brought from Rwanda was a ceremonial basket," she says. "I found a partner in Rwanda who pulled together about fifty women to weave. Now there are more than one thousand women employed and this group in Rwanda is also selling to large national retailers."

On that first trip to Africa, Liz also discovered unique products carved from Kenyan soapstone. "The group that makes the soapstone products was founded by a woman whose father was the village chief," Liz explains. "She was the first daughter in her family to learn to read and write and now she runs a company of about a thousand people."

Later, Liz met Phil from One World Projects at a conference. "He had started his company ten years earlier doing similar work in Latin America," she says. "We have been partners since that day. We sell everything together and have a few employees and a medium-size warehouse in western New York."

Three and a half years later, the two companies are selling products from twenty-four different developing countries around the world. "We import it all ourselves and understand the logistics, so I think we are well positioned to grow with the industry right now as the Fair Trade market is gaining momentum."

For her part, Liz loves having a job that lets her travel, uses her business skills, and helps people at the same time. "This is the hardest job I have ever had by far, but the experience has been incredible," she says.

Liz Wald's Advice to Corporate Escapees

"The corporate world will always be there. You can leave and go back and you will not be an anomaly anymore. People do it all the time."

PART III

GOING OVER THE WALL

TWELVE

Going Over the Wall

When you're finished changing, you're finished.
—**Benjamin Franklin**

Freedom lies in being bold.
—**Robert Frost**

So you've made your plans, you've explored your options, and you're ready to go over the wall. Congratulations. Before you know it, you'll be packing up your office knickknacks and planning your good-bye party.

Just keep in mind that there are going to be some bumps along the road to your dream career. The advice in this chapter will help you deal with all the annoying obstacles that may arise while you navigate your escape.

The Fear Factor

As you make your transition from a familiar career path to something new and different, you can expect to have a few moments of panic.

There's just no way around it. Change is scary—even if it's a change that you want so badly you can taste it.

Some people make the mistake of assuming that feeling scared means there's something wrong. They use the fear as an excuse to avoid taking action.

Certainly, it's important to pay attention to how you're feeling and to any danger signs that arise. Don't ignore your concerns. Just keep in mind that a little anxiety is normal even when you're on the right path.

"Fear is inevitable if you're awake," says Dr. Janet Scarborough, a Washington-based psychologist who specializes in counseling clients on career-related issues. "In fact, I worry about people who say they have no alarm whatsoever about making a serious life change like switching careers."

Whatever you do, don't let a perfectly routine case of the heebie-jeebies slow down your progress. Dr. Scarborough says that of her clients who make career transitions, the most successful are able to tolerate the fear and move forward anyway.

Fear of the Unknown

The most common fear—that of the unknown—is also the easiest to address. The research and planning steps that I have recommended throughout this book can help you to fight your fear with facts.

Often the worst-case scenarios that you torture yourself with are far more terrifying than any reality you will face. Allow yourself to feel the anxiety. What's the worst thing that could happen?

Then do your homework and decide if your nightmares have any basis in reality. If you're still worried, spend some time thinking through a Plan B and maybe even a Plan C so you know you'll have a safety net.

You owe it to yourself to explore your dream, even if the idea of the great unknown freaks you out.

Fear of Commitment

Dr. Jerald Jellison, a professor of social psychology at the University of Southern California and the author of *Managing the Dynam-*

ics of Change, compares the fear of career commitment to the anxiety you feel when you fall in love.

"These fears start coming up, but they don't mean that you don't love the person or aren't excited about your new career," says Jellison. "That terror is just a normal part of making a big commitment."

It's very possible that you'll experience a case of cold feet about your career change at some point along the way. That doesn't mean that you've changed your mind. It could just be the fear talking.

As you explore your new career direction, you may very well discover that it's not quite what you hoped it would be and decide to reevaluate. Don't dismiss valid concerns that arise, but don't blow your concerns out of proportion either. There's a big difference between making an informed choice to change your mind and wavering because you're afraid to put yourself out there.

Fear of Failure

The fear of failing stops many from ever really pursuing their dream careers. It's much less scary to stay in a job that you hate than to take a chance and risk looking like a fool.

However, those who never risk failure never attain great success. Beethoven's music teacher once declared him "hopeless" as a composer. Thirty-eight publishers rejected Margaret Mitchell's manuscript for *Gone with the Wind,* which went on to become one of the best-selling books of all time.

You can look at failure as a disaster or as a learning experience. Expect that failure is going to be a part of any great undertaking and vow not to take it too personally.

Nobody likes to fall on their face. But would you rather put up with a bit of ego bruising to achieve your dream or stay stuck in your rut?

"Even now, there are times when I am terrified," says Ralph Jovine, founder and CEO of the Atlanta-based technology firm

Grand Central Solutions. "I start to think about how much easier it would be to go back to a big company and let other people worry about it. But then I will go home, have a glass of wine, and realize that I'm overreacting. The fear thing is only temporary, but if I were to give it all up because of a little bit of fear and go back to Corporate America, that regret would last a lifetime."

If you find yourself paralyzed by fear at any point during the process of escaping from Corporate America, it may be because you've let yourself get overwhelmed by the grand plan instead of focusing on the smaller steps that will move you forward.

"Switch your focus to the specific things you can do today to move in the right direction," advises Dr. Jellison. "Focus on one step at a time."

What Will People Think?

You're not supposed to worry about what other people think. We've been taught that lesson by countless self-help books and after-school specials over the years.

Yet few of us are completely immune to the feelings of doubt that arise when the critics come out of the woodwork.

We crave approval and validation for our choices—especially the big ones. It's only natural to want the people in our lives to support us. The reality, however, is that not everybody will approve of your choice. In planning to escape from Corporate America, you are making a career move that some may see as impractical or even crazy. Often those who respond that way are projecting their own issues onto you.

Just because they may be comfortable in a cubicle doesn't mean you have to be. Everyone is different. You know as well as anyone that it would be far easier to stay where you are, but you've decided to take a chance on pursuing your dream.

The good news is that our worries about how people are going to react to our career change plans are usually far more stressful than their actual responses. We often create problems in our head that don't actually exist.

In fact, some people let fears about what other people will think prevent them from ever making a move at all. *What if Mom is disappointed in me? What if the guys at work think I'm a loser?*

"It is not shallow to care what other people think," says Dr. Janet Scarborough. "The trick is to acknowledge that you care, but not let it completely determine your decisions to the point that you are not being true to yourself."

Your Inner Circle

The people closest to you are likely to have the strongest opinions about your plans. Remember, your career change doesn't affect just you.

Your Partner or Spouse

Escaping from Corporate America will be a lot easier with a supportive partner in your corner. I know that I probably never would have made my move without the support and encouragement of my husband. When I was ready to give up, he was there to urge me on. When I didn't believe in myself, he was there to believe in me.

Our partners want us to be happy (if that's not the case for you, then your next book purchase should probably be from the Relationships section), but that doesn't mean we can automatically expect their unconditional support. After all, our career choices can have a big impact on our partners' lives. Our decision could raise practical and emotional issues for them.

Make a concerted effort to get your partner involved in your decision-making process. Respect any fears or issues that come up and work through them together.

Your Parents

Hopefully, your career decisions are no longer dictated by your parents. Still, parental disapproval can have a powerful effect on us no matter how old we get. When you decide to leave a corporate job to pursue something less stable, your parents' first reaction may be a negative one.

Their point of reference is from a different time, when a good corporate job meant security for life. They may think you're crazy to even consider quitting a good job at a big company.

Usually this response is motivated by love and concern. Your parents worry about you out in that big bad world, you know. They want to make sure you'll always have a roof over your head. Take their response for what it is, but keep in mind that your parents' perspective on corporate life could be severely dated.

Sometimes parental resistance is motivated by more selfish concerns. Your mother may have a lot invested in the notion of her son the executive or her daughter the vice president. Your father may enjoy bragging about your latest promotion at the senior center.

Of course you want to make your parents proud, but that's not a good enough reason to stay stuck in a job you hate. After all, you'll have plenty more opportunities to earn their pride in a career that you actually enjoy.

Your Friends and Co-Workers

Don't be surprised if your bold career moves attract attention from your friends and the people you work with. *Your* career change is likely to stir up a lot of *their* issues.

Many will be supportive, but there will inevitably be a few who seem to get some sort of joy out of bringing you down. In most cases, those who question or criticize do it in a sad attempt to feel better about themselves and their own choices. Try not to take it personally.

I know that's easier said than done. On bad days, a single off-hand comment from an acquaintance can be enough to make you start doubting yourself. That's why it's so important to build a support network of positive people whom you can rely on for reality checks, pep talks, and encouraging advice when the going gets tough.

YOU'RE DOING WHAT?: TYPICAL RESPONSES TO YOUR CORPORATE ESCAPE PLANS

- **"Wow, I'm so jealous."** When you announce that you're leaving, you may be surprised at how many people confide that they've been secretly harboring their own escape fantasies. You may just give someone else the kick start he needs to pursue his own dream.
- **"Wow, you're so brave."** Some people will respond as if you've just announced your plans to jump the Grand Canyon on a Segway. In some cases, that's because they've built up the dangers of such a move in their minds to justify their own career decisions.
- **"Are you sure you know what you're doing?"** There will be those who just don't get it. Some people are very content in the corporate world and can't understand why anyone would want to walk away. Others are good corporate soldiers who are conservative by nature. Remember, some of them don't buy pencils without getting a sign-off in triplicate.
- **"Can I have your office?"** Your career change is a big deal for you, but don't be too disappointed if all of your co-workers don't feel the same way. They may be more interested in pillaging your office supplies than discussing your plans. After all, they're not going anywhere and will still be dealing with the same old headaches long after your name has been removed from the corporate directory.

☕ Your Identity Crisis

You are not your job, but that doesn't mean your work doesn't have a huge impact on your identity. When you're escaping from Corporate America, you may feel like you're in limbo for a while. You're no longer that corporate prisoner (thank goodness), but you're not yet comfortable in your new role, either.

If you've grown accustomed to success and achievement, it can be discouraging to find yourself back in "wannabe" mode. Some people get freaked out by the feeling that they're losing an identity that they spent years building.

Try to remember that you are much more than your title. You're still the person who earned all those promotions or closed all those deals even if you have a different business card.

Adjusting to your new identity is a process. Don't be too hard on yourself if it takes you a while to get comfortable.

For most corporate escape artists, leaving the old identity behind is a freeing experience. "Going out on my own really helped me figure out who I am," says Lisa Bodell, founder of the innovation consulting firm Futurethink. "How good was I really? With my own company, my successes and failures are all up to me."

Aliza Freud, founder of the marketing research company SheSpeaks, found her new identity to be a much better fit. "In my corporate job, I knew that I was expendable. I knew that almost everyone at the company, including the CEO, was expendable. A lot of talented people could have done the same job I was doing. But at SheSpeaks, there is a lot of personal gratification in knowing that I am the one driving the business and making it what it is. That identity is a lot more important to me than the title I had at my old job."

DARING TALES OF CORPORATE ESCAPE

Making It Look Easy

Name: Robert Clauser
Former occupation: Partner at a top management consulting firm
Current occupation: Co-founder of Media & Entertainment Holdings

Robert Clauser's story is a unique one. He has managed to achieve success in almost all the different career paths discussed in this book. He has served as a lead partner at a major management consulting firm, launched his own nonprofit organization, produced films, took a sabbatical to accept a prestigious government fellowship, and finally—or at least most recently—started his own firm and took it public.

He is a living example that no career change is impossible if you are willing to work for it.

Robert was raised in a family of creative types and rebelled by going corporate after graduating from college. After two years traveling the world as an investment banker, he decided to pursue a career in consulting and went back to school for his MBA. He then went to work for a small boutique consulting firm and started producing movies in his spare time with a filmmaker friend.

"I would leave work at seven or eight at night to run out to the set to shoot scenes," he remembers. "I relied on a sleeve of Thin Mint Girl Scout cookies and a lot of Diet Coke for the energy to stay awake all night."

Eventually, he was recruited by Accenture to join its newly formed Media and Entertainment Division. "I spent about eight years at Accenture and by the end, I was their lead partner for the Americas for their media and entertainment strategy practice, working with companies like Sony BMG, MTV, Comcast, and Clear Channel."

At the same time, he helped to establish Accenture's not-for-profit practice, which did pro bono work for organizations such as the Metropolitan Museum of Art, the Tiger Woods Learning Center, and the NYC2012 Olympic campaign. Somehow he also found the energy to start his own nonprofit foundation with two friends. "We decided it was time for Hollywood to see other perspectives beyond the usual white guys making films," he says. The organization partnered with HBO to sponsor an annual screenwriting and production workshops to promote diversity in film.

How did he manage to juggle so many different projects? "You sleep on weekends," he says. "As Lucille Ball once said, 'If you need to get something done, give it to a busy person.' "

Eventually, however, Robert found that even his interesting side projects couldn't distract him from the fact that he wasn't enjoying consulting anymore. He was tired of influencing clients' business decisions and wanted to start making his own.

"On my thirty-ninth birthday, it occurred to me that if I was still consulting when I was forty, I would always be a consultant," he remembers. "To me, that would have been the beginning of the end. There were just too many other interesting things in the world that I wanted to do."

Fate seemed to step in when Robert applied for and was awarded a prestigious Rockefeller Fellowship, an unpaid thirteen-month program in public–private cooperation co-sponsored by the City of New York and the Rockefeller Foundation. "It was a great way to step back and have some time to think about what I wanted to do long-term," he says. By the time the fellowship ended, Robert had decided he was ready to start his career as an entrepreneur.

"I figured that even if it was a complete failure, it would still be a great story to tell and I could easily go back to work," he says. He teamed up with former clients and colleagues to form Media & Entertainment Holdings, a holding company that invests in and develops companies in the media sector.

"We filed with the SEC to take the company public in March of 2007 and raised $100 million on the American Stock Exchange," he says. As this book goes to press, Robert is having a blast evaluating potential acquisitions and preparing for his next challenge—running the New York City Marathon.

Robert Clauser's Best Advice for Career Changers

"If the thought of changing careers has crossed your mind, you owe it to yourself to at least investigate it. Meet with three people who have done what you want to do and find out how they did it. Remember, you can always go back—or forward."

Keep Moving Forward

Remember the law of inertia: A body at rest tends to stay at rest, and a body in motion tends to stay in motion.

As you move forward with your escape plans, you will definitely encounter obstacles. The key is to keep moving even in the face of fear, doubt, and negative people.

Action is the key to building the momentum you'll need to reach your destination. That doesn't mean that you have to make a major move before you're ready. Just keep taking steps—even if they're baby steps—every week.

THE BOOMERANG EFFECT

Why would anybody return to Corporate America after making a clean break? Sometimes there's a perfectly good reason—an amazing opportunity, a change in financial circumstances, or a shift in priorities.

Others may find themselves tempted to return to the comfort of the familiar when the going gets too tough or when fear of the unknown becomes overwhelming.

When David Kucher left his job as a music industry executive, his intention was to become a full-time writer. "I had saved enough money that I knew I could spend about six to eight months focusing on my writing career without having any income at all," says David. "I only spent about three weeks as a full-time writer, though, before I panicked. A former colleague offered a consulting opportunity and I decided to take it on. The assignment turned into ninety to one hundred hours of work a week for almost two years."

The downside was that David was lured back into the hectic corporate routine that he had vowed to leave behind. The upside was that he was billing $250 an hour and making more as a consultant than he had earned in his corporate job.

David eventually realized that the situation was making him miserable, even while it was building up his bank account, and he returned his focus to his writing career.

As you negotiate your own escape, beware of seemingly attractive offers that will take you off course or delay your progress. Don't give up before you've given your new career a chance.

Changing careers usually doesn't happen overnight. There is a lot of work along the way, and some of it is downright annoying. It's much easier to procrastinate, especially when life gets busy or a new season of *Project Runway* starts.

If you happen to get stuck in a rut, here are a few easy and painless ideas for getting your body in motion again:

- **Get some outside perspective.** Ask interesting new acquaintances to share their career stories and see if you can learn anything. You're not looking for the secrets of the universe here, just trying to stimulate some new thinking.
- **Rely on cheap fear tactics.** Ask yourself what will happen if you *don't* get your act together. Picture yourself still festering in your cubicle ten years down the road. That ought to be enough to get you moving
- **Look for inspiration.** Browse through a book or magazine article about somebody who overcame great odds to achieve great success. When your problems feel overwhelming, it's nice to see that they pale in comparison with the obstacles others have conquered.

- **Impose a deadline.** Set a deadline for completing the next task in your plan and ask somebody to hold you to it. Mark your calendar and commit yourself to making it happen.
- **Draft your resignation speech.** Think about exactly how you'll break it to your boss when it's time for you to move on. Close your eyes and visualize how you'll respond when she begs you not to go. Try to imagine the excitement you'll feel as you walk out the door for the last time.

SHOULD YOU HIRE A CAREER COUNSELOR OR COACH?

Some people find it helpful to hire a career counselor or a coach to guide them through the process of escaping from Corporate America. And why not? In the corporate world, the answer to any problem is generally, "Hire a consultant!" That's a very good thing for all of you aspiring solopreneurs.

A good career counselor or a coach can be useful in a number of ways. First, if you're still wrestling with the scary question of what you should do with your life (or at least the next few years of it), career counselors come armed with all kinds of assessments, personality tests, and other tools that can help you.

Even if you've already got your eye on the prize, a coach can be a great ally. He can help you fine-tune your plan, develop new strategies, or just provide a sympathetic ear when the going gets tough. What would Rocky have been without Burgess Meredith? Where would Kerri Strug have been without that scary Romanian guy who was always yelling at her?

Indeed one of the most valuable things a career coach can do for you is to serve as a royal pain in the butt. A good coach will encourage you when you're stuck, push you to dig deeper, and call you on it when you start slacking off (and you will at some point, believe me).

You may be able to recruit a friend to serve this purpose, but she probably won't be as effective. You don't want somebody who likes you too much and will let you coast.

What's the difference between a career counselor and a career coach? Generally, a counselor has a graduate degree in counseling and official NCCC (National Certified Career Counselor) credentials. On the other hand, there is no official license or credential required to practice as a career coach, and coaches come from a wide range of educational and professional backgrounds. There are many coach training programs out there, but not one that is considered the industry standard.

When it comes to choosing a professional to work with, look for someone with solid training and a successful track record helping people in situations similar to yours. Ask to see testimonials or client references to get a sense of what someone can do.

And keep in mind that even the most qualified counselor can't help you if you don't feel comfortable with him or his approach. If you're the hard-nosed practical type, you probably won't bond with the new-agey coach who wants you to get in touch with your aura.

Remember, a career coach isn't going to do your work for you. However, a little expert assistance may come in very handy if you get stuck.

The Power of Vision

I don't claim to understand all the mysterious forces at work in the universe, but I do know that interesting things start to happen once your vision becomes clear. I spent years halfheartedly searching for a more fulfilling career. But once I finally figured out a vision for the future that I could get excited about, something clicked. I just decided that I was going to make it happen—I could even picture myself walking into my boss's office to happily give my notice.

Almost immediately, I started to notice opportunities everywhere I looked. That mental click happened for me on New Year's

Eve, and I was working for myself full-time by March. Strangely enough, my resignation scene happened almost exactly the way I had been picturing it for months.

Some would say that I attracted the opportunities that came my way by asking the universe for them. Others would say that I simply opened my eyes to the potential that was already there. All I know is that my change in perspective led to dramatic changes in my circumstances.

Many of the corporate escape artists that I interviewed spoke of making the decision to go after their dream and suddenly hearing about the perfect job, meeting the ideal mentor, or stumbling upon a solution to their biggest obstacle.

Tracy Dyer, co-founder of handbag company Urban Junket, had a life-changing chance encounter when she traveled to Italy with her partner to research the leather market and determine if her business idea had potential. "We went to Florence without knowing much of anything except that everybody says you have to go to Italy if you want to know leather."

The only problem: They had no idea where to start looking for the suppliers they needed. "We were eating dinner at an outdoor café, talking about our search for leather factories and looking at our maps, and there was a man eavesdropping at the next table," she remembers. "We were shocked when he approached us and said, 'Excuse me, I own a leather shop. Do you need the names of some suppliers?' "

Talk about being in the right place at the right time. "From there, everything started to fall into place in a way," Tracy says. "We met four suppliers on that first trip."

You'll notice that Tracy didn't just hang out at home in Minneapolis waiting for Italian leather manufacturers to come knocking on her door. She had defined her vision and was out in the world working her butt off to bring it to life.

Why do good things start to happen once we get serious? Is it the law of attraction, the power of positive thinking, or just plain dumb luck? Tracy's father, Dr. Wayne Dyer, once wrote, "You'll see it when you believe it."

Could your intentions and beliefs really be so powerful? Oh, yes. But the right attitude will take you only so far. You also have to be willing to put in the work.

Bringing Your Vision to Life

When you encounter a particularly bumpy stretch on the road to freedom, try to remember that goals worth achieving are rarely easy. Stay focused on your vision for your future and don't give in to your insecurities. "If you were able to succeed in Corporate America, imagine how successful you can be doing something you truly love and believe in," advises Joshua Rosenthal, founder of the Institute for Integrative Nutrition.

The corporate escape artists that I spoke with had few regrets. "If I die tomorrow, I would be happy because I have already lived my dream," says Carolyn Hudson, the corporate marketing exec turned professional singer. "There is more to come, of course. But if I hadn't left my corporate job to pursue my music, I don't think I would have ever truly lived."

HAVE A NICE ESCAPE

Go confidently in the direction of your dreams. Live the life you have imagined.

—Henry David Thoreau

Only you can decide if you're really ready to escape from Corporate America.

The most important thing to remember is that you always have options. You deserve an inspiring, fulfilling career, and there's no reason you can't have one.

For more information, inspiration, and advice, visit the Escape from Corporate America website at www.escapefromcorporate.com. You can read more about the corporate escape artists that I interviewed, find exclusive content and resources, get answers to your questions, and connect with others who are planning their escapes.

I also invite you to share your personal corporate escape and/or dramatic career change stories. Please e-mail your story to me at mystory@escapefromcorporate.com or visit www.escapefromcorporate .com to learn more about how to contribute.

The following selected resources can provide additional support and guidance during your escape from Corporate America. Due to space constraints, it was impossible to include every helpful resource that I've discovered. Please visit this book's companion website at www.escape fromcorporate.com for an expanded, up-to-date resource guide and more stories and advice.

Finding Your True Calling

Career Tests

Online career tests can provide helpful clues in your search for your true calling. No generic career evaluation can give you a single, definitive answer regarding what you should do with your life. The idea is to come up with some ideas to explore based on the experiences of people with similar skills, interests, and values. Additional career and personality tests, such as the Myers-Briggs Type Indicator, are not available for free on the Internet, but can be explored and interpreted with the help of a career counselor.

- **Values Profile Quiz** (http://psychologytoday.psychtests.com/tests/values_ r_access.html). This *Psychology Today* quiz can help you prioritize your values and find out if they are in line with your current career.
- **The Career Key** (www.careerkey.org). This online career test is based on Holland's theory of six personality types and the work environments that suit them best. The ten-minute test costs $7.95 and will identify your dominant personality types and several possible career choices.

- **MAPP Assessment** (www.assessment.com). The MAPP Assessment helps to uncover career motivations and to find the most fulfilling types of work for you. You can complete the assessment online for free and receive a sample report and five career matches. More comprehensive assessments will cost between $9.95 and $129.95.
- **Skills Profiler** (www.careerinfonet.org/skills). This tool, sponsored by the US Department of Labor, allows you to inventory your skills based on previous job roles and see what other career paths you may be qualified for.

Helpful Books

The following books include exercises, guidance, and inspiration that may assist you in the search for your true calling.

- *What Color Is Your Parachute?* by Richard Nelson Bolles. This classic book is a great practical manual for career changers. It's chock-full of exercises to help you figure out your dream job, as well as job hunting advice.
- *Do What You Are: Discover the Perfect Career for You Through the Secrets of Personality Type* by Paul D. Tieger and Barbara Barron-Tieger. Identify potential dream careers through analysis of your Myers-Briggs Type.
- *I Could Do Anything If I Only Knew What It Was* by Barbara Sher. The exercises in this book can help you figure out what you're supposed to be doing with your life and what has been holding you back.
- *Working Identity* by Herminia Ibarra. This interesting book guides you through experimenting with new career identities.
- *What Should I Do with My Life?* by Po Bronson. Get inspired by these stories of people who have found their true callings.

Finding a Career Counselor or Coach

The best way to find a good career counselor or a coach is by referral. If you can't get a good recommendation, try looking in the directories listed below or contacting the career offices of your local universities. You can also visit www.escapefromcorporate.com for help in locating the right career counselor or coach for you.

- **Association of Career Professionals** (www.acpinternational.com). Find career service providers in your area with specialties from assessment to retirement planning.

- **National Career Development Association** (www.ncda.org). Browse through listings of accredited career counselors by state.
- **International Coach Federation** (www.coachfederation.org). A free Coach Referral Service will match you up with a career coach who fits your preferences.

Career Research

Find out more about the jobs and career paths that interest you—including necessary qualifications, compensation ranges, and typical daily duties—with these helpful resources.

- **O*Net OnLine** (http://online.onetcenter.org). This free online database provides a wealth of information on a wide variety of jobs and career paths. Job reports are based on data gathered from surveys of workers in each occupation.
- ***Occupational Outlook Handbook*** (www.bls.gov/oco/home.htm). This online handbook is published by the US Department of Labor and has information on more than 250 occupations.
- **Salary.com.** Find typical salary ranges and benefits packages by job role, industry, company size, and other criteria. Basic compensation info is free; enter your résumé details for a personalized report.
- **PayScale.com.** See typical compensation info for specific job titles, customized by experience, education, and location. For $19.95, you can sign up for a premium membership and see what real (anonymous) individuals are earning in that job role in your area.
- **PayScale's GigZig** (www.payscale.com/gigzig.aspx). See the most common career paths to your dream job and/or the most common next steps on your current path.
- **FabJob Guides** (www.fabjob.com). FabJob publishes a series of guides on breaking into dream jobs—from actor to motivational speaker to yoga teacher, and everything in between.
- **Roadtrip Nation** (www.roadtripnation.com). Watch footage of interviews with successful people from all walks of life.
- **Vocation Vacations** (www.vocationvacations.com). Spend your vacation test-driving a new career. For a fee, you can shadow someone in your dream job. Featured vacations include the glamorous (Broadway producer, baseball team manager) and the practical (caterer, dog trainer).

Financial Planning for Your Career Change

Finding a Financial Planner

A financial planner can help you with a comprehensive plan to support your career change.

- **How to Choose the Right Financial Planner** (www.fpanet.org/public/ tools/financialplannerhelp.cfm). Find out how a financial planner can help you and how to pick the right one for you.
- **The Financial Planning Association PlannerSearch** (www.fpanet.org/ plannersearch). Search for a qualified financial planner by location and specialization.
- **National Association of Personal Financial Advisors** (www.napfa.org/ consumer/planners). Search the NAPFA directory for fee-only financial planners.
- **New Means Financial Planning** (www.newmeans.com). The site for New Hampshire-based financial planner Sherrill St. Germain, who specializes in financial planning for career changers.

Finding Health Insurance

If your career change will mean walking away from a company-sponsored health plan, check out the following alternative resources for finding health insurance coverage.

- **eHealthInsurance** (www.ehealthinsurance.com). Get quotes and compare health insurance plans to find the right one for you.
- **GuidePoint Health** (www.guidepointhealth.com). Get instant online quotes from this insurance company, which specializes in the individual and small group markets.

To find a group plan, research professional associations and labor unions in your field. Associations offering group plans include:

- **Freelancers Union** (www.freelancersunion.org). Freelancers Union offers health insurance plans for freelancers in thirty states.
- **National Association for the Self-Employed** (www.nase.org). The NASE offers health insurance coverage for solopreneurs.

Finding a Corporate Job That Doesn't Suck

Researching Companies

- **Great Place to Work Institute** (www.greatplacetowork.com). The Great Place to Work Institute compiles the *Fortune* Best Companies to Work For list and offers additional information and research for job hunters.
- ***Fortune* Best Companies to Work For** (http://money.cnn.com/ magazines/fortune/bestcompanies). Research the top-rated firms and find information about their policies and employee benefits.
- **The Reputation Institute** (www.reputationinstitute.com). Read the results of the institute's annual online survey to measure the corporate reputations of six hundred of the world's largest companies in twenty-nine countries.
- ***Working Mother* 100 Best Companies** (www.workingmother.com). Learn more about the companies rated as most family-friendly by *Working Mother* magazine.
- ***Wall Street Journal Corporate Reputation Rankings*** (http://online.wsj .com/public/resources/documents/info-corprep070130-sort.html). See which firms' reputations ranked highest in a survey by *The Wall Street Journal* and Harris Interactive.
- **LinkedIn** (www.linkedin.com). At business networking site LinkedIn, you can connect with former employees of the firm you're researching.
- **Wetfeet** (www.wetfeet.com). Find industry and company profiles.
- **Vault** (www.vault.com). Read company profiles based on employee surveys and visit company message boards to read posts from former employees.
- **JobVent** (www.jobvent.com). Though most of the people who post at JobVent are there because they have axes to grind (all posts are anonymous), you may find it useful to read these unfiltered opinions from former employees of many large companies.

Job Listings

- Monster (www.monster.com).
- HotJobs (www.hotjobs.com).
- CareerBuilder (www.careerbuilder.com).
- Simply Hired (www.simplyhired.com).
- Craigslist (www.craigslist.com).

Featured Corporations to Check Out

- American Express (www.americanexpress.com).
- Best Buy (www.bestbuy.com).
- Booz Allen Hamilton (www.boozallen.com).
- Genentech (www.gene.com).
- Google (www.google.com).
- Intel (www.intel.com).
- PricewaterhouseCoopers (www.pwc.com).
- Salesforce.com (www.salesforce.com).
- SAS Institute (www.sas.com).
- Timberland (www.timberland.com).
- VistaPrint (www.vistaprint.com).
- Xerox (www.xerox.com).

Finding Recruiters

- **Recruiter Link** (www.recruiterlink.com). Find headhunters specializing in executive-level jobs.
- **SearchFirm.com** (www.searchfirm.com).Search a directory of executive recruiters by specialty, location, and other criteria.
- **Oya's Directory of Recruiters** (www.i-recruit.com). Another directory of executive recruiters and staffing firms.

Flextime, Part-Time, and Sabbatical Resources

- **Work Options** (www.workoptions.com). This site has downloadable proposal templates for telecommuting, job sharing, and part-time and compressed workweek schedules. Each template is $29.95.
- **Families and Work Institute** (www.familiesandwork.org). Read research on the latest trends and best practices in workplace flexibility.
- *The Savvy Part-Time Professional* by Lynn Berger. This book offers advice on finding part-time work and making a part-time schedule work for you.
- *Time Off for Good Behavior* by Mary Lou Quinlan. Although this book was written specifically for high-achieving women, it has plenty of advice for anyone seeking to take a sabbatical or leave of absence.
- *One Person/Multiple Careers* by Marci Alboher. Learn more about how to succeed in a portfolio career.

- *The 4-Hour Workweek* by Timothy Ferriss. Find out how to outsource more work and reclaim your life.

Finding a Job at a Start-Up or Small Company

- **JobKite** (www.jobkite.com). This online job board specializes in positions at small companies.
- **National Venture Capital Association** (www.nvca.org/members.html). Visit the venture capitalist websites to see if they are hiring for any of their funded companies.
- **Craigslist** (www.craigslist.com). Start-ups and small companies don't have big recruiting budgets, so you're likely to find many of their jobs listed on Craigslist, where it's much cheaper to post jobs than on the big job boards (and free in many cities).

Solopreneur Resources

- **Freelancers Union** (www.freelancersunion.org). Freelancers Union is an advocacy group for freelancers and independent professionals. It offers lots of resources, from job listings to networking tools and health insurance coverage.
- **Working Solo** (www.workingsolo.com). Learn more about starting and running a solo business.
- *Free Agent Nation: The Future of Working for Yourself* by Daniel H. Pink. This book was published in 2001, so some material is a little dated, but you'll still find lots of great information about the free agent movement.
- **IRS tax info for the self-employed** (www.irs.gov/businesses/small/article/0,,id=115045,00.html). Find out more about solopreneur taxes straight from the IRS.
- **Nolo tax and business advice for contractors and consultants** (www.nolo.com). Nolo, the legal information publisher, offers tax and business planning information for contractors and consultants.
- **Elance** (www.elance.com). Find and bid on freelance projects.
- **Guru.com** (www.guru.com). Post your profile and bid on freelance assignments.
- **VistaPrint** (www.vistaprint.com). Find low-cost business cards, stationery, and marketing materials for your solo business.

Entrepreneur Resources

Publications and Blogs for Entrepreneurs

- *Entrepreneur* **magazine** (www.entrepreneur.com). *Entrepreneur* magazine and the Entrepreneur website are great sources for information on all aspects of starting and running a business.
- *Inc. Magazine* (www.inc.com). *Inc. Magazine* and the Inc. website feature lots of great articles and columns for entrepreneurs.
- *The Wall Street Journal's Startup Journal* (startup.wsj.com). This online publication features articles and resources for entrepreneurs.
- **Guy Kawasaki's How to Change the World Blog** (http://blog.guy kawasaki.com). Read Guy Kawasaki's insights into entrepreneurship, innovation, and business trends.
- **About.com Entrepreneurs** (entrepreneurs.about.com). This comprehensive site features advice on all aspects of entrepreneurship.

Books for Entrepreneurs

- *The Art of the Start* by Guy Kawasaki. Kawasaki provides real-world-tested advice for launching any company or business project. He draws upon his personal experience as an entrepreneur, venture capitalist, and business guru to offer advice on everything from writing a business plan to hiring employees to building buzz for your new venture.
- *Before You Quit Your Job* by Robert Kiyosaki. This book by *Rich Dad, Poor Dad* author Kiyosaki focuses on ten real-life lessons for entrepreneurs who want to build a multimillion-dollar business.
- *Start Your Own Business* (Entrepreneur Magazine's Start Up) by Rieva Lesonsky. This comprehensive guide from *Entrepreneur* magazine offers practical information for every step along the path from idea to financing to running your business.

Mentors and Advisers for Entrepreneurs

- **SCORE** (www.score.org). SCORE (Service Corps of Retired Executives), a resource partner of the US Small Business Administration (SBA), offers free counseling for entrepreneurs via e-mail or in person at any of 374 chapters around the country. The SCORE website also has a wealth of information resources for entrepreneurs.

- **Small Business Development Centers** (www.sba.gov/aboutsba/sbaprograms/sbdc). The SBA also offers assistance to entrepreneurs and small-business owners through a network of Small Business Development Centers (SBDCs).
- **SBA Women's Business Centers** (www.sba.gov/services/counseling/wbc). The SBA's Office of Women's Business Ownership operates a network of Women's Business Centers that are designed to assist women in starting and running successful businesses.

Financing Your Business

- **Virgin Money** (www.virginmoneyus.com). Set up "friends and family" financing through a service like CircleLending to avoid misunderstandings and keep things business-like.
- **Prosper** (www.prosper.com). This online marketplace allows borrowers to connect with potential lenders.
- **Angel Capital Association** (www.angelcapitalassociation.org). Find angel investors and learn more about their preferences at the website of this association for angel capital investors.
- **National Venture Capital Association** (www.nvca.org). Learn more about the venture capital industry and the top VC investors.
- **GoBIG Network** (www.gobignetwork.com/small-business-funding). Post a request for financing and connect with potential investors.

Buying a Business

- **BusinessBroker.net** (www.businessbroker.net). Browse through a directory of almost thirty thousand businesses for sale and franchise opportunities.
- **Business Brokers Network** (www.bbnbrokers.com). Find a business broker in your area.

Networking Organizations for Entrepreneurs

- **Meet-up groups for entrepreneurs** (http://entrepreneur.meetup.com). Find networking groups for entrepreneurs in your area.
- **The Entrepreneurs' Organization** (www.eonetwork.org). This network of experienced entrepreneurs boasts sixty-six hundred members in thirty-eight countries.
- **Startupping.com** (www.startupping.com). This online community was created for Internet entrepreneurs by Internet entrepreneurs.

- **Count Me In** (www.countmein.org). Count Me In is a nonprofit organization that provides microfinance loans and business education for women entrepreneurs.
- **Ladies Who Launch** (www.ladieswholaunch.com). This national networking group focuses on women who are launching businesses.
- **LinkedIn** (www.linkedin.com). Find other entrepreneurs through business networking site LinkedIn.

Follow Your Creative Dreams

Books for Artists and Creative People

- *The War of Art: Break Through the Blocks and Win Your Inner Creative Battles* by Steven Pressfield. This inspiring little book is great for overcoming resistance and getting inspired.
- *The Artist's Way* by Julia Cameron. Keep your creative spirit alive with the exercises and advice in this classic book on creativity.
- *Career Guide for Creative and Unconventional People* by Carol Eikleberry and Richard Nelson Bolles. Get career management tips for creative personalities and browse through 207 occupations for creative types.

Classes for Creative People

Contact colleges, universities, arts organizations, and continuing education institutions in your area for information about local classes and workshops. Below are some online programs that may also be worth exploring in various disciplines.

- **Berklee Music** (www.berkleemusic.com/school/courses). Take online classes in songwriting, music theory, production, performance, and more.
- *Writer's Digest* **Online Workshops** (www.writersonlineworkshops.com). Take online writing classes with professional instructors in a range of genres.
- **Gotham Writers' Workshops** (www.writingclasses.com). Take online writing courses in memoir writing, screenwriting, children's book writing, and many other genres.
- **Hollywood Film Institute** (www.hollywoodu.com). Hollywood Film Institute's intensive 2-Day Film School is held regularly in cities

around the United States and in Toronto and London. If you can't make it in person, there are online and video film classes that you can check out from home.

Make a Difference

Finding Volunteer Opportunities

- **Idealist** (www.idealist.org). Find volunteer opportunities and non-profit job listings.
- **VolunteerMatch** (www.volunteermatch.org). Search for volunteer opportunities based on your interests.
- **Network for Good** (www.networkforgood.org). Donate your money or your time to worthy organizations.
- **Taproot Foundation** (www.taprootfoundation.org). Sign on to do pro bono projects for nonprofit organizations in your area of expertise.
- **BoardNetUSA** (www.boardnetusa.org). Search for opportunities to serve on a nonprofit organization board of directors.

Finding Nonprofit Jobs

- **Idealist** (www.idealist.org). Search nonprofit job listings.
- **Bridgestar** (www.bridgestar.org). Find job opportunities through this nonprofit recruiting firm.
- **Philanthropy Careers** (www.philanthropy.com/jobs). Search for nonprofit jobs and learn more about working in the nonprofit sector.
- **Guidestar** (www.guidestar.org). Research nonprofit organizations.

Alternate Teacher Certification Programs

- **The New Teacher Project** (www.tntp.org). Find out more about becoming a certified teacher through The New Teacher Project.
- **The National Center for Alternative Certification** (www.teach-now.org). Get comprehensive information about alternative routes to teacher certification in the United States.

Visit www.escapefromcorporate.com for additional resources.

ACKNOWLEDGMENTS

Thank you to all of the amazing corporate escape artists and brilliant experts who took the time to share their stories, advice, and inspiration. Because of you, writing this book was one of the most rewarding and educational experiences of my life (and a lot of fun, too).

Thanks also to my agent, Carol Mann, and her team at the Carol Mann Literary Agency, for making the whole experience possible.

I am eternally grateful to my editor, Jill Schwartzman, for her insight, support, and guidance. It has been a pleasure working with everyone at Random House throughout this process.

Sincere thanks also go out to the following people, who provided feedback, friendship, and special help: the Andrei family, Willie Asuncion, Lisa and Brian Bodell, Christa Bourg, Mark Fortier, Richard Fouts, Eliot Merberg and all of the counselors at SCORE NYC, Will and Tania Mulry, Andrea Reese, Beth Schoenfelt and the women of Ladies Who Launch, Dawn Seamon, Barbara Sher, Mary Shomon, and Sherrill St. Germain.

Words cannot express my gratitude to my family for teaching me to work hard, dream big, and never take myself too seriously. Thank you to Mary and Wes Skillings, Jeremy Skillings, and the rest of the Gannon and Skillings families. And a word of special tanks to Max "the Bear" Gannon, who knew I would write books way before I did.

Last, but certainly not least, there is my husband, Alex. Thank you for your enthusiasm, your feedback, your endless patience, your constant support, and for keeping me laughing even when I was on deadline. Without you, I never would have escaped from Corporate America or lived to write about it.

Find out more about the amazing corporate escapees and experts who told their stories and shared their advice for this book (or at least the ones who wanted to use their real names).

Scott Adams. Author, cartoonist, creator of *Dilbert* (www.dilbert.com), and co-owner of Stacey's Café in Pleasanton, California (www.staceys cafe.com).

Caroline Barlerin. Board member of the Taproot Foundation (www .taprootfoundation.org), a nonprofit organization that connects professionals with pro bono work for nonprofits.

Andrea Beaman. Chef, holistic health counselor, author, and TV host (www.andreabeaman.com).

Marc Benioff. Founder, chairman, and CEO of Salesforce.com (www .salesforce.com), a leading provider of customer relationship management applications and services.

Steve Bernstein. Founder and publisher, Zenbu Media (www.zenbu media.com), an integrated music media company with magazine and Web properties, a record label, and an events division.

Lisa Bodell. Founder and CEO of Futurethink (www.getfuturethink .com), an innovation consulting firm.

Michelle Boggs. Co-founder and CEO of McKinley Marketing Partners (www.mckinleymarketingpartners.com), an interim staffing firm.

Kim Brittingham. Writer.

Marcia Call. President of McKinley Marketing Partners (www.mckinley marketingpartners.com), an interim staffing firm.

Laura Cantrell. Musician and recording artist (www.lauracantrell.com).

Ben Cikanek. Executive director of operations for Kidrobot (www.kid robot.com), the cutting-edge art toy and apparel company.

Maxine Clark. Founder and Chief Executive Bear for Build-A-Bear Workshop (www.buildabear.com), the retail toy chain.

Robert Clauser. Co-founder, Media & Entertainment Holdings.

Andrew Coleman. Founder, LeadQual (www.leadqual.com), an online marketing and lead conversion company.

Cathy Detloff. Founder, Just Because Originals (www.justbecause orginals.com), an online specialty gift retailer.

Tracy Dyer. Co-founder, Urban Junket, a handbag design company.

Sally Fegley. Co-founder and co-owner, Tom and Sally's Handmade Chocolates (www.tomandsallys.com).

Mark Fletcher. Serial entrepreneur and founder of Startupping.com (www.startupping.com), an online community for Internet entrepreneurs.

Richard Fouts. Founder and CEO of Comunicado (www.comunicado .us), a marketing communications consultancy.

Aliza Freud. Founder and CEO of SheSpeaks (www.shespeaks.com), a market research firm.

Tevis Gale. Founder, Balance Integration (www.balanceintegration.com), a company that offers work–life balance training and resources for corporations.

Rich Gee. Founder, Rich Gee Coaching (www.richgee.com), an executive coaching practice.

David Hersh. Co-founder and vice president of business development for Multiply (www.multiply.com), the social networking community.

Perez Hilton. Blogger, Perezhilton.com (www.perezhilton.com).

Andy Hines. Futurist and director of consulting for Social Technologies (www.socialtechnologies.com), a global research and consulting firm specializing in foresight and innovation.

Carolyn Hudson. Singer, songwriter, and musician (www.carolynhudson .com).

Ralph Jovine. CEO, Grand Central Solutions (www.grandcentralsolutions .com), a software and development firm.

Alex Kay. COO, Word World (www.wordworld.com), a kids' entertainment and education company.

Jim Koch. Founder and chairman of the Boston Beer Company (www.bostonbeer.com), the nation's largest microbrewery.

David Kucher. Writer, editor, teacher, dramaturg.

Laurence Lederer. Founder and CEO of GuidePoint Health, a health insurance provider specializing in the individual and small-group market.

Georgia Lee. Writer/director/producer of the feature film *Red Doors* (www.reddoorsthemovie.com) and co-founder of Blanc de Chine Entertainment (www.bdcfilms.com).

Lynne Lerner. Founder, Pet Project Alliance (www.petprojectalliance.org), a nonprofit organization dedicated to promoting the human–animal bond.

Kenneth Lesley. Teacher.

Paul Lieberstein. Writer/co-executive producer/actor, *The Office* (www.nbc.com/The_Office).

Rob Malkani. Writer/executive producer of the feature film *Day Zero* (www.dayzerothemovie.com) and founder, Curbside Pictures (www.curbsidepictures.com).

Erika Mangrum. Founder and president, Iatria Spa and Health Centers (www.iatria.com).

Shannon McCaffery. Founder and chief implementation officer of McCaffery Communications (www.mccafferycomms.com), a marketing services agency.

Nicole Arslanian McCarthy. Founder and president of Talene Reilly (www.talenereilly.com), maker of stylish laptop bags and handbags.

Sarma Melngailis. Co-founder and owner of Pure (www.purefoodandwine.com), a popular Manhattan raw food restaurant, and One Lucky Duck (http://oneluckyduck.com), a retailer of raw food products.

Anthony Moody. Executive producer of the feature film *Day Zero* (www.dayzerothemovie.com) and founder of Indalo Productions (www.indalo.biz).

Tatiana Mulry. Senior vice president of product development for Teleflip (www.teleflip.com), a mobile communications company.

Daniel Nahmod. Singer-songwriter (www.danielnahmod.com).

Genevieve Piturro. Founder and director of Pajama Program (http://pajamaprogram.org), a nonprofit organization that provides warm pajamas and books to children in need.

Marcia Reynolds. Public speaker, author, and leadership coach (www.outsmartyourbrain.com).

Marie Elena Rigo. Founder and president, MER Life Design (www.fengshui-me.com), a feng shui and interior design consulting firm.

Jon Rochetti. Interim marketing executive for McKinley Marketing Partners (www.mckinleymarketingpartners.com) and travel blogger (www.thedctraveler.com).

Joshua Rosenthal. Founder and director of the Institute for Integrative Nutrition (www.integrativenutrition.com), an organization that trains professional health counselors.

Michael Sands. Founder and CEO of LesserEvil Brand Snack Co. (www.lesserevil.com), makers of healthier snacks.

Sharon Sausville. Full-time mom.

Jeremy Skillings. Founder and President, SEO Help Desk (www.seohelpdesk.com), a search engine optimization firm specializing in small businesses.

Julie Smith. Interim marketing executive for McKinley Marketing Partners (www.mckinleymarketingpartners.com).

Sherrill St. Germain, MBA, CFP. Founder, New Means Financial Planning (www.newmeans.com).

Richard Tait. Co-founder and Grand Poo-Bah, Cranium (www.cranium.com), the toy and game company.

Jeri Thorne. Interim marketing executive for McKinley Marketing Partners (www.mckinleymarketingpartners.com).

Cheryl Todmann. Director of community relations for the Brooklyn Bureau of Community Service (www.bbcs.org), one of Brooklyn's most prominent community service organizations.

Liz Wald. Founder and managing partner of EDImports (www.edimports.com), a company that imports handmade goods crafted by women in developing nations.

Tim Zagat. Co-founder, co-chair, and CEO of Zagat Survey (www.zagat.com), the survey publishing firm.

PAMELA SKILLINGS walked away from the security of a six-figure job and a twelve-year corporate career to start her own business in 2005. Her company, Skillful Communications, provides consulting and coaching on communication and career development issues for organizations and individuals.

Pamela frequently lectures around the country on career topics and is a regular contributor to About.com and print publications. She holds a bachelor's degree in journalism and a certificate in adult career planning and development, both from New York University.

Pamela currently lives in New York City with her husband. For more information, please visit www.escapefromcorporate.com.